Why National Standards and Tests ?

To John and Frances Jennings,
who gave me life and have been the most
important influence on making me who I am.

To Carl Perkins,
who showed me that one could have integrity
in political life and also be an effective advocate
for those less advantaged in our society.

John F. Jennings

Why National Standards and Tests?

Politics and the Quest for Better Schools

SAGE Publications
International Educational and Professional Publisher
Thousand Oaks   London   New Delhi

For information:

SAGE Publications, Inc.
2455 Teller Road
Thousand Oaks, California 91320
E-mail: order@sagepub.com

SAGE Publications Ltd.
6 Bonhill Street
London EC2A 4PU
United Kingdom

SAGE Publications India Pvt. Ltd.
M-32 Market
Greater Kailash I
New Delhi 110 048 India

Printed in the United States of America

Library of Congress Cataloging-in-Publication Data

Jennings, John F.
    Why national standars and tests?: politics and the quest for better schools /
by John F. Jennings.
        p. cm.
    Includes bibliographical references and index.
    ISBN 0-7619-1475-7 (cloth: acid-free paper) 1. Education—Standards—United States.
    2. Educational tests and measurements—United States. 3. Education and state—
United States. I. Title.
LB3060.83.J46 1998
379.1'58'0973—dc21   97-45327

This book is printed on acid-free paper.

    99 00 01 02 03 10 9 8 7 6 5 4 3 2

Acquiring Editor:	C. Deborah Laughton
Editorial Assistant:	Eileen Carr
Production Editor:	Sherrise M. Purdum
Production Assistant:	Denise Santoyo
Typesetter/Designer:	Marion Warren
Indexer:	Teri Greenberg
Print Buyer:	Anna Chin

Contents

Prologue

The common view today is that the public schools are not good enough and that something must be done to make them better. Setting higher academic standards is one way to raise the educational achievement of students. This book focuses on how national leaders encouraged this change through establishing national standards for the schools, proposing national tests to measure academic mastery by students, and aiding states and school districts to develop their own standards and tests.

This broad concept of establishing higher academic standards for the schools, once stated, seems simple enough, but it has been the subject of intense and fierce battling—especially after the idea of *national* standards and tests was introduced in the late 1980s by President George Bush, corporate leaders, educators, and the nation's governors.

Only now, in the later 1990s, are many states starting to implement high standards in their schools. In the process, however, many governors, state school superintendents, and other officials have made the point that they are implementing, not national standards, but rather the standards written for that particular state or school district. In other words, the battles over raising standards, and especially over establishing national standards and tests, were so fierce during the early and mid-1990s that afterward officials put a distance between themselves and the idea of national standards as they sought to raise the standards in their own states or local schools.

In 1997, however, President Bill Clinton revived the idea of national standards for education when he proposed the establishment of national tests to measure whether students had mastered reading skills by fourth grade and mathematics by eighth grade. His administration then set about the task of writing those tests, and the president appeared before various state legislatures and received the commitment of several states to administer those tests to their students in 1999. So in 1997, after all the battles over national standards and the apparent demise of that approach, the president raised the issue anew and used rhetoric similar to that of President Bush when he first proposed such standards in the early 1980s.

Why won't the idea of national standards and national tests go away? How did the country get on the road to establishing such standards in the first place? Why were there such fierce arguments during the late 1980s and throughout the 1990s over such standards and tests and over the idea of the federal government's helping states to establish their own standards? At first, the broad idea of raising standards and the particular concept of writing national standards and tests were supported by many political, corporate, and educational leaders and seemed to be accepted overwhelmingly by the public, yet as the debate evolved, strong and emotional opposition arose—why was this so?

This book will tell this story as it unfolded in Washington, D.C., from 1989 through 1997, with presidents, the Congress, and national business and education leaders debating how the country's schools ought to be improved and whether raising education standards was the best way to improve them. This debate is now being replayed across the country as state boards of education, state legislatures, and local school boards go about the work of requiring, writing, and implementing higher standards for students and schools. So reviewing the national dialogue may prove useful in under-standing the debate currently occurring in local communities and in state capitals.

A second important reason to tell this story is that sharp partisan divisions and a rupturing of bipartisan support for national programs aiding public schools were seen in these battles to use federal funds to encourage states and local school districts to raise their standards. These battles demonstrated a shift among Republicans toward supporting aid for private schools and a diminishing of support for public schools—an ominous development for American public education.

There is a third reason to tell this story: It is a very good example of how difficult it is to agree on a national policy for the United States. In a country of over 260 million people, with many different points of view and with a complex system of government, it is extremely hard work to achieve agree-ment on how we as a people ought to do anything. The saga of the national goals and of the Goals 2000 Act makes that point very clearly.

Americans, by large majorities, as shown by numerous polls, want higher standards in the public schools (Immerwahr & Johnson, 1996). But it is a long way from general agreement on that broad concept to finding specific means to implement it. Any serious effort to improve the public schools will take a long-term commitment to succeed; therefore, we must understand how we got on the road of raising standards and what we have to do to stay on it to ensure that American children are educated to be good citizens and to be gainfully employed.

Acknowledgment

I have always wanted to write a book. After five years of compiling resources, referencing, writing, and editing to produce this manuscript, while working full-time, I have fulfilled this aspiration, and extinguished any desire to go through this again. At least until enough time has passed so that I forget the birthing pains.

Once I was on my way to developing a manuscript, Mary Cowell was very helpful in educating me on how the publishing industry works; and I am appreciative for her wise counsel. Richard Jaeger of the University of North Carolina created the possibility for this printing by recommending to Sage Publications that they review my manuscript. At Sage, C. Deborah Laughton, the acquisitions editor, was very encouraging; and Eileen Carr, editorial assistant, and Sherrise Purdum, the production editor, were very easy to work with. Elisabeth Magnus was my instructor on writing proper footnotes, and I will never again neglect to write a page number on a newspaper article that I cut out. Mark Root created the two charts showing the votes in Congress on major education bills, and Kenneth Nelson made available the chart on the national goals for education. Thomas Wolanin, Michael Cohen, Christopher Cross, Susan Wilhelm, Ellen Guiney, Matt Alexander, and Marshall Smith were kind enough to read portions of the manuscript for accuracy. Thank you all.

When I retired three years ago from working for the U.S. Congress, Robert Schwartz, then with the Pew Charitable Trusts, was very helpful in securing funding for the policy center I established in Washington. Bob also invited me seven years ago to participate in the Pew Forum on Education Reform (now called the Pew Forum on Standards-based Reform), which has been a wonderful experience in deepening my understanding of American education. For the past decade Bob has been a major actor in helping public schools raise their standards for children.

Phi Delta Kappa International has earned my appreciation for supporting my writing over the years and for assisting in creating the policy center. Lowell Rose, Arliss Roaden, Ron Joekel, Sandy Weith, Janice Wampler, Donovan Walling, and Pauline Gough have all been wonderful people to work with at PDK. David Bergholtz, with the George Gund Foundation, has also been a key supporter over the years and an inspiration as he strives to improve our society and especially the schools in the large cities.

Toni Painter and I have worked together for twenty-seven years, first on Capitol Hill and then with the policy center. Toni is a dedicated person, and her loyalty and conscientiousness have made it possible for me to work full-time and also to write. Diane Stark-Rentner is another outstanding person who worked with me on Capitol Hill and now works at the center. Her competence in carrying out the center's activities has also given me the freedom to finish this manuscript.

Steve Molinari has been not only patient with my obsession with writing this book, but he has also been supportive daily of my struggle to find ways to use my professional life to improve education, especially for those who do not have strong advocates.

Lastly, I could not finish this section without commending all those who in their daily work strive to make public schools better. Despite a lack of due appreciation and the delivery of often undue criticism, what they are doing will make life better for millions of children and for the country. Thank you.

1

The Need to Improve the Schools

Why Raising Student Achievement Through Higher Standards Was First Proposed

When you learned to drive a car or to play the piano or the violin or to fly a plane, you were told what you needed to know. Then you were guided and corrected as you went along. If you did not drive or play or fly correctly, you were taught some more, and then you tried again.

What could be more logical than that as the way to learn something? It makes perfect sense that you would be told what you are to know, then helped along as you tried to master the material, and then given another chance to do it if you did not perform just right the first time.

That most sensible way to learn is *not* the way that American public schools now operate in many important respects. But it is the way that students will be educated once a major reform of elementary and secondary education that has recently begun is finally implemented. That reform is the subject of this book.

In American schools today, teachers explain material to students, help them to understand what they are doing right, and correct them when they are not mastering the material. And when teachers control the tests, they try to help students along so that they can do better the next time. But students, teachers, and the schools are often held accountable for performance on tests that students cannot learn to and teachers cannot teach to. Moreover, the results are not revealed to teachers or students, so there is no chance to learn from mistakes and work to do better next time.

Schools are caught in a "crapshoot" in which teachers are teaching in the dark and students are being tested in the dark. It amounts to a "gotcha" game. Students are not told exactly what they are going to be tested on; nor are they told afterward which questions they answered wrong so that they can learn the material for another time. Is it any wonder, then, that high school students are not motivated to learn? They do not see the relevance of what they are taught because that is not what they will be held accountable for.

Many important decisions about students' lives are made in similar fashion. An example that is easy to understand involves the SAT I, the country's most famous assessment, which is used every year to help determine the admission of hundreds of thousands of high school students to college.

A student cannot study for the SAT because the test prides itself on not being based on any one curriculum. A student can spend money to attend an SAT preparation course run by a private company, but all that company can do is to give some pointers on test-taking techniques and hazard some guesses as to the types of questions likely to appear on the test. No one but the Educational Testing Service, which writes the SAT, knows for sure what will be on that test. And those students who cannot afford the fees of those private courses are not even given the benefit of the educated guesses of the test preparation companies.

Admission to college is not the only matter decided in this fashion. Some states also require a student to pass a standardized test to graduate from high school, and some school districts require students to pass a test to proceed from one grade to the next. All of these major decisions are made on the basis of tests that cannot be taught because they consist of material that is unknown and whose results are not revealed afterward so that students can learn from their errors.

Does this seem like a strange system of education? If we were to learn to drive, play a musical instrument, or fly a plane this way, there would be many more car wrecks, discordant noises, and plane crashes than there are now. Imagine having to guess the right ways to drive, play music, or fly. Is it any wonder that the public schools are struggling so hard to improve and, in the popular opinion, not succeeding?

The irony is that public education has just been through a period of reform unmatched in intensity and length. During the late 1970s and throughout the 1980s, many states toughened high school graduation requirements, instituted professional testing for teachers and raised their salaries, and experimented with countless different ways of improving teaching and learning. But by the end of the 1980s, the general impression was that the schools had not improved very much, if at all. This view was based on the fact that SAT I scores had not increased substantially, that college professors were still complaining that students were not ready for postsecondary education, and that employers were asserting that high school graduates were unprepared for the workplace.

The American public is edgy and impatient with the schools and wants results, asserted Richard Riley (1993), the U.S. Secretary of Education, in a speech to the nation's governors. The country will be out of business if public education does not reinvent itself—and fast, according to Louis Gerstner, Jr. (1994), CEO of IBM. Gerstner went on to assert that just as American business had had to change to become competitive, so would American schools. However, he found chilling the combination of public apathy and bureaucratic obstructionism that stood in the way of the needed changes.

Since the late 1970s, public education has in fact undergone reform, and evidence in the early 1990s (Office of Educational Research, 1994) showed that more students were taking more difficult courses. Moreover, even though greater demands were being placed on students, the dropout rate had not increased. But there was also clear evidence from research studies that grade inflation had occurred and that a grade of C had crept up to a grade of B. It seemed that teachers and students, under pressure to improve and lacking objective measures of progress, had simply allowed grades to rise to show improvement.

Ironically, the school reform movement of the late 1970s and the 1980s, which created this pressure to improve, also helped to confuse the situation further because many states instituted or expanded testing systems without linking the tests to the curriculum. By 1994, 45 states had instituted or expanded testing programs for elementary and secondary education, but only a few had *any* type of mandated curriculum that would tell teachers and students ahead of time what they were going to be tested on and held accountable for.

In other words, there was no "truth in teaching or learning" in many schools. Teachers and students could only guess, sometimes with limited guidance, what they were supposed to know to be deemed successful. The reason for this lack of connection between the test and the curriculum was that accountability had been moved to the state level but the decisions on what ought to be taught had been left at the local level. The politicians—governors and state legislators—had responded to public displeasure with the public schools by instituting new tests in an effort to get better results from the schools. But few policymakers had moved to define first what results were to be expected from these tests: The academic standards had not been openly debated, defined, and disseminated.

The reason for this "disconnect" lies in our nation's history. The U.S. Constitution embodies the idea that government should be limited in its powers and that the closer the government is to the people, the better it will function. In education, this has meant that although states have authority over the schools, the power to determine the content of education has usually been delegated to local school boards. And because there are 14,000 or so school districts in the country, there is great variation in the education being offered to students.

In 1989, the National Academy of Sciences undertook a searching review of mathematics in the public schools because American students consistently rank below students in many other industrialized countries on international tests. Its report described the way the mathematics curriculum is typically fashioned in local school districts. It concluded:

> In the United States, with our traditional and legal decentralization of education, we go about things very differently [than in other countries]. Every summer, thousands of teachers work in small teams for periods ranging from one week to two months, charged by their school districts to write new mathematics curricula. These teacher teams usually have little training in the complicated process of curricular development, little or no help in coping with changing needs, and little to fall back on except existing textbooks, familiar programs, and tradition. The consequence usually is the unquestioned acceptance of what already exists as the main body of the new curriculum, together with a little tinkering around the edges. Many school districts simply adopt series of textbooks as *the* curriculum, making no effort to engage the staff in rethinking curricula; in those places, the *status quo* certainly reigns.
>
> The American process of curricular reform might be described as a weak form of grass-roots approach. The record shows that this system does not work. It is not our teachers who are at fault. In fact, teachers *should* play a dominant role in curricular decision-making. But teachers who work in summer curricular projects are being given an unrealistic task in an impossible time frame, with only the familiar *status quo* to guide them.
>
> In static times, in periods of unchanging demands, perhaps our grass-roots efforts would suffice to keep the curriculum current. In today's climate, in which technology and research are causing unprecedented change in the

central methods and applications of mathematics, present U.S. practice is totally inadequate. (pp. 77-78)

In other words, the decisions about curriculum that are made locally would seem to respect the country's tradition of local control whenever possible, but as the National Academy of Sciences suggested, this system may have outlived its usefulness in a rapidly changing world. And as already noted, the problem has become further complicated in that states have testing programs in mathematics and other subjects that do not match what teachers in local school districts teach. When the results of these state assessments come out later, the public believes that the students have not learned the material and that the schools have failed.

This does not have to be the way that education is provided. "We have a history of not training students in the material they will be tested on. Other countries don't hide the test from students," according to the New Standards Project (1994), which issued a report on the reasons that students in other countries do better in mathematics than American children. "That doesn't mean particular questions or answers of any one test are revealed to students. It means that teachers are able to gear what and how they teach towards the kind of questions that will appear on examinations" (pp. 1-2). In other words, students and teachers in other countries are told what they are expected to know and be able to do, and then they are held accountable for mastering that knowledge.

This kind of clarity in teaching and learning is a far cry from "the confusion that reigns in most [American] schools today where tests are generated by one vendor, textbooks by another and teachers are trained by people who don't know much about specific curriculums," according to Marshall Smith, then Undersecretary in the U.S. Department of Education, and Ramon Cortines, the former chancellor of the New York City school system (Smith & Cortines, 1993, p. A15). Again, this system of conflicting signals is about to change, and none too soon to help teachers and students do better than they are doing now.

The American public supports change in education when that change will make teaching and learning clearer in U.S. schools. Phi Delta Kappa-Gallup polls since 1989 have found an overwhelming majority of citizens in favor of a basic curriculum of subject matter for all schools—or what has been called in some of the surveys a "national curriculum" (Elam, 1995). Some 69% favored a standardized national curriculum in the local public schools in 1989

(Elam, 1995), and by 1994 this percentage had increased to 83% ("Phi Delta Kappa-Gallup Poll," 1994). But the desired change in education can be achieved without a national curriculum if states move to institute high standards for their schools—and do so openly so that students can master the material, instead of demanding accountability through tests whose content is not made known. Nonetheless, the poll results are interesting in that they show that the public is ready to go further than is absolutely necessary to bring about improvements in American education.

The process of openly instituting standards and making them high enough so that students learn much more is already under way. During the late 1980s, a movement began with the stated purpose of helping teachers know what they are to teach and helping students know what they are expected to learn. Learning and accountability are starting to be linked so that all the rules will be known ahead of time and students will be able to work toward achievable objectives *and* know much more.

This major change is generally labeled "standards-based" reform. It means that agreement will be achieved first on what students are to know and to be able to do—the standards. Then progress through school and graduation from high school will be determined according to mastery of this content. Teachers will know ahead of time what they are to teach, and students will know what will be expected of them.

The reforms of the late 1970s and 1980s led to this change because leaders began to recognize that the reforms made in that period too often focused on such things as instituting new testing programs without paying attention to the curriculum—or increasing course requirements without considering the quality of the education being offered. As the Consortium for Policy Research in Education concluded:

> Although students took classes with challenging titles as a result of the reforms, the titles did not ensure quality academic content. The increased number of tests only reinforced the poor skills and rote instruction that motivated the reform in the first place. Lessons learned from this experience led federal and state governments, as well as professional associations, to define content standards and expected student outcomes. (quoted in "Shortfalls," 1994, p. 6)

This movement toward reform based on defining high standards for education began among mathematics teachers and in some states that had strong educational leadership. In response to the report of the National

Academy of Sciences quoted above and to other such studies, the National Council of Teachers of Mathematics (NCTM) pursued an effort in the late 1980s to develop standards for mathematics. Those standards were issued by the NCTM in 1992. Meanwhile, Bill Honig, the state superintendent of schools in California, had already begun to develop curricular frameworks for the basic subjects in the early 1980s. Other teachers' associations and other states were encouraged by these experiences and initiated their own work on developing standards and frameworks.

The general public, the teacher associations, and some states were ahead of the country's leaders on this issue. But national politicians soon caught up. In 1989, President Bush and the nation's governors agreed on the idea of establishing national goals for education, the first ever to be adopted. This movement, which evolved into broad agreement on the need for voluntary national standards for education in order to pursue the goals, will be described in more detail in the next chapter.

One important development in this evolution from goals to standards was the appointment by the Bush administration and the Congress of a bipartisan advisory body to review the issue. The National Council on Education Standards and Testing (1992), whose membership was representative of a wide cross section of political views, issued its report calling for such standards in 1992. The report's depiction of American schools is important for understanding the motivation for this reform, so it too will be described in greater detail in the next chapter. But one summary quotation from the council's report would be helpful at this point:

> In the absence of well-defined and demanding standards, education in the United States has gravitated toward *de facto* national minimum expectations. Except for students who are planning to attend selective four-year colleges, current education standards focus on low-level reading and arithmetic skills and on small amounts of factual material in other content areas. Consumers of education in this country have settled for far less than they should and for far less than do their counterparts in other developed countries. (pp. 2-3)

That is the major reason that national and state leaders have coalesced around the need for defining content and student performance standards: The quality of American education must be improved, and the current system of relying on local decision making over curriculum is failing to bring about that improvement. Standards must be established to make clear what students ought to know, and those standards must be challenging if American students are to improve their educational achievement. As a result of this broad agreement, President Clinton, building on the work started by former President Bush, signed into law in 1994 the Goals 2000: Educate America Act, which placed the national goals into law, supported the certification of voluntary national education standards and national skill standards, and encouraged the states through grant aid to develop their own standards for education.

Even before the enactment of Goals 2000, however, the states were moving independently to develop their own agreements on what should be taught and learned, and they used the federal aid to accelerate this work. As of May 1994 (a month after Goals 2000 became law and before any funds were released), 42 states had already developed or were developing content standards, and 30 were developing or had already adopted student performance standards to measure mastery of content. By January 1995, 42 states had received Goals 2000 funding to help them in these efforts. By 1997, after the Goals program survived efforts in Congress to repeal it, all 50 states were participating either directly or through school districts.

With the federal government and many states moving in tandem, the effects of standards-based reform are already appearing in thousands of classrooms around the country, especially in the teaching of mathematics. By the end of the century, American education may be quite different from what it has been. Teachers will know what they are to teach, and students will know what is expected of them—and much more will be expected. But students, teachers, and the general public must understand why these changes are coming about because there is often a reluctance to change and a nostalgia for the "good old days."

The whole idea of having national goals for education is to focus the efforts of the country on improving the schools. Raising education standards is a major route to that improvement, and that is what many states, school districts, and the federal government have been trying to do since the late 1980s. Disputes along the way, including the debates over whether there ought to be national standards and tests, must not distract us from seeing the importance of this major, broad change in American education. The country is moving to a new way of schooling that will not only lead to a better education for children but also be fairer to both teachers and students in that they will now know what is expected of them: higher student achievement. The country is moving in the direction of truth in teaching and learning based on higher standards for students.

2

Origins of National Standards and Tests

How President Bush, Corporate Leaders, and Governors First Advanced the Idea of Raising Standards

Impatience With the Pace of Reform

In the early 1980s, President Ronald Reagan advocated sharply cutting back on any national assistance for education because he was a strong proponent of local control of government. By contrast, 10 years later, President George Bush (1991b), who had been Reagan's vice president, called for a "national crusade" (p. 648) to transform the country's educational system. The central elements in Bush's crusade would be national goals, national standards, and a national test to measure progress toward achieving those standards. These goals, standards, and tests were to be the first ever adopted for the United States.

What caused within the span of a decade such a sharp reversal in opinion between one conservative Republican president and another in their concepts of the national role in education? In advocating national goals, standards, and tests, Bush was clearly calling for a departure from the country's tradition of local control of schooling. Further, Bush's administration foresaw this new federal role as limited but also as one that would "be played vigorously" (U.S. Department of Education, 1991, p. 2). The U.S. Department of Education (1991) pictured the national role this way: "Washington can help by setting standards, highlighting examples, contributing some funds, providing some flexibility in exchange for accountability, and pushing and prodding—then

9

pushing and prodding some more" (p. 2). This was, needless to say, quite a departure from Reagan's views.

In essence, what brought about this change in perspective was an impatience with the school reforms of the 1980s. Bush (1991b) viewed them as "much too slow and too timid" (p. 648). Almost all the country's education trend lines were flat even after the states' reforms of the 1980s, according to the Bush administration, and the nation was spending far more on education without getting the results it should. Moreover, the rest of the world was not idly sitting by, waiting for America to catch up (U.S. Department of Education, 1991, p. 5).

By the end of the 1980s, 42 states had indeed raised their high school graduation requirements, according to the Educational Testing Service (1994). Over the decade, there were steady gains in the proportions of students taking what is called a "minimum academic program" (4 years of English and 3 years of social studies, science, and math). Only 13% of high school graduates had taken these courses in 1982, but by 1990, 40% of graduates had attained that level of education. At the same time, enrollments in remedial mathematics and elective vocational education courses had decreased.

On the basis of those numbers, it would seem that the nation was on the right track to educational improvement if one believed that students should be taking more academically demanding courses. However, even those statistics showing good progress in the 1980s made clear that 60% of American high school graduates in 1990 were still not taking a minimum academic program—and that was putting aside the questions of what happened to high school dropouts and whether some schools were retitling courses from "remedial" to "regular" course work, thereby showing greater improvement than may really have existed.

In addition to mandating that students take more academic classes, states had expanded testing to determine whether to promote students, had lengthened school days and years, had raised teacher salaries, had toughened teacher certification and entry requirements, and had more closely monitored school performance, according to the Consortium for Policy Research in Education (1994). Yet the sentiment as expressed by President Bush and others was that all these reforms were too timid and that progress was too little.

The nation's governors were in agreement with Bush that changes were not coming about fast enough, so they had begun in the early 1990s to seek wider, more systematic reform in the country's schools. In 1991, the National Governors' Association asserted:

We need many more examples of innovation and reform to serve as models for educators. But systemwide change is essential. Our challenge as Governors is to restructure the entire system to substantially raise the performance of *all* children and *all* schools in order to achieve the national education goals. (p. v)

In other words, the governors in their own states had tried to create change in the 1980s through enactment of many laws mandating more stringent high school graduation requirements and raising requirements for teacher qualification, and yet they had not attained the improvements they desired. Corroboration for the belief that progress was halting came from a study by the Educational Research Service (cited in Hoff, 1994), the most comprehensive study undertaken in decades of American secondary schools. It found that most of the nation's high schools as of 1993 had yet to install comprehensive reform plans and that the efforts undertaken were spotty, with few schools attempting to change systematically. "There's a lot of activity going on, but there have been very few high schools that have been able to put it all together," according to Gordon Cawelti, the study's director (quoted in Hoff, 1994, p. 1).

The business community voiced the same impatience as did the governors and President Bush over the pace of school improvement. Although some businesses during the 1980s had "adopted" schools and contributed time and resources to improving education in their communities, business leaders were becoming frustrated over the arguments about the effectiveness of reducing class size and about spending more money on the schools. Consequently, the U.S. Chamber of Commerce, the National Alliance of Business, the Business Roundtable, and other national groups pressed more and more for a results-oriented system and not one based on specifying all the requirements for a good education. In short, they advocated an "output" system and not one based on "inputs."

Another concern of many critics was that the schools lacked a way to motivate students to learn. In the past, colleges and universities had, in effect, set standards for high schools through their admission requirements. Donald Stewart, president of the College Board, noted that before the 1950s, colleges "exercised considerable influence over the standards of the secondary curriculum and indeed over the entire admission process" but that in the period between the 1950s and the 1990s, many more institutions of higher education were founded, and competition became more fierce among those schools to ensure adequate enrollments to fill their classrooms (College Entrance Examination Board, 1994, pp. 4-5). Today, with "open enrollment" policies and declining numbers of college-age students, it is not difficult for most high school graduates, and even for many dropouts from high school, to find a seat in a community college, state college or university, trade school, or private institution. This means that colleges and universities no longer have the influence that they once did to demand high standards from high schools, at least for those students who are college bound.

If most students can get into some kind of institution of higher education, then what is the motivation for those students to study hard in high school? Of course, those few students who want to get into selective 4-year colleges and universities will study to meet their requirements, but for the vast majority of students, there seems to be little motivation. Albert Shanker, the late president of the American Federation of Teachers, argued this point for years: American education is not fashioned in such a way as to motivate students, and this must be changed if the United States is to compete with other countries (Sontag, 1992). Stephen Heyneman (1990) of the World Bank made the same point: The lack of student motivation was the principal cause of ineffective schools and low-quality education in the United States. In contrast, developing countries, despite having far fewer resources, had highly motivated students and therefore a better return on the investment in education.

To summarize, by the early 1990s, all the reforms of the previous decade had not achieved substantial, measurable improvement in American elementary and secondary education, according to President Bush, the governors, many business leaders, and other critics. There were individual schools doing better. There were statistics showing more students taking more difficult courses. There was a continuing interest in trying to do better. But there was also something lacking, something missing at the core. It seemed that there had to be a stronger push for excellence, that change had to be undertaken in a more systematic and sustained way, and that there had to be goals or benchmarks against which to measure progress.

▨ National Goals for Education

In 1989, a few months after assuming office, President Bush convened the nation's governors to discuss education. This was only the third time in the history of the United States that a president had gathered the governors together for a substantive meeting, and it was part of Bush's effort to carry through on his 1988 campaign promise to be an "education president." That convocation, fueled by Bush's and the governors' impatience with change, led to agreement that the country should have national goals for education.

Those goals, which included preparing every child for school and seeking a 90% graduation rate from high school, were agreed on and adopted the next year by the president and the governors (including Bill Clinton, then governor of Arkansas). The act of establishing these goals was in itself very significant: For the first time, the nation had some agreement on what it wanted to achieve in education and could therefore measure its progress toward those ends.

The nation's governors, who are usually very jealous of protecting the rights of the states and suspicious of many federal actions, put those concerns aside as they became proponents of these national goals. The states could not improve education solely on their own, they said by their actions, so they were prepared to embark on a course that could lead to education operating differently than it had operated in the past. Even with some of the reservations that many of the governors must have had about opening this discussion at the national level, their willingness to do so marked a major departure from the extremely localized attitude that the United States had traditionally had about education. The adoption of the national goals by President Bush and the governors in 1990 was a new beginning.

▓ Bush's First Legislation

Before adoption of the national goals, Bush had sent Congress (then dominated by the Democrats) a bill (H.R. 1675, 1989; S. 695, 1989) to assist in school reform, but that legislation was very modest in proposing a few small programs, such as rewards for schools that raised their achievement and the funding of alternative systems for certifying teachers. None of these ideas were very different from other proposals considered before the national goals were adopted.

This legislative bill from the president did not contain any reference to national standards or a national test because it was sent to Congress before the adoption of the national goals. In addition, it took longer than a few months after adoption of the goals for Bush and the governors to evolve in their thinking to seeing the need for national standards and assessments. Also of note was the absence of any program encouraging vouchers to pay for tuition at private schools or for programs to allow parents to choose private schools over public schools. Those ideas had been favorites of some conservatives in

Goal 1: Ready to learn. By the year 2000, all children in America will start school ready to learn.

Goal 2: School Completion. By the year 2000, the high school graduation rate will increase to at least 90 percent.

Goal 3: Student Achievement and Citizenship. By the year 2000, all students will leave grades 4, 8, and 12 having demonstrated competency over challenging subject matter including English, mathematics, science, foreign languages, civics and government, economics, arts, history, and geography, and every school in America will ensure that all students learn to use their minds well, so they may be prepared for responsible citizenship, further learning, and productive employment in our Nation's modern economy

Goal 4: Teacher Education and Professional Development. By the year 2000, the Nation's teaching force will have access to programs for the continued improvement of their professional skills and the opportunity to acquire the knowledge and skills needed to instruct and prepare all American students in the next century.

Goal 5: Mathematics and Science. By the year 2000, United States students will be first in the world in mathematics and science achievement.

Goal 6: Adult Literacy and Lifelong Learning. By the year 2000, every adult American will be literate and will possess the knowledge and skills necessary to compete in a global economy and exercise the rights and responsibilities of citizenship.

Goal 7: Safe, Disciplined, and Alcohol- and Drug-free Schools. By the year 2000, every school in the United States will be free of drugs, violence, and the unauthorized presence of firearms and alcohol and will offer a disciplined environment conducive to learning.

Goal 8: Parental Participation. By the year 2000, every school will promote partnerships that will increase parental involvement and participation in promoting the social, emotional, and academic growth of children.

Figure 2.1. The National Education Goals

SOURCE: The National Education Goals Panel (1255 22nd Street, NW, Suite 502, Washington, DC 20037). NOTE: The six original National Education Goals were created at the first Education summit held in Charlottesville, Virginia, in September 1989. There the President and the nation's Governors agreed that establishing National Education Goals would capture the attention of Americans in order to better our schools and increase our expectations for student performance. In July 1990, the National Education Goals Panel was created to monitor education progress and report to the American public. On July 1, 1994, Congress added Goals 4 and 8.

the past, but they were missing from Bush's first education proposals—a noteworthy omission because the inclusion of aid to private schools was to play an important part in Bush's second set of reform proposals, as were standards and tests.

When Congress considered Bush's reform legislation, several congress-people and senators expressed discontent that the goals had been adopted without broad consultation with the public and with teachers—or with Congress, for that matter. The other major criticism, especially from Democrats, was that Bush's programs were too modest in concept and in resources, involving around $700 million, and that such small programs would not be of much assistance to the states and school districts in achieving the national goals.

The Democratically controlled Congress, therefore, broadened the scope of the legislation to include additional programs costing several hundreds of millions of dollars more, especially aid for teachers to be retrained (H.R. 5115, 1990). The national goals were also included in the legislative bill with statements that the federal government ought to fund more fully some of its programs, such as Head Start, if it was to provide real assistance to the schools in achieving the goals.

This legislation passed both the House of Representatives and the Senate, although in different forms. A conference committee composed of representatives and senators reconciled the differences between the two bills and sent this agreement back to be repassed by the House and the Senate before it could be presented to the president for his signature. With Bush's support, that final bill passed the House, but then it ran into trouble in the Senate. Several conservative Republican senators opposed the new programs added by the Democrats to aid in implementing the national goals because they thought that this was an undue expansion of the federal role in education, so despite Bush's endorsement, they began a filibuster. Because Congress was in the last days of the session of 1990, that opposition killed the conference report, so no bill was sent to the president.

Bush's first school reform legislation showed the tensions that would result from the country's dealing for the first time with the idea of trying to improve education through the use of goals and through the exercise of more vigorous national leadership. During the 1960s, President Lyndon Johnson had led the country in initiating several major national programs to improve educational opportunities, but due to the context of the times, most of these programs were aimed at assisting the less advantaged—children who were poor or disabled, could speak little English, or had migratory farmworker parents. Therefore, during the 1960s and 1970s and through the 1980s, most of the federal programs aiding elementary and secondary education had an equity purpose and were not aimed at most children.

What Bush, the governors, and the business community were concerned about was improving education for *all* children, not just the 25% or so who were at some risk of not succeeding due to family circumstances. This was a much broader purpose than the one the federal government had been focused on since the mid-1960s.

In addition, most of the federal programs had aimed to provide some additional services for disadvantaged children, following the theory that such extra aid would help them to make up for the deficiencies in their family backgrounds or individual circumstances. The new, broader national role in improving education did not seem to fit that mode, but no one knew what it should be: Should it be to provide some incremental aid to the states based on their raising their test scores, should it focus on teacher retraining, or should it encourage the creation of different schools? The uncertainty over the broader purpose and the lack of understanding of how to accomplish that purpose were real obstacles to involving the national government in assisting the states and local school districts to achieve the new national goals.

Another complicating factor was that the federal government did not have much additional money to spend. When President Reagan assumed office in 1981, the national debt was about $900 billion, but when President Bush took the oath of office 8 years later, that debt had mushroomed to nearly $3 trillion due to the tax reductions enacted during Reagan's administration as well as to the increased spending for military activities he had achieved and the failure to rein in spending on other purposes. Consequently, in the early 1990s, the national government did not have much money to place behind any efforts to help to attain the new national goals for education.

A final factor that started to become apparent during the consideration of Bush's first school reform legislation in 1990 was that very conservative individuals, commonly known in political terms as the "far right," were not comfortable with any expansion of the federal government's role in education. President Bush called himself a conservative, as did most of the national business leaders and many of the governors who called for the national goals in education. But this advocacy by conservatives of a new national attitude toward improving education did not allay the fears of the far right that any expansion of the federal government's role in education was perilous to the citizenry. Therefore, several very conservative senators who had been out-voted on Bush's bill earlier in the congressional session took advantage of the time pressures at the end of the congressional year and killed Bush's legislation through a filibuster.

Those three factors—the undefined nature of the new national role in raising standards, the lack of substantial federal funding to back up the national goals, and the opposition of the far right—were to recur at each stage of the fashioning of this new approach to improving the schools. Other factors would also appear, but those were the most obvious as Bush's first legislation initiated the opening of the debate.

As states and school districts now go about the work of writing their own higher standards for students, they are facing these same three factors. At what level should curriculum decisions be made: by the state, by the school district, or by the school? Will funding be provided to refashion curricular materials and retrain teachers? And how adamant will groups such as the far right be in opposing these changes in public schools? Thus, the debate about raising standards that occurred at the national level in the early and mid-1990s is continuing with the same issues at the state and local levels in the later 1990s.

▨ America 2000

Lauro Cavazos had been the secretary of education at the end of President Reagan's second term in office, and President Bush kept him on for almost the first 2 full years of his administration. In late 1990, however, Bush decided that he needed a more aggressive secretary, probably due to the defeat of his new program, so he fired Cavazos and appointed Lamar Alexander. As governor of Tennessee, Alexander had helped to enact a major school reform initiative in that state as one of the governors who responded to Reagan's urging in 1983 that the states, not the federal government, improve education. In accepting the appointment as U.S. secretary of education in 1991, Alexander was implicitly acknowledging that the federal government also had a role to play in reforming education, mimicking Bush's own change of position.

Alexander threw himself into his job, leading the *Washington Post* to comment: "If the Education Department seemed to move in slow motion under Lauro F. Cavazos, the maligned agency has shifted into fast forward since Lamar Alexander succeeded him as education secretary three weeks ago" (Cooper, 1991, p. A4). A major reason that Alexander was able to move so fast once he assumed office was that he had begun to draft a school reform plan for Bush as soon as the president asked him to accept the appointment, which was late in 1990.

Alexander worked with Chester Finn, a professor at Vanderbilt University, and with several other education experts. While they were writing their plan, two reports were issued by conservative groups advocating the initiation of national testing for schoolchildren. Lamar Alexander, who was then president of the University of Tennessee, served on the first of these panels, and Chester Finn served on the second.

The first group, a presidential advisory committee composed of business people and educators, recommended to Bush on January 16, 1991, the creation for the first time of national examinations of elementary and secondary education students (De Witt, 1991). Paul O'Neill, chief executive officer of the Aluminum Company of America (ALCOA) and chair of the group, asserted that teachers should teach to standards and that having national tests would be the only way to reach the national goals.

Two weeks later, an education group chaired by the former Republican governor of New Jersey, Thomas Kean, proposed that all high school seniors be required to take a national examination of their knowledge and skills. One approach that was discussed was for the federal government to mandate such a test and to pay the costs of its administration. Finn, as a member of the panel, told the press that a national test would "sort of" lead to a uniform curriculum but that one created partly by textbook publishers already existed. He further asserted, "We ought to acknowledge that we have a national curriculum that is doing us no good at all" (quoted in Cooper, 1991, p. A4).

Finn's remarks echo the description offered by the National Academy of Sciences of the setting of mathematics curricula by local teachers (see Chapter 1 of this book): There is an appearance of local control, but the reality is that, due to restraints of time and expertise, teachers often choose to use materials prepared by national textbook publishers and curriculum development companies. Furthermore, there is a tendency to uniformity in the use of these materials and books because two states, California and Texas, that represent about 20% of the population have had for years state practices for adoption or certification of textbooks. This means that the publishers have tried to satisfy those two states and then sold those same books to school districts in most of the other states that did not have state adoption or certification of textbooks.

In drafting their plan for the president, Alexander, Finn, and others drew on their experiences on those two advisory panels and began their new work by starting from the premise that the United States "must construct an entirely new and radically different education system over time" (Alexander, 1993, p. 7). Alexander (1993) believed that "developing world-class standards of achievement in core subject areas, and encouraging voluntary national examinations to determine progress in reaching these standards, will be essential to reaching the National Goals for Education" (p. 6). A plan based on these beliefs was presented to the president, and he accepted it.

On April 18, 1991, President Bush (1991a) announced his new education plan at the White House. He stated his belief that the time had come to establish world-class standards for what children should know and be able to do in five core subjects: English, mathematics, science, history, and geography. A system of voluntary examinations would also be developed for all fourth-, eighth-, and 12th-grade students in these five core subjects. The issue of report cards showing the academic performance of all schools, school districts, and states would be encouraged (Office of the Press Secretary, 1991). These elements of national standards and examinations were the fundamental building blocks for the Bush-Alexander plan to "construct an entirely new and radically different education system over time" (Alexander, 1993, p. 7).

In addition to national standards and assessments, 535 "new American schools" would be funded to "break the mold" of existing school designs, and business would be asked to contribute to a new, nonprofit corporation that would fund other innovative schools. Bush's plan also sought more flexibility in the use of federal education funds, promotion of parental choice of schools through incentive funds to local school districts, improvement of the training of teachers and principals, and encouragement of alternative routes to certification of teachers. New funds would be requested to assist industry to develop national job skill standards, and various other initiatives would be undertaken (Office of the Press Secretary, 1991, pp. 3-9).

Bush and Alexander sought to deflect criticism, especially from conservatives, that their plan advocated an expansion of national influence over education through statements they made asserting that America 2000 was "a national strategy, not a federal program" (U.S. Department of Education, 1991, p. 2). Repeatedly, they stated that this plan "honors local control, relies on local initiative, affirms states and localities as the senior partners in paying for education and the private sector as a vital partner, too" (p. 2). The federal government's role was to help by setting standards, providing some funds and flexibility, and "pushing and prodding—then pushing and prodding some more" (p. 3).

The initial reaction to America 2000 was mostly favorable. Albert Shanker, then president of the American Federation of Teachers, called it "a turning point in American education" (quoted in Jennings, 1992, p. 304). A month later, when the administration submitted its legislation to Congress, the bill was introduced in the House (H.R. 2460, 1991) by the Republican leadership and in the Senate (S. 1141, 1991) by two Democrats, Edward Kennedy and Claiborne Pell, who chaired the full committee and subcommittee with jurisdiction over education in the Senate. Thus, the bill had bipartisan cosponsorship, although Kennedy did, on introducing the bill, express some concern over the proposals to subsidize parental choice of private schools, create national testing, and fund 535 experimental schools. Kennedy also said that he wanted to add his own ideas to Bush's before moving the legislation (Yang, 1991).

Kennedy's comments show a conditional endorsement of Bush's ideas, and the Bush administration in turn was wary of the Democratically controlled Congress dealing with the development of national standards and of national examinations. Although America 2000 endorsed the development of national standards and tests, the legislation that was submitted by Bush to Congress did not ask for legal authority to create such standards and assessments. The bill that Kennedy and Pell cosponsored authorized only 18 relatively modest new federal programs, such as the new "break the mold" schools and the training programs for teachers and principals.

Instead of asking for the enactment of a law for standards and assessments, the Bush administration took the back-door route of merely notifying the congressional appropriations committees that it was going to fund the development of those standards and tests with monies it already had requested (letter from Lamar Alexander to Cong. William Natcher, April 23, 1991).[1] This tactic was a clever way to avoid the problems of congressional debate over these issues and the delay that would accompany those considerations, but it did show a distrust of Congress that was to later plague the passage of the America 2000 legislation as it worked its way through the congressional process.

▓ National Council on Education Standards and Testing

Bipartisanship on the issue of school reform, with some wariness on the part of both the Democratic Congress and the Republican administration, prevailed for some time once America 2000 was announced and the legislation introduced. But it was a bipartisanship that had to be worked at because the American system of government is based on the idea of competition between the two political parties and thus tends to push the debate toward showing the differences and not the agreements between the politicians.

In May, Secretary Alexander drafted a plan to appoint a council to advise the administration about how to carry out the development of the national education standards and examinations, and he expected to get this council up and running without any input from Congress. But Congressman Dale Kildee, the Democratic chair of the Subcommittee on Elementary and Secondary Education in the U.S. House of Representatives, contacted Alexander and suggested authorizing this council by statute so that it would have more legitimacy in performing its duties. Alexander agreed, so a bill to create that council was introduced by Kildee in May (H.R. 2435, 1991), quickly passed by both the House and the Senate, and signed into law by the president 5 weeks later (National Council on Education Standards and Testing Act, 1991). This unusually fast pace for the legislation was possible because the Republican administration and the Democratic and Republican leadership in Congress were trying to keep education a bipartisan issue.

The work of the council, once it was appointed and functioning, also showed that such bipartisan cooperation was possible. By the time the bill formally creating the council was introduced, Alexander had already appointed the overwhelming majority of the members of the group; his appointments included a broad array of several dozen individuals, Democrats as well as Republicans, liberals as well as conservatives. The cochairs were Carroll Campbell, the Republican governor from South Carolina, and Roy Romer, the Democratic governor of Colorado. The bill, which passed Congress and which Bush signed into law, gave Congress some additional appointments to the council to be made by the Democrats and the Republicans. Thus, in the end, the council was ensured balanced representation in terms of partisanship and ideology.

The legislation included an important change from Alexander's original plan. The council had to review the desirability of such standards and assessments for the country instead of simply advising on the mechanics of establishing specific national standards and a national test. Congress signaled in this bill that it wanted an open debate on the appropriateness of such concepts and not just a drafting of a plan to implement such standards and tests.

The council was very diligent in its work, beginning its hearings as soon as it was appointed and concluding its task and issuing its report 7 months later. The credibility of the council was high because it was brought into existence jointly by the administration and Congress, because its membership was diverse, and because it reached out to many different points of view in its hearings and through the work of its task forces. The council's conclusions, therefore, carried more weight than did the recommendations made early in 1991 by the two groups referred to above: the presidential advisory committee appointed by Bush and the task force headed by former governor Kean, both of which had recommended a national test.

The chief recommendation of the National Council on Education Standards and Testing was expressed in its final report of January 24, 1992. Although that statement in part has already been quoted in the preceding chapter, it is important enough to repeat. It asserted:

> In the course of its research and discussions, the Council concluded that high national standards tied to assessments are desirable. In the absence of well-defined and demanding standards, education in the United States has gravitated toward *de facto* national minimum expectations. (p. 2)

In those two sentences, the council crystallized the concerns of the governors, the business community, various education experts, Secretary Alexander, and President Bush and pointed the way to how school reform would be encouraged from the national and state levels. Further, that report gave legitimacy to the Bush reform plan, America 2000, and helped to solidify support for its core recommendation for national standards.

The council's report also pointed out that the country's debate over improving education was going in a new direction. There was occurring "a fundamental shift of perspective among educators, policymakers, and the public from examining inputs and elements of the educational process to examining outcomes and results" (National Council, 1992, p. 8). The council commented that it had changed its perception on a key issue: It had initially discussed standards and assessments as a way to help measure progress toward the national education goals, but now it had come to see the movement toward high standards as a means to help achieve the goals. In other words, the development and use of education standards was a way to bring reform to the schools, not merely a means of measuring progress.

The council gave three major reasons for the necessity of this monumental change in American education. National standards were necessary, according to the council, to ensure educational opportunity for all Americans, especially those not now doing well in school because they are held to low expectations.

Second, standards were needed to enhance the civic culture, especially because the population was growing increasingly diverse. And third, raising standards would enhance America's economic competitiveness through improving the quality of human capital. The council emphasized that its conception of standards was that they would contain high expectations and not minimal competencies, that they would provide focus and not a curriculum, that they would be national and not federal, that they would be voluntary and not mandatory, and that they would be dynamic and not static.

In issuing the report, the cochairs, Governors Campbell and Romer, referred to the inadequate way in which progress is measured in American education: Tests assess the comparative performance of students but do not let students know the curriculum ahead of time so that they can study it and be told how much they have achieved. In other words, the way the system is operated now, there is no truth in teaching or learning. The governors said:

> We presently evaluate student and system performance largely through measures that tell us how many students are above or below average, or that compare relative performance among schools, districts, or states. Most measurements cannot tell us whether students are actually acquiring the skills and knowledge they will need to prosper in the future. They cannot tell us how good is "good enough." (National Council, 1992, p. i)

In the view of the council, the country had to define "good enough" by developing standards; then the assessments would follow to measure how far students had advanced in learning this knowledge. If the country was to raise the quality of educational achievement, the system of tests that merely measured comparative progress of students had to be changed to one in which the content of knowledge was specified first and then student progress was measured against how much of that knowledge had been acquired. As simple as that may sound and as commonsensical as it may appear, that one recommendation called for radical change in American education.

The council did depart from the Bush administration in recommending a system of assessment and not the single national test advocated by the president and Secretary Alexander in their America 2000 program. The principal reason for this change was that the council came to believe that a single test would lead to a national curriculum because the subject matter of the test would have to be defined ahead of time and this would comprise the elements of a curriculum. Therefore, it was recommended instead that a system of assessments be developed so that states could adopt different curricula. The governors made explicit this point in releasing the report: The council was not proposing a national curriculum; rather, they wanted to set in motion mechanisms that would "result in *local* commitment to high *national* expectations for achievement for all students" (National Council, 1992, p. ii).

Those statements made clear that the council was very sensitive to the issue of federal control, and its other recommendations confirmed this. For instance, the report suggested that a national, not a federal, coordinating structure be put in place to advance standards setting and assessment development. This structure would include a politically balanced National Education Goals Panel that would have heavy representation from the states as well as the legislative and executive branches of the federal government. Under the Goals Panel, there would be a council to perform the work of coordinating the standards and assessments tasks, and its membership would be composed of educators, public officials, and the general public. The issue of the powers of this council would prove to be controversial later in the consideration of the Bush and Clinton legislative proposals in this area.

Another issue of great controversy would be whether there ought to be standards to determine whether schools were providing the appropriate educational opportunities for students to learn the content standards. During the deliberations of the council, intense debate occurred on this issue, and after much struggle, the council recommended that school delivery standards be developed by the states and not at the national level, unlike the development of the national content standards and the assessments. Everyone said they agreed that "all children must have the opportunity to learn the material that new standards will indicate they should know" (National Council, 1992, p. 38), but the argument was over whether these school standards ought to be on the same national plane as the content standards. On the council, there was a close division of opinion, but finally the Bush administration representatives weighed in forcefully on Governor Campbell's side of the argument, which was that this was not a matter for the national level and should be left to the states. That decision of the council was not the final one on this issue, and votes were to occur in Congress for the following 3 years on whether there ought to be national standards to ensure that all children had the opportunity to learn the new national content standards.

The National Council on Education Standards and Testing performed a notable service to the country in defining the new approach to improving the schools that was called for by implication when the national goals for education were adopted. The council's hopes for reform based on the development of national standards and of a national system of tests were to prove too optimistic, however. Many of the national standards that were later developed were too complicated and too ambitious for easy adaptation by the states and local school districts. The national system of tests was contingent on the national standards, so it too proved easier to discuss than to implement. But the council's discussion of raising standards in the schools and its efforts to achieve a bipartisan and ideological consensus agreement on the issue were very helpful in stimulating the states and school districts to change their curriculums, assessments, and teacher training. It is sufficient at this point to note that the main objectives of the council were not directly achieved as they were contemplated but that they were achieved in effect because the country accelerated its efforts to raise standards in the public schools.

▦ Congressional Action

While the National Council on Education Standards and Testing in 1991 was holding its hearings on those issues and writing its report, action began in Congress on the administration's legislative package incorporating the other elements of America 2000. The Senate proved to be cooperative with the Bush administration, and the House of Representatives combative—establishing a pattern that was to appear again when President Clinton in 1993 sent up his school reform legislation.

During the spring and summer, the House Committee on Education and Labor held hearings on the administration's proposal. There was debate on whether using standards and testing as a lever for reform was the appropriate way to improve the schools, but there was also some deference to the national council because it was holding its own hearings on that same issue at the same time. An important linkage was that the ranking Republican on the committee, William Goodling, and the Democratic chair of the Subcommittee on Elementary and Secondary Education, Dale Kildee, were congressionally appointed members on the council for the House of Representatives and thus kept their colleagues on the committee apprised of the council's deliberations.

On the House committee, the main critics of the standards and assessment approach were the Democratic liberals, especially those from the largest cities, who centered their argument on the use of tests and seldom discussed standards development. Their main concern was that the results of testing were predictable (generally related to the socioeconomic status of the students) and that poor results for students in the largest cities and in other economically disadvantaged areas rarely led to substantive assistance from the states or from other more advantaged areas to help to bring about improvement. In other words, the use of tests as a means to bring about school reform was just an exercise in "blaming the victim"; the real answer was to increase aid for the schools so that students could be helped to do better.

The other potential opponents of the Bush program were the more conservative members of the Republican minority, who were concerned about an expansion of the national role in education but who for the most part held their fire because they did not want to be perceived as attacking their own president. When the liberals in the committee hearings raised their concerns about tests and their uses, the conservatives countered that students and the schools had to be held more accountable and, further, that money was not the answer. The conservatives, like the liberals, did not focus at first on the idea of national standards; instead, they talked mostly about testing and accountability.

Many Democrats also criticized the president's proposal for not providing enough money for education reform. They especially belittled the idea that funding 535 schools would lead to substantial change because this would affect about 0.5% of American schools. The Republicans responded that the schools had to be substantially changed and that this was a way to "break the mold," as Bush and Alexander put it.

The House committee decided that there should be a different approach for reform than the one suggested by Bush's proposal for funding New American Schools and 17 other small categorical programs. The leadership of the committee became interested in the "systemic reform" approach that was being undertaken in states such as California and Kentucky. The Consortium for Policy Research in Education was closely following this development and providing technical assistance to several states that were trying to implement it. Marshall Smith, who subsequently became a top official in the Clinton administration, and Jennifer O'Day from Stanford University were especially active in articulating the philosophy behind this reform (O'Day & Smith, 1993; Smith & O'Day, 1991).

The basic idea was the one that the National Governors' Association had described in their 1991 report *From Rhetoric to Action*: Small experimental programs were not achieving the large-scale change that was needed, and instead the entire educational system within a state had to be changed in a coherent and coordinated fashion. Furthermore, the focus had to be on teaching and learning and not on other issues such as governance or vouchers, and all the changes brought about within a state had to buttress the development and use of a curriculum incorporating higher standards for all children.

As Smith and O'Day explained it, reform of a state's entire educational system began with the development of these high standards for academic content, then led to the definition of the levels of achievement that students at different ages ought to attain, then led to the alignment of the assessments to this content and to these performance levels. The revision of textbooks to reflect these agreements on content and performance and teacher training and retraining to incorporate the same matter were the next steps. The rationale for this approach was that American students would never achieve well in the current system because it was so disjointed (as described in Chapter 1 of this book by the National Academy of Sciences and by Smith and Cortines), with curricula set in different ways by thousands of school districts, textbooks fashioned in still other ways by the national publishers, assessments set by the states in still other ways, and the teacher training institutions going in still other directions.

The House committee was impressed with this view. Thus, it wrote its bill based on this approach for reform of the whole system because such an approach seemed to complement what several states were undertaking on their own and seemed more likely to bring about broad reform than did the experimental schools approach of the Bush administration (H.R. 3320, 1991). Some of the liberals on the committee, however, were still unhappy because they felt that this approach, although better than the administration's, nonetheless pivoted on standards and assessments. In the liberals' view, the criticism that students in different school districts were being provided educations of greatly varying quality due to the relative wealth of the areas had not been answered by this new approach any better than by Bush's program.

These equity concerns of the liberals became focused on the idea of providing for national school delivery standards—the same issue that had been debated in the National Council on Educational Standards and Testing. These measures (later called "opportunity-to-learn standards") would supposedly describe the conditions that would have to be present for students to have the opportunity to learn the content standards. For example, students could not be expected to master chemistry unless they had access to a science laboratory. The liberals argued that there had to be national opportunity-to-learn standards if there were going to be national academic content standards.

The House committee therefore included in its bill a requirement that states had to have such school delivery standards if they wanted to receive a grant for systemic reform, an amendment adopted as the means of securing the grudging support of some of the liberals on the committee. The Republicans on the committee were not happy with this amendment, but they did not make it a major point of contention because they were trying to secure the enactment of their president's program. However, as we shall see, when it came to the same type of amendment being added to the Clinton proposal in the following year, the Republicans adamantly opposed the entire bill and claimed that its adoption would lead to federal control of education. This is an example of how issues and politics intertwine: What may not bother a legislator at one point may turn into a major battle later because the political circumstances have changed.

The Bush administration was not very happy that its experimental school approach and use of small categorical programs were being so drastically changed by the House committee into an approach putting all the funds into a single grant to a state for systemwide reform. But because the administration did not have enough votes, with the Republicans then being in the minority on the House committee, it did not vigorously oppose that change, and it hoped for better support from the Senate for its point of view.

A major obstacle arose, however, when the committee faced the issue of choice. Although Bush's first school reform proposal had not included aid for private schools, America 2000 asked for several hundreds of millions of dollars to encourage states and school districts to offer programs to parents so that they could choose the public or private school they wanted their children to attend.

The national organizations representing public education did not object much at first to those proposals because they did not know how serious the administration was about them, for Bush had not previously proposed vouchers or aid to private schools. But as Alexander fought hard for choice as a principal part of the administration's program, they became more concerned and began to voice opposition. By July 1991, the *New York Times* reported that Bush's plan was coming under increasing fire and that "the presidents of the country's two major teachers' unions have sharply attacked his plan after earlier praising it" (Chira, 1991, p. A12). Shanker of the American Federation of Teachers, who had earlier warmly praised America 2000 because he thought that it was proposing solutions for the lack of student motivation, issued a warning about the choice issue that proved to be very accurate: "If they want to pick a fight, they've picked one. This is a terrible tactical error. If they don't find a way to get off this, it will destroy the program" (quoted in Chira, 1991, p. A12).

Although such opposition to choice because it represented competition for the public schools might be expected from the teachers' unions, the concept was receiving, at best, tepid support from national business groups, such as the Business Roundtable and the National Alliance of Business (Chira, 1991). For instance, Owen Butler (1991), chair of the Committee for Economic Development and formerly chair of Procter and Gamble, wrote a column in the *New York Times* advising that "the nation should not be rushing headlong down the path of private school vouchers until we know how the system might work in practice" (p. A8).

Despite Shanker's warning and the coolness to the idea of private school choice from the national business community, Secretary Alexander was unperturbed by the storm, saying, "It doesn't bother me one bit—the debate is engaged" (quoted in Chira, 1991, p. A12). It was indeed, and the contention surrounding that issue was to delay the legislation so long and cause so much ill will that it ultimately killed the bill.

The House committee tried to find a compromise on the choice issue but failed. In September 1991, it voted to allow states to use funds for choice under the systemwide reform plan if state law permitted such use. At the time, only two states permitted use of public funds in private secular schools, and none allowed direct state funding of religious schools ("In the Name of Choice," 1991). In effect, Congress was proposing to defer to the states on the issue of aid to private schools.

That committee vote was very contentious and caused consideration of the bill to be delayed until the following year due to the opposition of the major public education organizations, which feared any signal from the national level about the acceptability of aid to private schools. When work was resumed in 1992, a new bill was introduced (H.R. 4323, 1992). Because the new legislation deleted the provision permitting a limited use of funds for choice, several Democratic members, including the chair of the committee, changed their votes and supported the bill. The delay, however, meant that funds that had been set aside for the program were redirected to other programs and that the bill was slipping closer to the end of the legislative term, which always makes chancier the voyage through the legislative shoals.

Work on the bill dragged on until May 1992, when it was finally approved by the House committee, but only after everyone was unhappy. Secretary Alexander was upset about the deletion of the choice provision and the elimination of the New American Schools and said, "This bill is worse than awful. The only ones who should be happy are those who want schools to stay forever just as they are" (quoted in Zuckman, 1992, p. 1451). Congressman William Ford (Dem.-Mich.), the chair of the committee, expressing the sentiments of the liberals about the use of standards and tests to reform the schools, responded to Alexander by saying, "It's all cliches and show business. It's not going to revolutionize anything" (quoted in Zuckman, 1992, p. 1451).

In August, the full House of Representatives took up the bill and voted on many of the same issues as the committee had. During the debate in the House, an amendment that would have restored the earlier compromise on choice was defeated, and attempts to restore the administration's experimental schools approach to reform were repulsed. Because the House considered the bill after the issuance in January of the report of the National Council on Education Standards and Testing, its version of the legislation included a limited authority to fund national standards development and to experiment with testing tied to these standards, but these were not central provisions, so they were not much debated. Instead, the issue of parental choice of private schools, the funding of New American Schools, and other amendments consumed the attention of the members of Congress.

The final vote approving the bill in the House of Representatives was 279 to 124, with all but one of the opponents being Republicans. Even with conflicting views and many reservations about the legislation, the overwhelming majority of the elected representatives was reluctant in the end to be opposed to a school reform measure.

While the House committee was resuming its work on the bill in January 1992 and fighting over the choice issue, the Senate moved ahead and approved the legislation (S. 2, 1991) with bipartisan support. The Senate defeated an amendment permitting use of federal funds to pay for choice by parents of private schools for their children, even though that amendment had the support of the president. Instead, the Senate permitted federal funds to be used for parental choice among *public* schools. The Bush administration was happier with the Senate on other issues because it retained the approach to reform based on funding of experimental schools. The Senate did, however, add to the bill several new programs encouraging other innovations.

The Senate bill was considered the same month that the National Council on Education Standards and Testing issued its report calling for the development of national standards and a system of assessments. Although no amendments were offered to deal directly with funding such developments, Senator Jeff Bingaman (Dem.-N.Mex.) did offer a provision implementing the recommendations to refashion the National Education Goals Panel and to create a subgroup that would monitor the development of standards and assessments. That amendment was adopted by voice vote, showing a deference to Senator

Bingaman, who served with Senator Orrin Hatch (Rep.-Utah) as a Senate representative on the council. There was very little debate on this issue.

Before the bill could be approved by the Senate, opposition from very conservative members had to be overcome because they still opposed any expansion of federal aid to education. The Senate did vote them down and passed the legislation by a vote of 92 to 6. Comparing the two bills, the Bush administration was happier with the Senate's than with the House's version, despite the loss of its private school choice provision.

Because the House and the Senate had passed different bills, a conference committee had to meet to reconcile the differences. During those meetings, the Senate negotiators accepted the House's systemwide reform approach, including the requirement for school delivery standards, as well as the limited authority to fund standards development and to experiment with assessments. The Senate representatives, led by Senator Kennedy, knew that the enthusiasm for the bill was tepid among the House liberals and felt that these concessions were the only way to secure the bill's approval. On its part, the House accepted a version of the Bingaman amendment that furthered the push for national standards by strengthening the National Education Goals Panel and creating a subcouncil to oversee the standards and testing development. The final agreement did not contain any funds for choice involving private schools, but it did permit use of funds for parental choice among public schools.

When the conference agreement was brought back to the House, it was easily approved because it was so similar to the bill earlier approved by that chamber, but then the legislation ran into a filibuster in the Senate from the more conservative Republican senators who were still opposed to any major expansion of the federal role in education. Because it takes 60 votes to overcome a filibuster, it is relatively easy for a small group of opposing legislators to kill legislation, particularly in the last days of a congressional session when every minute counts.

Helping the conservatives was the tepid—and mixed—support for the final bill. The Bush administration was in favor of the bill but not avidly fighting for it because the development of New American Schools was not the centerpiece of reform and because there was no authority for funding private school choice programs. Some Democrats, especially those in the House, were likewise for the bill, but not enthusiastically because they had some doubts about the standards and testing approach to reform and because the presidential election was only a few weeks away and they were not happy about the prospect of Bush's signing a school reform bill during the campaign. Some other Democrats, however, especially Senator Kennedy, were strongly in favor of the bill because they saw it as a way to improve education and expand federal aid. Some Republicans also favored the bill because Bush had proposed it, but the more conservative ones had doubts about the expansion of the federal role. Given these cross-currents of views, it was not surprising that a small group of senators was able to torpedo the bill by mounting a filibuster.

While Congress was debating the parts of America 2000 that were submitted as legislation, the Bush administration moved ahead on funding the development of national standards to define the content of what children should know and be able to do in the major curriculum areas. The administration had notified the congressional appropriations committees that it was going to use discretionary funds for this purpose, as mentioned earlier, and had not met with any disapproval, so it went ahead with this work. The U.S. Department of Education, the National Science Foundation, and the National Endowments for the Arts and the Humanities provided funds for grants to various organizations of teachers and others to begin to develop standards for the sciences, history, the arts, civics, geography, English, and foreign languages.

Thus, as President Bush was preparing to run for reelection in 1992, he had lost both his modest first and his more ambitious second legislative packages, but his administration was moving forward on developing, for the first time in the United States, national standards for education. The idea of having national goals for education had evolved into having national standards for what children should be taught and also into support for a national system of tests to measure their attainment of that knowledge.

▓ A Historic Development

The Bush administration's encouragement of national education standards "launched what may well be a historic development in American education," claimed Diane Ravitch (1993, p. 153), an education historian and assistant secretary for research in Alexander's Department of Education. As she explained, "Unlike most other modern societies, this nation has never established explicit standards as goals for student achievement; those nations that do have such standards view them as an invaluable means of ensuring both equity and excellence" (p. 153). Ravitch's observations about the importance of what Bush proposed are right to the point, and the failure of Bush to achieve enactment of his school reform legislation should not diminish the significance of this accomplishment.

Bush and Alexander made a great strategic error in brushing aside Shanker's warning and pushing increasingly in 1992 for school choice involving private schools, for that decision led to the undoing of their legislation. If that issue had been put aside, a school reform bill would have been on the president's desk sometime in 1992, and the federal government would have joined the states in trying to raise the quality of the public schools. Instead, the debate over choice delayed the bill and gave conservative Republicans the opportunity to kill it. It then took a new president to push national school reform legislation through Congress.

President Clinton, however, could not have done what he did unless President Bush had opened the door. Just as it took a conservative Republican president, Richard Nixon, who was a staunch anticommunist to reopen relations in the 1970s with communist China, so it was necessary that a conservative Republican be the one to begin a debate in the 1990s on reaching national agreement on what should be taught in the schools.

In the past, the Republicans had been the ones alleging that Democrats wanted to have greater federal control of education because Democratic President Lyndon Johnson had proposed in the mid-1960s most of the federal programs to aid education and because Democrats were usually more strongly in favor of such federal aid to education than were the Republicans. But when the Republicans advocated national standards for education and began funding their development, that issue was muted. National standards for all children certainly implied more influence over education from the national level than did programs aiding the 25% or so of all children who were at risk—the beneficiaries of then-current federal aid programs.

Putting aside the partisan implications, the real significance of Bush's proposing national standards for education was twofold. First, it meant that the country as a whole, acting through the national government, should be concerned about the education of *all* children. Second, it meant that the quality of public education ought to be discussed at the national level. President Bush and Secretary Alexander were too optimistic—as was the National Council on Education Standards and Testing—that developing national standards would improve education. But viewed more broadly, their advocacy of higher standards focused the nation's attention on the need for improvement in education.

▓ Note

1. Throughout this chapter and those to follow, letters, memos, and other such documents not published anywhere but circulated in Congress or in committees or subcommittees (e.g., official correspondence of cabinet members, letters from lobbying organizations, "Dear Colleague" letters) are noted in the text by sender(s)' and receiver(s)' names, title of document if any, and date but are not listed in the references. Copies are in my own files and, presumably, the files of the organizations or individuals from whom they were sent.

3

The 1992 Presidential
Campaign and the Transition
to a New Administration

*How Bush and Clinton Differed
on Education, but How Clinton
Continued the Fight for Higher
Standards That Bush Began*

The Presidential Campaign

The presidential campaign of 1992 was extraordinary in several ways. There were three candidates instead of the usual two major party nominees, and the third candidate, billionaire Ross Perot, added spice to the race because no one knew from moment to moment what he was going to do or say, yet he attracted considerable popular support.

The campaign was important from the point of view of education because George Bush, Bill Clinton, and Ross Perot all endorsed the development of national standards for education and of national examinations for schoolchildren (Miller, 1992). Never before in a presidential campaign had there been such agreement. In fact, it seems that never before had even one major party presidential candidate espoused the creation of such standards. As with the national goals for education, this congruence of opinion in 1992 showed a very significant departure from the two-centuries-old American tradition of local control of education.

An unfortunate side effect of this unusual agreement was that there was little debate among the candidates about national standards and tests. In political campaigns, those vying for office often try to highlight their differences and gloss over their similarities; therefore, there was little discussion in 1992 of the need for such standards and assessments. In retrospect, it would have been healthier for the country to have had a full debate over the need for such a shift in education and of the merits and demerits of such a change. Such a debate would have better educated the citizenry and the country's leaders about the issue.

As already noted, President Bush came to this position on national standards primarily through the influence of business leaders and of his second secretary of education, Lamar Alexander. As a consequence, the president proposed a comprehensive program to bring the federal government into school reform, using standards and examinations as the core element. His main achievement at the end of his term was that the funding had begun on the development of the national academic content standards and that the debate had moved a considerable distance toward accepting what would once have been a radical idea.

President Bush's failing was that he could not develop broad bipartisan support for America 2000 or organize the national public education organizations behind his program. This failure resulted from two factors. First, Bush tended more and more as the presidential campaign progressed, again under the influence of Lamar Alexander, to put aid to private schools at the center of his reform initiatives, causing endless controversy and delay. Bush, who had been silent on that issue for the first 2 years of his presidency, was advocating in his last year that three fourths of all aid for school reform be earmarked for "G.I. Bills for Students" that would be available for attendance at private schools.

The second reason that Bush failed in education was that he did not put the effort into achieving his agenda. As the *Wall Street Journal* (Stout & Murray, 1992) noted, the president devoted "scant time and energy to pushing those ideas . . . [and] put little steam behind the America 2000 proposal. Consequently, major elements of it have remained stalled, or have been diluted into ineffectiveness" (p. A14). The irony was that the president who had started his term in office with almost no domestic agenda had fleshed out by the end of this period a very respectable one for education and had in fact asked for more funding for those ideas than the supposedly more generous Democratic Congress was willing to grant (Scully, 1993). But Bush did not work to achieve his agenda, so it failed.

Commitment to education was not missing from the Democratic candidate for president, Bill Clinton. He had "expended considerable political capital in pushing education issues in Arkansas," again according to the *Wall Street Journal* (Stout & Murray, 1992, p. A14). He had also served as the head of the Education Commission of the States (a coordinating body for the states on education) and had been the point man for the Democratic governors in developing the national goals for education. Clinton seemed to revel in attending meetings on education and talking about it.

Clinton put his agenda for education, as well as for other social areas, into a publication called *Putting People First: How We Can All Change America* (Clinton & Gore, 1992). Decorated with the usual campaign rhetoric, that book set forth his ideas for improving education. Prominent among them was "establishing tough standards" through work with educators, parents, business leaders, and public officials to create a set of national standards for what students should know and to create a national examination system to measure students' and schools' progress in meeting the national standards (pp. 84-88). Another objective was to achieve the national education goals that he had helped to write with President Bush.

The *Wall Street Journal* had it right when it concluded that "there are actually some striking similarities" between Bush and Clinton on education (Stout & Murray, 1992, p. A14). It stated:

> To varying degrees, both men support national student standards and a national examination system. Both support report cards to measure states' progress. Both favor expanding Head Start, increasing the freedom for parents to choose their children's school, increasing the flexibility of teacher certification and creating academies for teacher training. (p. A14)

That newspaper, which is known for its conservative bent, went on to say, "Even education experts close to the administration admit that Mr. Clinton has been one of the best governors in addressing education" (p. A14). However, this degree of concurrence of opinion should not becloud important differences that existed between the two candidates, and those differences demonstrated how differently the two political parties would come to approach other issues in education.

Lamar Alexander, during the campaign, attacked Clinton by saying that he was the captive of the teachers' unions. Alexander alleged, "In order to get the nomination, he has had to make the NEA [National Education Association] happy, and the NEA only likes people it can control. They want a president with their agenda, instead of an agenda for change" (Stout & Murray, 1992,

p. A14). Without accepting Alexander's characterization of Clinton, one can readily see that the influence of the NEA on the Democratic party was substantial, with its delegates being the single largest block of votes at the Democratic convention in New York in the summer of 1992.

The Democratic party platform, reflecting this influence, called for more money for education, expressed opposition to the Bush initiative "to bankrupt the public school system" through private school vouchers, and deplored "the savage inequalities [in financing and services] among public schools across the land" ("Party's Statement," 1992, p. 62). Additional funding was urged for Head Start and for child care, and site-based decision making and public school choice were endorsed. Youth apprenticeship programs and community service opportunities for individuals to earn funds for postsecondary education were also included in the platform. There was little in the Democrats' platform that public school teachers—or most advocates for public education—would oppose.

In contrast, the Republican party platform had a far different tone. The schools were not educating children, it asserted, and therefore Bush was commended for his "bold vision to change radically our education system" ("Party Stresses Family Values," 1992, p. 2562). Furthermore, the Democratic leadership in the House and the Senate were lambasted for thwarting the will of the people for radical change. The America 2000 strategy "languish[ed] in the Democrat Congress . . . opposed by special-interest unions that have a power grip on the failed policies of the past" (p. 2562). It was true enough that the teachers' unions vigorously opposed Bush's tuition vouchers proposal, but it was also true that very conservative Republican senators who were opposed to any expansion of federal aid were the ones who had administered the coup de grace by filibustering and thereby killing both of Bush's education bills in 1990 and 1992 after the Democrats had accepted them.

The biggest differences between the Democratic and Republican platforms dealt with aid to private schools and with social issues. Unlike the Democrats, the Republicans proposed $1,000 scholarships for parents to pay for private school tuition, endorsed home schooling, opposed birth control or abortion services in schools, insisted that sexual abstinence be taught, advocated the recitation of the Pledge of Allegiance in schools, and endorsed voluntary student prayer in schools and the right to offer prayer at commencements or other occasions. Alexander may have been correct in saying that public school teachers had a say in drafting the Democratic party platform, but it is also clear that the ideological and religious right wielded great influence when it came time to write the principles on which the Republicans wished to be judged.

Despite this rhetoric, there were commonalities between the Democratic and the Republican party platforms reflecting the common views held by Bush and Clinton, as already noted by the *Wall Street Journal* (Stout & Murray, 1992). The Democrats insisted on results from the schools and endorsed world-class standards in mathematics, science, and other core subjects, as well as tests to measure the progress made in meeting these standards. The Republicans likewise called for the establishment of tougher standards and assessments for what children should know and for a loosening of the strings tied to current federal aid programs. Also like the Democrats, the Republicans endorsed the idea of a youth apprenticeship strategy to help students meet high standards and learn job skills.

An important point is that when the Democrats and the Republicans endorsed the concept of national education standards and assessments, they were not espousing the same testing as used in the 1970s and 1980s. There was an understanding, at least on the part of some leaders, that the basic concept behind standards and the assessments aligned to them was quite different. For instance, Clinton said that he favored a meaningful national examination system, not "norm-referenced tests that you give two or three years and then every American is making above the . . . average" (quoted in Baumann, 1992, p. 3).

In other words, the idea of testing is not to compare students but rather to measure how much content contained in the standards each student has mastered. Testing is not meant to be a competition where some are doing better than others, although none may be doing well. Instead, the idea is that the knowledge to be mastered ought to be identified and then each student ought to be given an opportunity to learn that material, followed by an assessment to determine how far he or she has come in mastering it. There ought to be truth in teaching and learning based on high standards.

So there was agreement between the parties on the issue of standards and assessments, but the battle lines in other areas of education were clearly drawn for the 1992 presidential and congressional elections. The Democratic party and Clinton allied themselves openly with the teachers' unions and implicitly with the other public education organizations. The agenda was to reform public education through the development of national standards and examinations, public school choice, retraining of teachers, community service programs, and other means. The education groups also hoped that there would be much more federal aid for education.

The Republicans positioned themselves as advocates for radical change in education. They wanted to re-create public schools through the development of New American Schools, but they also increasingly presented themselves as advocates for private schools. They also wanted to bring "moral fiber" back into education through prayer, teaching of sexual abstinence, forbidding condom distribution to students, and permitting parents to teach their children at home. Last, Republicans advocated national standards and assessments as a means to upgrade the quality of the curriculum in public education. But as with many points of similarity in campaigns, that issue was slighted, and the more emotional and contentious ones were highlighted.

▓ The Transition to a New Administration

In November 1992, Bill Clinton won the presidential election, and the Democrats retained their majorities in both the U.S. House of Representatives and the Senate. Public school advocates were gleeful that they had rebuffed the challenge from Bush and his party to make vouchers or private school choice programs integral to American education. The defeated Republicans were bitter, as shown by an article in the *Wall Street Journal* entitled "The Education Empire Strikes Back" (Finn, 1992). It depicted the public school "empire" as renewing its grip on American education, beginning with Clinton because he would be so indebted to the NEA for his election.

The national public education organizations naturally saw the picture differently. As the National School Boards Association's Michael Resnick later said, the biggest difference between the new Clinton administration and the out-going Bush administration was that "this administration operates more on the premise that public schools are where the children are and changes are going to happen within the current system" (quoted in Jordan, 1993, p. A19). That was precisely the point of differentiation, and the Clinton team was working on ways to reform, not abandon, the system of public education.

Even before the election, several groups tried to influence how a Clinton administration might attempt to carry out its ideas. One particular effort came from Gordon Ambach (1992), executive director of the Council of Chief State School Officers, with the assistance of Michael Cohen, who had worked with the nominee on writing the national goals for education when Clinton was a leader in the National Governors' Association, and Marshall Smith, who was dean of the Graduate School of Education at Stanford University. His *Transi-*

tion Guide for the "President's Program for Education" laid out a detailed agenda for education and advocated that the first education bill to be introduced ought to be the one that had died in the last Congress.

During the presidential campaign, it was unclear how much funding Clinton would ask for education if he were to be elected, but many congressional Democrats and representatives of the national education organizations expected a strong commitment from him. The Democrats on the Hill felt that Reagan had ravaged support for federal programs and that Bush had gotten considerable mileage from his America 2000 program without putting much new money into implementing it. As the *New York Times* (Clymer, 1991) put it, Bush's proposal was "a bid not only to change American education but also to seize the Democrats' best political issue" (p. I1), and more galling to the Democrats was that he was doing it on the cheap by not requesting much funding.

Clinton and Richard Riley, his nominee for Secretary of Education, however, wanted to be perceived as "new Democrats" and not as Great Society liberals. In the late 1980s, Clinton and Riley, as well as many others in the new team, had joined the Democratic Leadership Council (DLC), which had as its purpose redirecting the Democratic party away from what were seen as overly liberal, Washington-based, big-government solutions to problems. These reform Democrats distrusted those who had spent many years in the nation's capital working on education and other social issues, especially those who had served in Congress since the 1960s or 1970s. Those congressional Democrats were seen as the old guard wedded to the ways of the past. In the view of the DLC, the Democratic party was having so much difficulty in winning the presidency and was losing ground in other national, state, and local offices because these Washington officials were setting the tone for the party and because that message was not selling among the voters.

The national education organizations were not the targets of the same dissatisfaction as were the senior Democratic members of the House and the Senate, but the positions of those organizations were very similar to those of the Democratic leadership in Congress, with whom they had worked for decades to create and expand federal aid to education. The major public elementary and secondary education groups wanted the federal government to mount large programs offering general aid to education as well as aid in school construction, technology acquisition, and teacher retraining. The major postsecondary education groups wanted a vast expansion of the Pell Grant program and other forms of student aid, as well as greater assistance for graduate education, library book acquisition, and research.

Clinton and Riley thought that these schemes smacked too much of trying to spend large amounts of federal money on problems without identifying first what the results were going to be. On the basis of their experiences as governors, they thought that the public would not accept this kind of spending without far greater accountability than ever demanded before from the federal level. They also felt that these ideas were conceived in isolation from what was happening in the states and at the local level and that any new federal programs had to support state and local efforts and not be created as separate structures to operate on their own without acknowledging what the other levels of government were trying to do and without trying to blend the federal efforts into their programs or at least to support those efforts.

Richard Riley had been a state legislator in South Carolina; he then became governor and was the first to be reelected once the state constitution was changed to permit consecutive gubernatorial terms. He had conceived and battled for a major school reform program that, when implemented, put South Carolina near the head of the list of the states in changing its public schools. Riley also believed that the federal programs, as helpful as they were to a state as poor as South Carolina, were not in the forefront of school reform. In fact, he believed that in too many instances they were peripheral in the schools and even detrimental to reform because they caused such a focus on rote learning.

Those experiences and views led Clinton and Riley to see the world differently than their allies in Congress and among the Washington-based national education groups. That is why Riley said in April 1993, in justifying his budget request for education, "My vision is one of fundamental change" (quoted in "Clinton Proposes," 1993, p. 1). He also stated at the same time, "The Clinton budget is a budget for change. It's a new way of doing things" (quoted in "Clinton Proposes," 1993, p. 1).

At the end of January, after Clinton was inaugurated, the new administration announced that the Goals 2000 legislation (the successor to Bush's America 2000) would be the first bill submitted to Congress. The point was that a new framework for federal aid had to be created and a new role fashioned for the national government, and thus that business would not go on as usual, with the administration asking Congress simply to revise and extend the current array of programs.

The congressional Democrats who were not enthusiastic about Bush's legislation and the national education organizations that shared that lack of enthusiasm generally took the news with resignation. Their hopes were still high that Clinton's administration would not only be better than Bush's on the issue of vouchers but also eventually come through with more funding for the current programs. It was difficult, however, for some Democratic members of Congress to shift from being free agents who could lambaste Bush for his program to being team players expected to follow a president who was advocating for the same ideas as had Bush.

Congressman William Ford, the chair of the Committee on Education and Labor, had been one of the harshest critics of Bush's America 2000 proposal, saying that it was all show business and would not bring about any real change; now he faced the task of guiding Clinton's Goals 2000 bill through Congress when that bill was modeled after Bush's and the Democratic variation of it, the Neighborhood Schools Act. Ford's response was:

> What you're doing is trying to take a football team that's only ever played defense and asking them to play offense. I'm telling them, "Let's don't launch any great offensive and start running our own plays until the coach tells us what he wants to do." (Cooper, 1993, p. A8)

Senator Edward Kennedy, the chair of the Labor and Human Resources Committee, adopted the same attitude as Ford, following "coach" Clinton. But their views were not shared by all the Democratic members of Congress, as we shall see in the next chapter, and that boded poorly for swift passage of the Goals 2000 bill.

Ford and Kennedy were clearly among the congressional leaders whom the DLC believed had led the Democratic party too far to the left of the political spectrum. But Ford and Kennedy had served in Congress when the last Democratic president, Jimmy Carter, was in office between 1977 and 1981, and they knew firsthand how destructive to Democrats had been the poor relationship between the Carter White House and the Congress. In fact, Kennedy had even challenged Carter for renomination in 1980, thereby weakening support among Democrats for Carter. Ronald Reagan was elected, and Bush succeeded him, so the Republicans held the presidency for 12 years and even gained effective control of Congress for some years. Understanding these consequences, Ford and Kennedy were willing, despite their own strong personalities and more liberal views, to make themselves into followers—with a few deviations by Ford, as we shall see. If Kennedy and Ford had not been generally willing to follow the president, Clinton's program for education would not have been enacted, and that program had enough trouble as it was because others did not model themselves on Ford and Kennedy.

Goals 2000 in the U.S. House of Representatives

How Liberals Expressed Concerns About the Fairness of Standards, and How Conservative Opposition to the Idea Grew

Preparing the Legislation

Once the Clinton administration decided definitely in January 1993 to send separate legislation to Congress dealing with standards-based reform, it began the process of shaping its policy. In Washington, the usual procedure in forming policies is for the president's advisers to draft a proposal, then to consult informally with Congress and with significant public and private groups as they flesh out their ideas, and then to submit a legislative bill to Congress and work with congressional and organizational supporters for its passage.

In February, Secretary Riley sent his aides to Capitol Hill to consult with the Democratic members of the House and Senate education committees, the members of Congress whom he would be working with most closely to achieve this new policy. Because consultations frequently begin at the staff level, Riley's aides met with the staff of the Democratic members of the Senate education committee and received a generally good reception for their ideas for reform and for the strategy of a separate school reform bill. These positive reactions reflected Senator Kennedy's support—a very important factor because he was the chair of the Senate committee and the leading Senate Democrat on the issue of education.

On the House side of the Hill, the story was different. The congressional aides for the Democratic members of the education committee complained about the administration's proposal to move separately on the school reform legislation; this reflected the more tepid support among many House liberals for the idea of standards-based reform. The Democratic aides also criticized the lack of substantial new funding for education and noted that these ideas were very similar to Bush's.

Later in February, Secretary Riley himself met with the Democratic members of the House committee in a closed caucus. He heard some mild complaints about the lack of a large increase in spending for education in the new administration's description of its bill, but he did not encounter from the elected representatives any specific criticisms of the administration's strategy to submit separate school reform legislation as its first order of business or of the general ideas discussed in that package of changes. At this early point in the year, the general feeling of the congressional Democrats toward the new administration was one of goodwill and cooperation. Congresswoman Patsy Mink (Dem.-Hawaii), who was not at the meeting, later sent a letter to the secretary (February 27, 1993) expressing some concerns, but that was not what Riley heard at the caucus.

After receiving a positive reception on the Senate side and after this generally supportive meeting with the members of the House committee, the administration logically assumed that the complaints it had encountered at the staff level in the House did not reflect the members' concerns, except possibly those of Mrs. Mink. Therefore, the administration kept on track with its strategy of a separate bill and with the concept of building on standards as a way to improve education.

In March, the congressional budget committees began to write the outlines for the government's budget. The House budget committee, controlled by the Democrats, cut back on increased funding for education and other social programs and instead placed a greater emphasis on reducing the deficit. These actions showed that there was a stronger congressional sentiment for deficit reduction than for new spending. But the liberals on the House committee on education had thought that Clinton's election signaled increases in spending for education, and now they saw that possibility evaporating.

When it became clear to the Democratic members of the education committee that deficit reduction was assuming a higher priority than the creation of new programs or the expansion of older ones, they began to get restless about the direction of events. Meanwhile, the U.S. Department of

Education was continuing with its drafting of the new school reform bill and was trying to balance many interests: governors and chief state school officers, business groups and educational organizations, House and Senate Democrats, and Republicans. The liberals on the House committee had been told that they would be asked to take the lead on the legislation, but as they saw that their interests were being lumped together with many others, their unease grew.

In mid-March, 11 of the Democratic members of the House committee took the highly unusual step of sending a letter to Chairman Ford asking that the administration's bill not be rushed through the legislative process and that they be afforded sufficient time to consider the bill (letter from Cong. George Miller et al. to Cong. William D. Ford, March 16, 1993). As a rule, members of Congress communicate orally with one another, especially if they are on the same committee and even more so if they are members of the same party. So this letter could only be perceived by the chair as a strong warning that he should not make any rash promises to the administration about the bill.

Ford had already told the press and everyone else that he thought that his role was now one of following the president—the "coach"—and that he would do all he could to get the president's entire program enacted, including his proposals for education (Cooper, 1993). This letter made clear that the other Democratic members of Ford's committee did not share that enthusiasm.

Another troubling aspect of this episode for Ford had to be that the letter originated from a senior member of the committee, Congressman George Miller (Dem.-Calif.). It is very unusual for a veteran member to challenge a chair, implying an attempt to assume a leadership role among the members of the committee in opposition to the chair's own presumed role. Miller, a very aggressive and liberal member from California, was generally assumed to have understood this implication because he was a chair in his own right, of the Committee on Natural Resources.

Ford called a caucus of the Democratic members of the education committee and invited Riley back to talk to them.[1] Before Riley appeared, Ford told the members that he was upset by the letter as an affront to him as chair but that nonetheless he had now reconsidered his support of the administration's bill and would not cosponsor it as it was now drafted. That shift of position by the chair pleased the other Democrats, so when Riley came into the caucus, he met almost uniform criticism of the draft bill and of the strategy of submitting separate reform legislation.

The Democrats voiced major and minor complaints to Riley about the administration's draft bill. In particular, they argued that students could not be expected to meet high curriculum standards unless they had a fair chance to learn the material and that too many school districts lacked resources to provide that opportunity (this became the argument over "opportunity-to-learn" standards). Further, they argued that there was not enough money requested for the new federal program to have a major impact on improving education so as to provide such opportunities. In their eyes, it was backwards to test first to see if students knew the content; instead, real change ought to be secured through better funding of education, and only then should testing occur.

Another shortcoming they saw in the administration's draft bill was that there were not strong enough enforcement mechanisms if a state chose not to follow the requirements of the bill. They wondered why these ideas for school reform could not be combined with the renewal of the current federal programs under the Elementary and Secondary Education Act because those programs were already in nearly every school district. The members also stated that the bill was too similar to Bush's, that they were not being consulted enough, and that the administration was tilting too much toward the states and especially toward the governors.

Secretary Riley was taken aback by all of this discontent, especially because he had encountered such goodwill from the same people—his allies—a mere month before. He responded by pointing out that the administration's draft bill was based on the legislation that had passed the House education committee in the previous Congress and thus that he did not quite understand the members' opposition.

Chairman Ford, in his new role as leader of the malcontents, countered that the Democrats had had to pass something last time: Their leadership told them that they had to have a bill to counter Bush's and that the Democrats could not merely oppose Bush's ideas. Therefore, Ford contended, that sequence of events should not lead people to believe that the House members had no problems with Bush's approach of using standards and tests to improve education.

Riley responded to these assertions by noting that the federal government had not had a role in school reform for the past 12 years and that this draft bill would create one based on standards and improving education for all children. He did not understand why the Democrats were afraid to seize the issue of raising standards.

Riley also felt that the federal government could work in partnership with the states only if the states determined the problems and then the U.S. Department of Education tried to help. He said that he heard loud and clear the concerns about assessments and standards measuring the opportunity to learn but that the federal government ought not to mandate the conditions of education—even through a set of assurances that all children had the opportunity to learn more. Furthermore, he emphasized that the current federal programs were not adequate to improve education and that the Congress had to go beyond Chapter 1 (which was the largest current federal program).

After hearing the intense arguments of the members, Riley told them that he now better understood their concerns and would request that the committee not proceed to hearings on the administration's bill, as had been planned for that week. Further, because there were clear problems with this approach, he would bring the members' concerns directly to the president.

Although party caucuses are meant to be private or "off the record," this particular meeting was reported in the press almost as if a transcript had been released. The reporters were abuzz about it for weeks because it was one of the first incidents showing the conflict between the views of the "new" Democratic Clinton regime and the "old" Democratic leanings of the more liberal members of Congress. *Education Week,* the prime national newspaper in the field of education, reported on "a stormy meeting" (Miller, 1993, p. 26) that Riley had had with the committee Democrats, after which he had decided to delay indefinitely the release of the administration's school reform bill and to begin meetings with them and with the major education groups.

A more acid commentary came from the *U.S. News and World Report* ("The Faces," 1993):

> Liberal Democrats, not Republicans, have fired a shot at education reform that could portend big fights over Bill Clinton's "re-inventing government" agenda. . . . Some House education committee members upbraided Riley for his approach, . . . unhappy with the emphasis on reform at the expense of more aid to the disadvantaged through existing programs. . . . Says . . . a spokesman for the secretary: "We're trying to carve a new role for the federal government in education. Change is difficult." (p. 10)

The administration had learned through this difficult meeting that the prime concerns of the liberals, and of many national education organizations, were adequate funding and equity: namely, ensuring somehow that all students had the opportunity to learn the content of any new curriculum standards. But Riley and Clinton did not want to back down from their basic position that a new way had to be found to improve education and that simply adding funding to the current federal programs would not achieve that result.

As if to underscore these points, the administration's proposed budget for the next year ("Clinton Proposes," 1993), released a few weeks after the argumentative caucus meeting, requested a minimal overall increase of 1% in spending for education. Also proposed were cuts in funding for 89 programs and the elimination of 24 more programs. The funding saved by these cutbacks was shifted to the yet-to-be-submitted school reform initiative. Secretary Riley stated, in justifying the budget request: "My vision is one of fundamental change" (quoted in "Clinton Proposes," 1993, p. 1).

In early April, negotiations were conducted by Riley, with Congressmen Ford and Kildee representing the Democrats on the committee.[2] The congressional leaders asked that national opportunity-to-learn standards be developed and that no testing denying grade promotion or graduation from school be encouraged. Such changes were needed, they argued, to ensure a fair chance for students before they were held to higher standards. Ford and Kildee also asked for limitations on the powers of the governors in the process of establishing national standards because the liberals felt that the governors would not encourage strong opportunity-to-learn standards, which would lead to greater state funding of education. Last, Ford and Kildee asked for a substantial increase in funding for education from the federal level.

Riley agreed tentatively to the requested changes dealing with the opportunity-to-learn standards and the prohibition on testing that would lead to major consequences for children (called "high-stakes testing"). Regarding the other requests, Riley said that he had to consult with the president. When that meeting occurred in mid-April, Clinton supported Riley on his agreements but refused to accede on the other points. Clinton also urged Riley to meet with the Republicans on the administration's ideas because he had learned through experiences on other legislation that they could not be ignored.

As a result of these negotiations, most of the House Democrats signed on to cosponsor the administration's bill, but they also secured a promise from Ford that they would have a chance to amend the bill in committee to include the changes they had wanted but that the administration had rejected. Riley and his aides were very disappointed with that attitude because they had accommodated major concerns of the liberals, at the risk of losing the support of the governors, the business organizations, and some others.

During the negotiations with the House Democrats, the administration had been in constant contact with the National Governors' Association (NGA), the major business groups, the American Federation of Teachers, and many others. Riley's chief aide for school reform, Michael Cohen, who had worked for the NGA when Clinton was a governor, was the person charged with balancing all these interests. Every time the House Democrats demanded a change, Cohen tried to respond in a fashion that would accommodate that concern while not driving away these other actors. It was a difficult balancing act, and in the end a number of these others were unhappy. For instance, Shanker of the American Federation of Teachers was upset about the prohibition against high-stakes testing because he believed that such testing was necessary to motivate students.

Some of this discontent made its way into the press. Morton Kondracke (1993c), a conservative columnist for several newspapers, including *Roll Call,* the main paper for Capitol Hill, wrote in early April that college students were not adequately prepared and that the nation needed higher standards for achievement but that "House liberals may be forcing the Clinton Administration onto a path that will delay implementation of such standards for years" (p. 6). He accused Ford and Kildee of getting a commitment from the administration for equal emphasis on opportunity-to-learn standards "such as per pupil spending and teacher education levels that will slow pupil testing indefinitely" (p. 6). According to Kondracke, liberals "think it's unfair to test children unless they are first given adequate learning resources" (p. 6), but in his view, money certainly was not the reason that college students did not know much.

An editorial in *The Wall Street Journal* in mid-April ("Rolling Riley," 1993) commented that it was "hard to govern like a genuine New Democrat" and pointed to Riley's "rough time in a meeting last month, [with House Democrats] sending him back to write a bill more to their liking" (p. A12). Seeking a villain, the editorial accused Marshall Smith, a high official in the Department of Education, of masterminding a plot to force opportunity-to-learn standards into the administration's school reform bill with the intent "to block any student testing until schools are equal in such things as salaries, teacher credentials (as the unions define them), facilities and the like" (p. A12). The newspaper sarcastically opined: "The episode shows how hard it is for even a well-intentioned Democrat to break free of the cartels that control public policy in Washington. We almost feel sorry for Mr. Riley" (p. A12).

Taking a somewhat different perspective, *Business Week* (Del Valle, 1993) editorialized that Clinton's new reform plan was "payback time" for the teachers' unions due to their support during the campaign and that it therefore would not contain radical reform ideas (p. 43). In particular, school choice would be only mentioned and not emphasized, as it had been under Bush.

Some newspapers, however, saw the situation differently: The fact that the negotiations were occurring was a sign that the legislation had a good chance of being enacted. Julie Miller (1993c) in *Education Week* said that prospects were brightening for the administration's reform bill due to the changes that Riley and his aides had agreed to in their meetings with the House Democrats. *The Wall Street Journal* (Sharpe, 1993a) pointed out that "with the choice controversy removed from the debate, the administration may have an easier time passing its package" (p. B1) but also cautioned that the opportunity-to-learn standards could turn into legislative minefields.

While all this was occurring in early April, the senior Republican members on the House and Senate education committees, including Senator Nancy Kassebaum (Rep.-Kans.), Senator James Jeffords (Rep.-Vt.), and Congressman William Goodling (Rep.-Pa.), sent a joint letter to Riley (April 2, 1993) supporting the Clinton administration's initial leanings. These members pointed out that "many of the features of Goals 2000 resemble President Bush's America 2000 proposal" and that they supported many of the concepts embodied in both those proposals. Though not supporting a national curriculum, they endorsed the development of national content standards and encouragement to the states to develop their own standards. The Republicans opposed, however, the development of federal opportunity-to-learn standards and any requirement on the states to develop their own such standards.

Riley met with the Republicans on the House committee and briefed them on the draft of the administration's bill that contained the agreements with the House Democrats. The next day, the Republicans sent him a letter saying that he was headed in the right direction with trying to create "a results oriented education system that values outcomes over structure" but expressing a concern that the provisions for opportunity-to-learn standards went too far in trying to balance "results with a concern for fairness" (letter from Cong. William Goodling et al. to Secretary Richard Riley, April 21, 1993).

Despite agreeing with the thrust of the Clinton reform bill, the bottom line from the House Republicans was that none of them were willing to cosponsor the administration's proposal. Although their reservations about the opportunity-to-learn provisions were real, another factor in their declining to cosponsor was that intense partisan fights were occurring at that very time on Clinton's budget deficit reduction bill, and the Republican leadership did not want to do anything in any area to appear to be aiding the president. This shows how the general political atmosphere is important in understanding the different motivations of members of Congress.

▓ Goals 2000: Educate America Act

Now the action shifts from behind the scenes to full view on the stage of public policy. After finally securing substantial Democratic support in the House, President Clinton (1993a) sent Congress the Goals 2000: Educate America Act. In a press release from the U.S. Department of Education on April 21 describing the need for the bill ("Clinton Sends Congress Goals 2000: Educate America Act"), Secretary Riley said:

> We need high standards. In an international marketplace and an information century, countries that meet world-class standards will have the edge. This bill will help to establish internationally competitive standards so communities and states can, if they wish, gauge their curriculum and instruction against those that are world class. (p. 1)

Riley also stressed the need for comprehensive, systemic, and sustained school reform as the key to improving schools and student performance. Goals 2000, he said, would aid bottom-up state and local school reform and increase accountability for results while reducing red tape. The end result had to be to motivate students to achieve to higher standards.

Goals 2000 proposed to set into law the six national goals for education that President Bush and the nation's governors had agreed to in 1990 and established by law the National Education Goals Panel to monitor the implementation of those goals (H.R. 1804, 1993; S. 846, 1993). This panel, with substantial representation from the governors, would also approve national content and opportunity-to-learn standards. Approximately $400 million was requested for grants to states that chose to improve their schools by adopting their own state standards for content and their own opportunity-to-learn standards. Last, national job skill standards would be developed through a council representing business, labor, and education.

In an attachment to the April 21 press release ("How 'Goals 2000: Educate America Act' Will Work"), the Department of Education put forth its rationale for using standards as the linchpin for school reform:

> All students can learn more than they do presently. Too many children and youth receive a watered-down curriculum and suffer from expectations that are too low. The Nation needs clear standards of what all students should know and be able to do and clear statements of what it will take to provide all of them the opportunity to meet these standards. (p. 2)

The major national education organizations joined with the most important business groups in sending a letter to Congress supporting this program (letter from Chamber of Commerce of the United States et al. to Congress, "Organizations Supporting Goals 2000: Educate America Act," April 22, 1993). The Clinton administration had been successful in keeping on board all the important education and business associations, including the Chamber of Commerce of the United States, the Business Roundtable, the Committee for Economic Development, the National Alliance of Business, and the National Association of Manufacturers. The education/business letter urged that the bill be passed with strong bipartisan support because its enactment was essential for achieving school reform based on rigorous education standards and assessments ("Organizations Supporting Goals 2000," 1993).

Noteworthy by its absence from this list of endorsing organizations was the NGA. The *New York Times* (Chira, 1993) noted that the governors had not taken a position as yet on the bill because of concern about the opportunity-to-learn standards that the House Democrats had insisted on including in the bill. A spokesperson for the NGA was quoted as saying that because the states paid for 94% of the costs of elementary and secondary education, governors were wary of provisions calling for federal oversight. She added, "This is a pretty substantial shift in relations between the federal government and education. It's always been a state game" (Sullivan, quoted in Chira, 1993, p. A18).

The *Times* (Chira, 1993) also noted that the Clinton plan retained key features from former President Bush's school reform plan, most notably the development of voluntary national curriculum standards and national testing, but that it dropped the centerpiece of the Bush strategy, vouchers for private school tuition. The *Wall Street Journal* (Sharpe, 1993b) likewise commented that the Clinton education legislation was a continuation of Bush's plans but that it also contained some controversial items, especially the opportunity-to-learn standards, which some Republicans opposed because they feared that these could lead to federal interference in the daily operation of the schools.

A later article in the *New York Times* (Celis, 1993) said that although there were doubts about the bill's giving states too much authority and about the lack of large sums of money attached to the legislation, "even skeptics of the plan said they supported the Clinton package because it gave a national umbrella for the national movement to restructure schools and stressed job training" (p. A20) through the creation of the job skill standards. The Bush administration, it noted, had begun initiatives in both these areas, but the Clinton plan went beyond those proposals.

The *Washington Times,* which is generally perceived as more conservative than the *New York Times,* put a different spin on the story. The Clinton administration's education reform bill, Carol Innerst (1993) wrote, "appears to weaken the national push toward assessing what students have learned" (p. A4) because it strengthens the focus on spending through the incorporation of the opportunity-to-learn standards. Congressman Goodling was quoted as saying that he was concerned because there was more emphasis on resources than on results.

The *Washington Post* ("Administration's Proposal," 1993) described the plan's provisions for voluntary national standards and for grants to states and local communities to design their own strategies for meeting the national goals. It concluded that the essence of the idea was to rely "on public pressure to force schools to improve" (p. A28).

Similarly, Jill Zuckman (1993a) noted in the *Congressional Quarterly* that the Clinton administration hoped that "by laying out a framework of what is expected of all students and schools, both will rise to the challenge" (p. 1027). But she jabbed the Democrats for criticizing Bush for not proposing enough money for education and then having to "swallow those words as they praised a new school reform bill" (p. 1027) from Clinton that contained less money than Bush's—$420 million as compared with $690 million. She also noted that Riley had had a rocky journey bringing the bill to the Hill and had had to appease the House Democrats by emphasizing the opportunity-to-learn standards. Goodling was quoted saying that Riley "got beat up pretty badly by the majority" (p. 1028) and had been pushed too far in stressing those standards, but other Republicans were quoted as being smug that a Democratic administration was now pushing an initiative begun by Bush.

Robert Samuelson (1993), an economics columnist for the *Washington Post,* castigated the Clinton proposal as a continuation of "a tradition of national hypocrisy" (p. A19). He asserted that the main reason that most American students do not do as well as they might is that they do not work very hard and that the Clinton bill would discourage harder work by prohibiting the use of tests for high-stakes purposes, such as graduation from high school. He urged that the federal government could help to stimulate student motivation by tying the receipt of aid for postsecondary education to passage on a qualifying test.

These news accounts show the cross-currents as national policy is fashioned. Clinton and Riley continued on the same path as Bush and the governors with the idea of using high standards as a way to improve the schools. But being advocates for the public schools, they did not propose vouchers for private schools as had Bush and Alexander, and thus their approach did not appeal to conservatives. Instead, they tried to placate the liberals by upgrading the treatment of equity issues, as shown in the inclusion in their legislation of the opportunity-to-learn standards addressing the conditions of education. But in bowing in that direction, Clinton and Riley ran the risk of angering the governors, who were afraid of federal regulations that would require them to raise state spending on education. Further, the president and his secretary did not completely satisfy the liberals because, as "new Democrats," they were seeking a new path for school reform and were not enthusiastically endorsing the current federal programs or major new spending on education.

In setting policy, there are so many different points of view that it is never possible to satisfy them all. The art of politics and government is in sticking to your principles, while assembling a coalition that will secure enough support to get something done. Clinton and Riley were to succeed, but before that occurred, they would face many trials.

Subcommittee Action

On April 22, Secretary Riley appeared before the House committee to testify in favor of the administration's proposal (*Hearings on H.R. 1804,* 1993, pp. 1-42). He stressed the important role that education played in the national economy and in the ability of the country to compete abroad and asserted that schools must possess strong curricula and high expectations if students are to do well. The Goals 2000 bill helped in this effort, he said, by supporting state and local reform efforts through "seed funding" of reform.

Riley received mild treatment at the committee's hands, reflecting the weeks of work he had put into persuading the Democrats to support the bill and explaining its provisions to the Republicans. Although Republican Congresswoman Marge Roukema (Rep.-N.J.) expressed the fear that national opportunity-to-learn standards and national skill standards would lead to a national curriculum and national funding standards and although Democratic Congressman George Miller asserted that the opportunity-to-learn standards in the administration's bill were not strong enough, in general, there were no difficult questions for the secretary.

In the legislative process, the amending and voting on the wording of the bills usually begins at the lowest level: the subcommittee of the committee that has jurisdiction over the area of activity. Therefore, in this case, the writing of the school reform legislation was to start in the Subcommittee on Elementary and Secondary Education of the Committee on Education and Labor of the House of Representatives.

On May 6, that subcommittee met to consider the administration's bill. An amendment proposing a seventh national education goal regarding the preparation and training of teachers was accepted by the subcommittee when it was offered by Congressman Tim Roemer (Dem.-Ind.), and other amendments were also adopted that would direct more funds to local school districts and would require that disabled children be included in state school reform plans.

A last-minute controversy regarding the authority to set the national job skill standards was averted by delaying that discussion until the full committee. A fight over vouchers was settled quietly when the advocates let the issue be decided by a voice vote, which went against them. And the widely expected battle over the opportunity-to-learn standards was avoided by a compromise between Congressman Goodling and Congressman Major Owens (Dem.-N.Y.). The two congressmen had agreed on a limited list of factors that would have to be included in those standards, and both sides seemed satisfied.

Then Congressman Jack Reed (Dem.-R.I.) offered an amendment that states had to take specific corrective action if the opportunity-to-learn standards were not being carried out in local school districts. This amendment had not been circulated earlier, although Reed had frequently stated his concern that the administration's bill did not contain effective enforcement provisions.

Congressmen Goodling and Steve Gunderson (Rep.-Wisc.) vehemently opposed the Reed amendment and called it a "deal breaker" because they felt that they had gone about as far as they could with the opportunity-to-learn standards in their agreement with Owens and now were being faced with an amendment that pushed them further. The Democrats, however, rallied around the Reed amendment, arguing that it was the only way to ensure that the bill meant anything—a position that showed their lingering doubts about standards-based reform.

After a heated debate, the Reed amendment was adopted on a party-line vote. A vote to approve the entire bill, including the Reed amendment, then followed, with all the Democrats voting for the bill and all the Republicans voting against. The issue of school reform was being considered in a very dry forest, and the smallest flame led to a full-blown firestorm ("Bipartisan House Education Coalition," 1993; Hoff, 1993a).

Riley and other members of the Clinton administration were extremely upset: They felt that they had gone the extra mile to get the liberals behind the bill and to keep the Republicans informed but that the liberals had then pulled an amendment out that no one had seen, and its approval had driven the Republicans away. Further, although the NGA had sent a letter to the committee before the mark-up showing a division of opinion about the bill (letter from Governors Roy Romer and Carroll Campbell for the National Governors' Association to Secretary Richard Riley, May 6, 1993), the passage of the Reed amendment was bound to prove to the governors that the Congress wanted to micromanage the schools within the states.

The full committee did not take up the Goals bill for another 6 weeks, and that time was filled with controversy regarding the bill, especially centered on the Reed amendment. In late May, after the subcommittee mark-up, President Clinton and Secretary Riley began to speak out publicly about their views on what the House had done to their original ideas. At a White House ceremony, Clinton said, "[Goals] will facilitate fundamental reforms in our schools. And I must say that's probably why some people don't like it all that well, including some members of my own party in the Congress" (quoted in "Clinton, Riley," 1993, p. 1). He added, "We can't raise standards and achievement, either by leaving things the way they are, or simply by piling on more particular programs and mandates from Washington" (p. 2). Therefore, he urged Congress not to change the package that he had sent them.

Riley told a business group during the same month that he was trying to keep Goals tied to the lessons that had been learned in school reform but that "in Congress, we're being pulled by the extremes . . . good people, but people who have a more extreme view" (quoted in "Clinton, Riley," 1993, p. 2). Some in Congress, he added, would "load it down with a 'Christmas tree' of things" (p. 2). He pled for the help of business to keep the legislation focused on goals and results.

On June 3, President Clinton sent a letter to Chairman Ford urging support for the bill as it had been presented to Congress. In particular, he opposed the Reed amendment because national leadership must be balanced with recognition of the fact that education is primarily a state and local responsibility. He added:

> Amendments which require states, as a condition of federal support, to commit to specific corrective actions for schools that fail to meet [opportunity-to-learn] standards go too far. These requirements will impede states' efforts to focus accountability on results. In addition, they will require states to commit to specific actions even before the nature of the problem is known. For these reasons, this type of requirement will be a disincentive for states to

participate in reform efforts. I urge you not to support amendments that
expand the definition or role of opportunity-to-learn standards.

Clinton's letter caused a stir among the committee members because it is
very unusual for a president to send any communication under his name while
a committee is considering a bill. Normally, the work of influencing legislation at the early stages of drafting is left to the secretaries of the departments
and to informal communications, especially if the same party controls the
executive branch and the legislative branch of government. It was obvious to
the members that both the president and Secretary Riley were quite concerned
about the action of the subcommittee, and it was equally obvious that the
governors had been able to convey their opposition to the Reed amendment
directly to the White House.

On the other side of the issue, Keith Geiger, president of the National
Education Association, asserted that the inclusion of the opportunity-to-learn
standards was a "forthright statement that if we expect improved learning
outcomes, we must improve learning conditions" (quoted in "Grading Goals
2000," 1993, p. 6).

Most voices raised in the debate, however, supported Clinton and Riley's
view. The American Federation of Teachers, the other teacher organization,
did not agree with the National Education Association. Al Shanker told the
NGA, "It's totally wrong to hold the development of content and performance
standards and stakes hostage until you solve all of the equity issues, or most
of the equity issues, or even some of the equity issues" (quoted in Rothman,
1993, p. 20). Shanker argued that students in poor schools would never be
exposed to a curriculum of high quality if equity was first pursued.

Chester Finn, who as an assistant secretary of education in the Reagan
administration was involved with drafting America 2000 for Lamar Alexander, wrote in the *Washington Times* that the Goals 2000 bill was "not worth
enacting" because it portended a huge increase in federal regulation and
control (quoted in "Grading Goals 2000," 1993, p. 6). Congressman Goodling
(1993) wrote in *Roll Call* that the committee Democrats were just pushing for
more money for education through the device of the opportunity-to-learn
standards and that he did not believe that this view was in keeping with Riley's
or Clinton's ideas on what was really ailing American education.

On June 15, Governors Roy Romer and Carroll Campbell wrote to
Congress on behalf of the NGA, saying that all the governors were concerned
that the opportunity-to-learn standards could be changed from a voluntary
mechanism to "an attempt to mandate priorities at the state and local levels."

The Business Roundtable also wrote opposing the amendments regarding those standards because they believed that the federal government's role was to set goals and not to impose mandates (letter from Joseph T. Gorman, on behalf of the Business Roundtable, to William D. Ford, June 14, 1993).

Continuing the drumbeat against the bill, several columns appeared in the *Wall Street Journal* saying that Goals 2000 meant "more government from Washington, and with it, more money, more lawsuits, and more bureaucracy strangling states and communities" (Manno, 1993, p. A14) and that the original Clinton bill had a "Different Democrat design" when first drafted because it was based on the idea of standards, tests, and consequences but that the "liberal congressional Democratic barons" had taken the proposal and "amended, diluted, and transformed" it (Wattenberg, 1993, p. A16).

The *U.S. News and World Report* concluded, "Just when it looked as though we would get a serious school-reform bill through Congress, House Democrats have moved in and mugged it beyond recognition" (Leo, 1993, p. 19). That magazine said that the Reed amendment converted voluntary opportunity-to-learn standards into mandatory ones because states would have to take corrective action if school districts did not meet those criteria.

Except for the National Education Association, the House Democrats were alone. No articles appeared in major publications giving the reasons for the Reed and other opportunity-to-learn amendments, nor were any public arguments made in the news media about the need to improve the quality of schools if a standards and testing approach to reform was to be adopted. The forces that usually argued for additional and fairer funding for education decided, for whatever reason, to leave the battleground to others, and therefore the opponents had a field day.

▓ Full Committee Action

Once a subcommittee approves a piece of legislation, it proceeds up to the full committee, so the next action on this bill was to occur in the Education and Labor Committee of the House of Representatives. As the full committee prepared in mid-June to consider the bill that had been approved by the subcommittee in May, the pace of activity quickened.

Congressmen Reed and Goodling met several times to try to resolve their differences, but it seemed that the loud opposition from outside Congress to the opportunity-to-learn standards made Goodling more adamant against them, so no compromise proved possible. Congressman Richard Armey

(Rep.-Tex.) began to circulate letters in favor of an alternative to the Clinton bill that would be based on choice programs involving private schools and would not have any reference to any type of standards.

Ford and Kildee, who were concerned that Democratic support for the bill was still too soft, urged the administration to adopt an attitude of accepting any Democratic amendments they could, with the hope that any difficult changes could be scuttled later in a conference committee with the Senate because that body seemed inclined to adopt a much less controversial version of the legislation. Riley listened to this advice and thus eventually quietly acquiesced to some amendments that Clinton had asked the committee to delete.[3]

On June 23, the full committee met to consider the bill. The transcript of the committee's deliberations (U.S. House of Representatives, 1993) shows that the meeting began quietly enough, with the adoption of a package of 18 amendments that resolved many of the minor concerns that Democratic and Republican members had had with the legislation, such as retaining too much money at the state level. Then Congressman Armey offered his substitute for the bill, which emphasized the conservative approach of using vouchers for private school tuition. The Clinton approach would reform nothing, he contended; it was an "education establishment dream bill" that would further entrench the status quo (U.S. House of Representatives, 1993, p. 10). Armey said that his substitute would achieve results because it would delete all the provisions dealing with standards—content, opportunity, and job skill—and instead would make the funds available to states and school districts only for merit schools, model schools, site-based management, and choice programs.

Ford argued against Armey and said that a similar choice provision "had sunk" the Bush administration's reform efforts ("House Panel Close," 1993, p. 4). The Armey substitute was defeated, with 7 members in favor and 35 opposed. The proponents were the more conservative Republicans, and the opponents included all the Democrats and the more moderate Republicans. Armey's approach had been too radical for the moderate Republicans because it rejected entirely the idea of using standards to improve education. In other words, Armey was arguing that Bush's idea of using standards for reform was no better than Clinton's.

The Republicans were more united in supporting amendments to change the provisions of the bill regarding the development of national job skill standards. Some business organizations felt that the bill did not give business enough of a voice on the panel that was to choose job clusters and coordinate the work of skill standards development, so Republican amendments were offered to create a stronger role for business and, failing that, to delete entirely the provisions for skill standards. Those Republican amendments were defeated.

After those votes, the committee adopted several amendments offered by Democrats that weakened the power of the governor-dominated National Education Goals Panel and that made other changes in the administration's bill. The Republicans noted that the president opposed those amendments, but the Democrats ignored this in voting for their own amendments.

Congressman Goodling then offered an amendment to delete the Reed amendment, contending that it would lead to unfunded mandates on the states. As an example of the effect of the amendment, he said that if the opportunity-to-learn standards set a certain ratio for the number of teachers to students, school districts would have to find the money to reduce their class sizes to conform. Goodling urged instead that the whole effort be focused on what children learn (U.S. House of Representatives, 1993).

Congressman Reed countered that the issue was whether the country was going to be serious about reform or "continue to make noise about reform and use rhetorical flourishes and not confront the hard questions" (U.S. House of Representatives, 1993, p. 99). He argued that the country was moving to raise academic standards but that unless some basic resources were provided, those standards would never be achieved. It was not intellectually honest, he said, to adopt a standards approach to reform without addressing what to do if a state did not provide the resources that a child needed to succeed. Reed, however, acknowledged the sincerity of Goodling's opposition and offered to modify his amendment to say that a state would not have to guarantee any particular course of action but would simply have to adopt procedures to address the issue of resources.

Goodling rejected the change offered by Reed and said that the amendment would still be an unfunded mandate on states if they participated in the program. Gunderson joined Goodling in rejecting the amendment, saying that he was willing to accept opportunity-to-learn standards as long as they were voluntary on a state but that now the Reed amendment, even as revised, made them mandatory or would discourage states from applying for funds.

Reed countered that without his amendment, the bill would be "a paper exercise, another sort of feel-good bill that doesn't make anything better" (U.S. House of Representatives, 1993, pp. 115-116). Congressman George Miller joined the debate, saying that governors and local school officials should not say that they wanted to raise standards and then not help schools to deliver on the content because many schools cannot do that now. He urged public officials to

> come clean with the American public on how many children don't have the textbooks to convey the content to meet the standards, how many children don't have qualified teachers by training to convey the content so that they can meet the standards. (U.S. House of Representatives, 1993, p. 122)

Goodling, pounding the table, responded to Miller, "We heard a lot of rhetoric, we heard a great speech, but we didn't send one penny to any school district in this country. We just heard a lot of hot air. . . . No money went out, just the mandates" (U.S. House of Representatives, 1993, p. 122).

Reed responded that there was indeed a lot of rhetoric used in the committee's debate but that there would be a lot more in the years ahead if his amendment was deleted because there would not be any real reform. He also pointed out that his amendment was supported by the National Parent Teachers Association and by the American Association of School Administrators and that those groups were not partisan and were interested in real reform.

The vote on retaining the Reed provision was 28 in favor and 15 opposed, with all the Democrats favoring and all the votes against being Republican. The entire bill was then accepted by the committee by the same partisan vote. So nothing had really changed from the subcommittee: The liberals insisted on significant changes in the administration's bill, and the Republicans were either extreme conservatives totally opposed to the whole idea of using standards for reform or were moderates who favored raising standards but were against anything that seemed to require states to spend more money on education.

The *Congressional Monitor* ("Democrats' Amendment," 1993) reported the next day that the Reed amendment had caused angry protests from Republicans and that Goodling, who had been furious about the amendment, had concluded, "This bill is a disaster. I don't think the Senate will fall for any of this junk" (p. 3). The *New York Times* (Clymer, 1993) reported that while the Clinton bill on educational standards was advancing, Gunderson had said that it would "nationalize education," and Reed had countered that all he wanted to do was to require states to think about how they would make their schools better (p. A19). Clinton's school reform bill was following the same pattern as Bush's, with partisan, fist-banging fights marking its progress, concluded the *Congressional Quarterly* (Zuckman, 1993c). The committee's

Republicans often sided with the Clinton administration against the efforts of the committee's Democrats to alter the National Education Goals Panel and to strengthen the opportunity to learn standards, wryly noted *Education Week* (Pitsch, 1993b).

Rochelle Stanfield (1993) in the *National Journal,* another magazine covering the events on Capitol Hill, asserted that Riley and his top aides in the Department of Education, though having real-life experience in state and local government, lacked experience in dealing with Congress, "particularly the House, which requires a delicate touch" (p. 1515), and that this deficiency was beginning to show. The prime example cited was that the school reform bill was drafted "without much consultation with Congress or with the education lobbyists who were expected to support it" (p. 1515) and that this early isolation in decision making was the root of the later bickering over the details of the reform bill.

The inexperience of Riley and his crew showed further in the weeks following the full committee mark-up when they began to consider bypassing the committee and instead working directly with Republicans and with Democrats who were more conservative than the committee's members.[4] The idea Riley toyed with was to have a coalition of these members offer the administration's original bill as an amendment to the committee-approved bill when the full House of Representatives considered the legislation.

Ford and Kildee expressed to Riley their opposition to this strategy. A major argument they made was that the administration had several other important bills pending before the same committee, such as Clinton's prized national service bill, and that the liberal Democrats, if defeated on the school bill, would not cooperate with the administration on other legislation.

After seeing the long-term problems that this approach would create in dealing with the committee, Riley agreed that it would be better for him not to pursue it. The secretary, however, was very frustrated with the liberals. In his view, the business community, the governors, and the major education organizations were all supportive of the administration's initial bill, and the only opponents were the liberals on the House committee, yet these people were succeeding in slowing down the bill and maybe even defeating it. This seemed to confirm the worst fears of Riley, Clinton, and the others who had formed the Democratic Leadership Conference that liberals were driving the agenda of the Democratic party and that their ideas were out of step with the majority view in the country.

After flirting with the idea of beating the liberals in the House with the support of a Republican-conservative Democratic coalition, Riley channeled his frustrations in a more positive direction when he adopted the suggestion of Congressman Kildee and of a key legislative aide in the department, Thomas Wolanin, that he work on changing eight particular amendments that the administration opposed. Riley, who was known in South Carolina for his patient persistence and dogged determination, undertook this task and worked at it for the next several months.

In July, at the annual convention of the National Education Association, Clinton (1993b) acknowledged the "Herculean efforts" of Riley in working for passage of Goals 2000 and spoke out against any efforts amending the bill to "water it down, weaken it or divert it" from being framed to assist local communities and the states. He added, "We cannot run the schools of this country from Washington, D.C. We need to empower you to run them" (p. 1268).

Riley (1993a) also began to speak more publicly about the legislation and the need to enact it. In a letter to the *Wall Street Journal,* he stated that a column that had appeared in that paper contained "deliberate distortions" of the administration's bill because challenging content standards were still at the heart of the bill even as it was moving through Congress and because the opportunity-to-learn standards were not a recent creation but had originated with the National Council on Education Standards and Testing appointed in 1991 by the Bush administration and the Democrats and Republicans in Congress (p. A13).

Although the states have the basic responsibility for education, Riley told the American Federation of Teachers in July, there must be national goals and world-class standards set at the national level, and these would be "the lighthouse . . . as the goals for states to look to" (quoted in "Riley Pledges," 1993, p. 5). But then the states would set their own content and performance standards, opportunity-to-learn standards, and assessments, and local schools would have creativity to reach those state standards. He added, "I think that's where industry's going to decide to put new businesses—those states that have high standards, and that they know people are reaching upward, in terms of education" (p. 5).

At the same meeting, Riley pointed to his experiences as governor in South Carolina, where he had pushed for a school reform plan based on high standards. People had told him that it could not be achieved because there were so many poor people in the state, but he had persisted nonetheless, and the reform bill had passed. He insisted that high standards made a difference for all young people regardless of wealth and that in the new economic era people must understand that "children are not born smart—they get smart, through hard work, study, and opportunity" (p. 6). Goals 2000 was meant to help in that effort.

A far different vision of the legislation, however, was beginning to appear from conservative opponents as the bill awaited further action in the House during the summer of 1993. The Heritage Foundation (1993), a Washington-based think tank, asserted that the bill would stifle grassroots education reform by establishing federal standards for school spending and teacher salaries, increasing bureaucratic control of education, establishing an intrusive federal role, and creating mandates that would force state and local governments to raise taxes. The foundation argued that the Armey substitute that had been defeated in committee ought to be passed instead because it encouraged school choice and did not create any standards that would lead to enhancing "the power of bureaucrats, enabling them to block real reform" (Tucker, 1993, p. 7).

In July, Congressman Armey and then-Minority Whip Newt Gingrich (Rep.-Ga.) announced that GOP conservatives would offer their own substitute to the Clinton bill when Goals 2000 was considered in the House. Armey said that the alternative "takes away from the liberals control of the nation's schools" (quoted in "Armey," 1993, p. 3) and that the reason his substitute had lost in the education committee was that the panel was a "wholly owned subsidiary of the National Education Association" (p. 3), with Republicans not even representing the broad range of views among the House GOP.

In late July, members of Congress received a letter from Beverly LaHaye of the Concerned Women for America (July 22, 1993) endorsing the Armey substitute because that amendment "would prohibit the use of funds for sex clinics and the controversial 'outcome based education'" and because the committee's bill would offer "no flexibility, no choice, and no accountability" and would set into motion "a dangerous trend towards national standards, national curriculum, and a national school board." Phyllis Schlafly of the Eagle Forum also wrote to the Congress (July 21, 1993) to endorse the Armey substitute because the committee bill would incorporate "the education establishment in all aspects of life from conception until after one enters the work force." The Free Congress Foundation (1993) wrote calling the committee bill "business-as-usual" (p. 1) but then contradicted itself by alleging that it would create "an engine for broad social change and redistribution of wealth" (p. 3).

In August, Concerned Women for America expanded on its earlier criticism of the bill, saying that "Goals 2000 strives to use schools to increasingly replace the family" (LaHaye, 1993, p. 4). A publication of that group called the Bush America 2000 legislation "the stealth bomber of reform" because it "called for a heightened level of involvement by the federal government" (p. 5). Bush, according to the publication, had wanted a "revolution" in American public education, and Clinton had intentionally used a similar title for his bill because a consensus had "been reached by the nation's governors and the political sense is that there will be bipartisan support at the federal level for this 'revolution' " (p. 6).

This was the beginning of the far right's inflammatory rhetoric against Goals 2000 and national involvement in standards-based reform; from it was to emerge a full-blown campaign to depict this school reform effort as a destroyer of families. The quiet opposition of conservative Republican senators to Bush's school reform bills was being transformed by far-right groups in the summer of 1993 into a battle against "mind control" of children and other nefarious schemes. And as shown by the material published by Concerned Women for America, former President Bush was being blamed for first leading the country onto this path.

While all this criticism was coming from the political right, Riley went from office to office in Congress, trying to convince the Democratic members of the education committee, who were on the political left, that they had to change their amendments for the bill to pass the House. Finally, in August, he had some success. Julie Miller (1993b) reported in *Education Week* that the House liberals were becoming more willing to negotiate "as it became clear that a coalition of Republicans and moderate Democrats—possibly with the support of the administration—might be able to amend the bill on the House floor" (p. 36).

To underscore this possibility, Congressman David McCurdy (Dem.-Okla.), a leader of the more conservative Democrats, sent a letter to Chairman Ford on September 9 expressing opposition to the Reed amendment as an unfunded federal mandate and hoping that the administration's original language would be offered as an amendment on the House floor. An interesting aspect of McCurdy's letter was that he said he and many of the more conservative Democrats enthusiastically supported the establishment of national education goals and standards as proposed in Clinton's bill. This showed that the political far right was not having an effect on these more conservative Democrats with its criticisms of national standards.

During August and September, the governors and the business community continued their attacks on the Reed amendment. The National Alliance of Business (Kolberg, 1993) said that "the House bill would serve as an impediment rather than an incentive to school reform" (p. A20) because of the federally mandated opportunity-to-learn standards. At its annual summer meeting, the NGA said that "the states, not the federal government, should assume the responsibility for creating an education delivery system that enables all students to achieve high standards" (quoted in Hoff, 1993b, p. 1). At that meeting, Secretary Riley faced criticism from Republican Governor Campbell that the House bill would make the states "subservient to a committee of the Congress" (quoted in Hoff, 1993c, p. 1). Riley (1993b) sought to reassure the governors that the bill was voluntary and furthermore that he was working with the committee "in a spirit of cooperation" and expected favorable results in terms of changing the offending provisions.

Riley (1993b) told the nation's governors that he and President Clinton were "fully committed to reinventing the federal government's role in education" because current programs are "outside of, and irrelevant to, the overall reform process." He added that the situation would soon get worse if those programs were not changed because the states were moving on changing assessment systems and other aspects of education and would soon run into federal requirements blocking such reforms. Continuing with the same theme, Vice President Albert Gore announced in September his "re-inventing government" plan, which called for the elimination or consolidation of 40 education programs. According to Mark Pitsch (1993b) of *Education Week,* he appeared "to single out the Education Department, which has been repeatedly faulted for poor management in recent years" (p. 23).

In the face of these criticisms and the possibility of defeat on the House floor, but especially due to Riley's persistence going from congressional door to congressional door, most of the committee Democrats agreed to change their amendments weakening the National Education Goals Panel and strengthening the opportunity-to-learn standards. Most notably, Congressman Reed agreed to insert in his amendment that no other federal aid would be conditional on compliance with the Goals legislation, so that a state could avoid any corrective action on improving the conditions of education by simply declining funding from the new Goals program.

Because all the offending amendments were going to be deleted or weakened, President Clinton sent a letter to Ford on September 23 expressing satisfaction with progress on the bill, particularly regarding the opportunity-to-learn standards and the Goals Panel. However, the president said that the administration was still troubled by some of the bill's provisions and would work in the conference committee with the Senate to achieve a bill based on his principles and meriting bipartisan support. Clinton, therefore, urged the House to support the bill at this stage.

Clinton and Riley deserve credit for sticking to their principles on education, concluded Morton Kondracke (1993a) in *Roll Call* as he described the negotiations between Riley and the Democrats during the summer and the resulting removal or modification of the offending amendments. He asserted that Clinton was ready to veto his own program if it limited the flexibility of states to improve their schools and that this implicit threat had helped to convince the committee members to change their provisions. Mark Pitsch (1993a) in *Education Week* reported that this agreement between the administration and the members meant that the way was paved for the bill to go to the House. *CongressDaily* quoted a Republican aide saying that the GOP members of the House were "pleased with the progress" that the Democrats and the administration had made ("House Panel Democrats," 1993, p. 3).

On October 1, the National Education Goals Panel released its second annual report on how far the nation had come in meeting the six goals established by President Bush and the governors in 1990; its conclusion was that the results had "been wholly inadequate" (quoted in Jordan, 1993, p. A2). Secretary Riley commented, "It is time for America to get serious about our children and our future. The federal govenment can no longer stand on the sidelines as we slip further away from reaching these goals" (quoted in Jordan, 1993, p. A2). Due to his hard work and that of Michael Cohen, Thomas Wolanin, and other aides, the House was ready to consider Goals 2000 as a way to help with that reform.

▨ House Consideration

As it became clear in early October that Goals 2000 would soon be brought before the House for debate and amendment, different forces started to generate letters and materials trying to influence the outcome. Secretary of Education Riley and Secretary of Labor Robert Reich wrote to members of the House on October 1 urging support of the bill because its central purpose was "to fundamentally improve teaching, learning and occupational skills throughout America" through the development of academic and occupational skill standards.

National education groups lined up behind the legislation. The Council of Chief State School Officers, for instance, sent letters to every member of the House pointing out that since the time that the national goals for education had been adopted, there had been no federal action to help carry them out (letter from Gordon Ambach to Representatives, October 4, 1993). Shanker of the American Federation of Teachers, despite his concerns about the prohibition against high-stakes testing, wrote to the members of the House (October 12, 1993) urging passage of the bill because it recognized the federal government's "legitimate role in stimulating educational excellence" and because the bill would be amended to allow the development of content standards to proceed without having to wait for opportunity-to-learn standards to be set.

The nation's major business groups also supported the legislation. Their letter of endorsement (from William Kolberg, President, National Alliance of Business, and Co-Chair, Business Coalition for Education Reform, to Cong. William Ford, October 12, 1993) noted that the Goals Panel report showing wholly inadequate progress toward achieving the national goals demonstrated once again the need for voluntary national standards describing what all children should know and be able to do. "The bill's emphasis on comprehensive reform, high standards for all children, and world class occupational standards to guide workers and education and training programs is a significant step in securing the nation's future economic vitality," they asserted. However, the business groups expressed two reservations about the bill: The opportunity-to-learn standards ought to be developed at the state level, and there needed to be a greater business role in establishing the job skill standards. Among the groups in this business coalition were the Chamber of Commerce of the United States, the National Association of Manufacturers, the Business Roundtable, the National Alliance of Business, and the Committee for Economic Development.

With the nation's major education and business organizations aligned behind the legislation, it would seem that its passage would be easy, but a fierce attack came from the political right. The Family Research Council (1993), for instance, alleged that the bill would create additional bureaucracy, including a "*de facto* national school board" (p. 1).

Congressman Armey, in leading the charge in the House for the conservatives, sent out a series of "Dear Colleague" letters to members repeating the accusations about the "national school board" ("Here Comes the National School Board," October 1, 1993) but also adding that the bill would require political correctness for textbooks ("Political Correctness Police Bust Kindergartners?" October 4, 1993), would lead to welfare offices being put into schools along with health clinics that would refer students for abortions ("Creating the Spaghetti Sauce Schools of Tomorrow," October 4, 1993), and would lead to outcome-based education's going national ("How Do You Spell Outcome-Based Education? G-O-A-L-S 2-0-0-0," October 6, 1993). Armey described outcome-based education (OBE) as shifting schools from how much students know to how well they are socialized, holding "smart children back to the pace of the slowest learners," and weaning "children from their parents' values to instill in them politically correct, secular-left values" ("How Do You Spell . . . ?" October 6, 1993). Armey concluded that the legislation was "no mainstream bill"; rather, it was "radical, unprecedented, and dangerous," and if it were to pass, "three and a half centuries of local educational liberty in America [would] effectively be at an end" ("Here Comes the National School Board," October 1, 1993).

The Clinton administration circulated materials to refute Armey's charges linking Goals to OBE (U.S. Department of Education, 1993). There was no affiliation between the legislation and OBE, it asserted, because "Goals 2000 focuses exclusively on academics" and "does not, as some state OBE programs do, endorse non-academic outcomes" (p. 2). The allegation about changing children's values could not be further from the truth, according to the administration, because the bill encouraged parents to play a greater role in their children's education and in fact was endorsed by the National Parent Teachers Association. Smart children would not be held back because all children would have their educational achievement lifted, and the current system of low expectations, low standards, watered-down curriculum, and schools that failed to educate would be ended. Last, the new national council had not been given any powers to be a national school board, or it would never have been recommended by the National Council on Education Standards and Testing, which had been appointed by the Bush administration and Congress.

Thus, the charges and countercharges went back and forth. The administration also circulated several articles from newspapers endorsing the concepts in Goals. For example, *U.S.A. Today* in April had strongly supported the idea of national education standards, saying that "those unequivocal standards can give parents and educators benchmarks to measure their schools against" ("Make Schools Better," 1993, p. A12), and a *Dallas Morning News* column in August (Kondracke, 1993b) had criticized Republicans for "waffl[ing] on education" (p. A13)—being in favor of standards when Bush recommended them and then opposing them when Clinton suggested the same thing.

Governor Roy Romer of Colorado sent a letter to Ford (October 7, 1993) endorsing the bill as it was to be amended and urging further work during the conference with the Senate to produce final legislation that would accord with Clinton's principles. Romer sent his letter seeking "speedy passage" of Goals in his capacity as an individual governor instead of as a representative of the NGA because Governor Campbell and several others would not agree to a letter endorsing the bill.

As all these letters of praise and damnation of the legislation were being circulated and read by the legislators, the Committee on Rules of the House met to consider the terms under which the bill would be sent to the floor for debate and amendment ("Goals 2000," 1993). In the House of Representatives, unlike the Senate, most major bills can be considered only after the time for debate and the format for amendments is set by a "rule" that is approved by that committee and then voted on in the full House.

Originally, during the week of October 4, the Rules Committee was set to approve a rule permitting an unlimited number of changes to be proposed to the bill, but then the National Education Association, the National Parent Teachers Association, and several other groups protested that an entirely "open" rule would produce a chaotic situation on the floor, especially regarding amendments dealing with choice, vouchers, and other ways of aiding private schools. Therefore, the Rules Committee agreed to delay the bill for a week and to require that all amendments be printed in the *Congressional Record* before they could be considered for inclusion in the rule.

By the following Monday, 14 amendments had been submitted. The committee met on the following day and approved a rule making in order 10 of those amendments. The committee explained that two of the four others were duplicative, and it did not permit those amendments that dealt with extraneous social issues, such as an amendment that would have required that nothing in the bill could encourage homosexuality, bisexuality, or transsexuality.

When the House considered the rule on Wednesday, October 13, the Republican members of the Rules Committee argued against its acceptance on the ground that all amendments ought to have been permitted, but when the motion was offered to approve the rule, they let it be adopted on a voice vote, thus avoiding a nasty fight. In the ways of the House, this meant that the Republicans would not fight the bill tooth and nail and that some Republicans would support the legislation. If an all-out fight had been brewing, every procedural motion would have been challenged, including a demand for a vote on the rule.

Finally, that same day, the school reform bill was before the House for debate and amendment. Congressman Kildee, the floor manager of the legislation, emphasized that Goals called for systemwide reform as advocated by the governors and many school reformers and that this reform would be fashioned through a process developing a national consensus. Kildee was followed by many of the Democratic members of the committee who offered their support, although some had raised concerns earlier in the process.

Congressman McCurdy, who had written to Ford in September asking for an opportunity to vote on the administration's original bill, said that he now supported the compromises worked out by Secretary Riley with the committee members because these moved the bill closer to the introduced legislation; therefore, he would vote for the bill. Thus, it seemed that the liberal and conservative Democrats were all lining up behind the legislation.

Congressman Goodling, the Republican point man on the bill, gave an important speech detailing how the bill that was being brought before the House was different from the bill that the committee had approved. Goodling said that almost all the problems the Republicans had found with the bill as it left the committee had been worked out, such as the issue of unfunded federal mandates and the voluntary nature of the program. He also reminded the members how the whole process had originated with President Bush and the governors.

Congressman Gunderson backed up Goodling, calling Riley's work a "minor miracle" in producing such agreement on the bill ("Goals 2000," 1993, p. H7743). He said that he supported the concepts of the bill because Americans were so mobile and should have some assurance through voluntary standards that the education their children were receiving was somewhat similar as they moved from school district to district. A few speeches were made against the bill by conservatives, including Congressman Cass Ballenger (Rep.-N.C.), who argued that the bill was too bureaucratic and cost too much. But there was not great heat or angry rhetoric.

The first amendment offered was one from Goodling to forbid any federal mandate, direction, or control of a state's, local school district's, or school's curriculum, program of instruction, or allocation of resources. Congressman Gary Condit (Dem.-Calif.) supported Goodling's amendment because he became interested in the bill due to the controversy about the Reed amendment and a fear about unfunded mandates being imposed on the states. Goodling's amendment meant, he said, that no state would have to reallocate state funding due to the receipt of Goals funds.

Kildee, as floor manager of the bill, accepted this amendment pursuant to a prior agreement with Goodling. Nonetheless, a record vote was demanded because all the publicity about the Reed amendment had created such a stir. The result was 424 in favor and none against. The controversy about the Reed amendment and the opportunity-to-learn standards was thereby laid to rest— but only for the time being.

The second major amendment was offered by Congressman Armey and was the same substitute that he had offered in the committee: namely, an elimination of any requirements for the development of any education standards and instead the imposition of a new requirement that any state that received federal school reform funds had to spend at least 25% of those funds on choice programs that could involve private schools. Armey's substitute also forbade the use of any of this money for schools to coordinate their programs with other social and health services.

Armey argued that his amendment would avoid the development of a national curriculum by a new national school board through a top-down bureaucratic approach to reform, that it would lead to choice programs for the poor, and that it would not lead to the inclusion of health clinics and welfare offices in the schools. He cited the support of two former secretaries of education, Republicans William Bennett and Lamar Alexander, and of the Citizens for Educational Freedom, the Christian Coalition, the Family Research Council, the Eagle Forum, the Concerned Women for America, and the Christian Action Network. Several Republican members spoke up in favor of Armey's proposal.

Kildee opposed Armey on the grounds that he would limit school districts to four activities that could be funded for reform and thereby would restrict local flexibility in seeking the best way to change the schools; further, the restriction on use of funds for coordination of social and health services meant that children could not be helped to be better prepared for school. Goodling opposed Armey because he thought that involving the federal government in funding private schools would ultimately lead to government control over those schools. Reed, Mink, and other committee Democrats rallied against the Armey substitute and in favor of the committee bill.

The Armey substitute, supported by the political far right, was defeated, with 130 in favor and 300 against. Almost every vote in favor was cast by a Republican, and the votes against were from the Democrats, who were joined by a number of more moderate Republicans.

After considering a few other minor amendments, the House voted on final approval of the legislation. Almost anticlimactically, after all the intense arguments and votes on the bill over the course of many months, Goals 2000 was approved by the House by a vote of 307 to 118. Two hundred and forty-nine Democrats voted in favor and only two against, and 57 Republicans voted in favor and 116 against. The only politically independent congressman also voted in favor of the bill.

Secretary Riley triumphantly announced:

> This vote moves us one step closer to once again making "excellence" the single most important value in the American education system. Goals 2000 is not a liberal or a conservative solution to this nation's education ills. It is a

pragmatic reform built around what has been shown to work: involving parents, raising standards, and overhauling teacher education. ("U.S. House Passes," 1993, p. 6)

The *Washington Post* ("Schools and Standards," 1993) commended Riley for his steady leadership in steering the bill to passage between the shoals of Republican fears of federalization of education with national standards and Democratic concerns that low-performing groups and struggling public school systems would be written off if they failed the new standards. The same editorial also hailed the adoption of the Goodling/Condit amendment because it put to rest the fear of federal control and because national standards would only lead to improvement "by force of example, not by force of federal law" (p. A22).

Jill Zuckman (1993b) in the *Congressional Quarterly* reported, almost with surprise, that "in noticeable contrast to the partisan fights that marked committee consideration of President Clinton's Goals 2000 education reform bill, the measure sailed through the House October 13" (p. 2817).

Thus, Goals 2000 made its way through the House from the first days of February 1993, when it was described to a skeptical congressional audience, to the middle of October, when it passed overwhelmingly. A major crisis had involved the caucus with the Democratic members in March when Riley had had to refashion his ideas just to get them introduced and supported by his own party, but the real crunch had come when the more liberal Democratic members of the committee pushed the bill even further toward requiring the states to take action to correct inequities in educational opportunity and had run into staunch resistance from all the Republicans, the administration, the governors, the business community, and others.

It had taken all of Riley's skills moving the Democrats back toward the political middle to put the bill on the way to overwhelmingly accepted passage, but he had succeeded only because of aid from Goodling, who was willing to buck the majority of his own party to pass a federal school reform bill, and from Reed, Mink, Owens, and Kildee, who in the end saw that it was more important to support the president to secure agreement on the idea of national school reform than to stick to positions that they believed in but that would not prevail.

After this important step in the process, the outline of the national role in assisting in school reform became clearer: urging higher standards for students, with some financial assistance being provided to states and school districts in this task. An attempt by liberals to have the federal government or a national body such as the Goals Panel prod the states to secure more equitable funding of education or to provide additional dollars was rebuffed. Likewise, an effort by conservatives to eliminate all standards and to substitute vouchers as the alternative means of school reform was rejected.

In this debate in the House, the liberals had peaked in terms of their influence on the legislation. Although they did not get everything they wanted, the bill as passed by the House still funded the development of national opportunity-to-learn standards and required states to write their own such standards if they wished to receive federal school reform dollars. But conservatives were homing in on the whole idea of standards-based reform as exemplified by Goals 2000 and were becoming more fixated on the perceived evils of this approach. Their greatest influence was yet to come, with one result being that the liberals were to lose much of what they had gained.

Because any bill must pass both houses of Congress, the action now shifts to the Senate and to the House-Senate conference committee that fashioned the final legislation. As we shall see, different battles had to be fought in those forums, but the three major factors were constant: fashioning a new approach to school reform based on higher standards, an embarrassment that the federal government could not back up this reform with substantial dollars of its own or require states to spend their own dollars to improve the schools, and an increasingly strident attack from the political far right.

▨ Notes

1. The following account of this caucus, at which I was present, is from my notes.
2. The following account of these negotiations, to which I was a party, is from my notes.
3. I was present at these meetings; the descriptions are from my notes.
4. The following account of Riley's meetings discussing strategy, at which I was present, is from my notes.

5

Goals 2000 in the Senate and the Conference Committee:

How the Concept of Raising Standards Triumphed, but Only After Liberal Concerns About Equity Lost and Increasingly Strident Conservative Opposition Was Overcome

The advocates of Goals 2000 stumbled and bumbled on their way through the House of Representatives and then sprinted to the finish line for a magnificent ending, passing the legislation by a vote of more than two to one. Most of the debate in the House centered on the perceived strengths and weaknesses of setting higher standards as the way to raise the academic achievement of students.

In the Senate, the supporters of the legislation had an easier time of it regarding the core concept of using high standards to help improve the schools. In that chamber of the Congress, however, the bill became embroiled in major controversies concerning unrelated social issues, especially efforts to permit prayer in the public schools. Once the bill passed the Senate, the conference agreement resolving the differences between the House and Senate bills faced the same difficulties on social issues as had the Senate.

These events represent an important turning point in the debate on Goals 2000. The idea of using high standards as a means of raising students' academic achievement was gaining broad acceptance, so the opponents from the political far right shifted tactics. Although opponents continued to snipe at the idea of any greater national influence over education, their main energy became directed in Congress to loading down the legislation with a range of social amendments. The objective was to kill the legislation through controversy over these contentious social issues and, failing that, to weaken the supporters of the legislation for the upcoming election in the fall of 1994 by having them vote against popular social issues.

▨ The Senate

During the Bush administration, Senator Kennedy, the chair of the Labor and Human Resources Committee and one of the country's most prominent political liberals, had introduced Bush's school reform bill, America 2000. In fact, Kennedy was the principal sponsor trying to secure enactment of that legislation in the Senate, in cooperation with the Republican leadership. Kennedy's role was in sharp contrast to the position of many of his fellow liberals, the House Democrats, who at first were extremely skeptical of the Bush bill and then only reluctantly supported it.

Consequently, when President Clinton in 1993 sent his Goals 2000 proposal to the Congress, Kennedy was able to gain the support of many Republican senators by arguing that it was similar to the Bush bill that both he and they had supported. In other words, a spirit of bipartisanship had been created in the Senate on the issue of school reform during the Republican administration, and that feeling continued during the first days of the new Democratic administration.

The tension between the liberals and the conservatives that permeated the House was further defused in the Senate because Kennedy, one of the most liberal senators, was advocating positions very close to those of the governors and of many Republicans. Kennedy advocated for the idea of higher standards and related assessments as a means of improving the schools and also for increased flexibility for the states and local school districts in administering federal aid programs.

In February 1993, Secretary Riley appeared before the Senate committee on the broad topic of education goals and standards and received generally easy treatment. At that hearing (*Education Goals and Standards,* 1993), Senators Christopher Dodd (Dem.-Conn.) and Paul Simon (Dem.-Ill.) raised the liberals' concerns about the need to address the financial resources devoted to schooling as part of any debate on standards. Riley emphasized instead the need to concentrate on teaching and learning. He stressed how hope had to be brought to poorer communities through setting higher standards and having greater expectations for poor children and that this would help people to pull themselves up.

At that hearing in February, Riley promised Kennedy that the administration's bill would be sent to Congress within a few days. But then Riley became enmeshed in all those problems with the House that were described in the last chapter and in particular faced that difficult caucus with the Democrats after which the administration had to change its proposal. Consequently, Riley's promise to Kennedy was broken while he dealt with the cantankerous House.

By May, when the legislation was finally submitted, the controversy from the debate in the House had seeped over to the Senate. As a consequence, when Riley returned to testify before the Senate committee on the new legislation, he faced more difficult questioning from the senators than he had experienced in February.

Most of the Democratic senators praised the bill, following Chairman Kennedy's leadership, but echoing the opportunity-to-learn controversy in the House, liberal Senator Paul Wellstone (Dem.-Minn.) urged that national standards be set to help states achieve funding equity among school districts. Restating his position as expressed in the House, Riley quickly rebuffed a national-level concentration on equalizing resources and instead urged a focus on learning and teaching.

Also reflecting the controversies in the House, the Republican senators were much more aggressive in raising their concerns about the proposal than they had been in February. The ranking Republican, Senator Nancy Kassebaum of Kansas, said that she wanted to relax the requirements with which a state would have to comply to receive funds. Senator Orrin Hatch of Utah wanted to know if standards-based reform would force his state to adopt federal priorities. Senators Judd Gregg of New Hampshire and Daniel Coats of Indiana asserted that the bill gave too much power to the federal government and criticized the Clinton administration for not endorsing aid to private schools through vouchers or choice programs.

Riley responded to the Republicans by saying that the national standards were all voluntary: Nothing was mandatory, so no state would have to adopt any standards it did not want. A state had to have standards, but "how they do it is up to them" (Hoff, 1993a, p. 3). In answer to Gregg and Coats, Riley said the administration simply disagreed with them on the need for vouchers for private schools, believing that aid should go only to public schools.

An issue that was to prove important later in the legislative process in securing Republican support was whether the secretary of education had the authority to approve state-set standards. In other words, what did it mean that a state had to have standards but "how they do it is up to them"? Kennedy and the Democrats later amended the administration's bill to remove any implied power on the part of the federal government to approve state standards. This amendment further strengthened bipartisan support for the legislation in the Senate.

Even with this sniping from the political left and right at the Senate hearing, Riley and Goals 2000 received kinder treatment at the hands of the senators than they had in the House. A controversy did arise, however, concerning the job skill standards. This issue had arisen in the House, but it had greater visibility in the Senate's debate on the legislation.

The Bush administration had funded research on defining the skills that workers would have to master for various jobs. The idea was that once these skills had been identified by job or by industry, schools and training centers could concentrate on developing them systematically in trainees. Support for the idea came from business and industry, which felt that applicants for jobs were not being adequately prepared. Clinton's Goals 2000 called for the creation of a national board that would coordinate the development of these job skill standards (*National Skills Standards,* 1993).

Senator Kassebaum and some other senators advocated that the business community have a greater role in developing these national job skill standards than was called for in the administration's bill. The National Association of Manufacturers and other business groups asserted that the national skill standards would be useless unless business was the central force in shaping them and was in control of the national board that was to coordinate the development of those standards, as envisioned in Goals 2000.

Kennedy temporarily side-stepped that issue by removing from consideration the provisions dealing with the skill standards and then convening the full Senate committee to vote on the rest of the bill—the education part. At that meeting in mid-May, Senator Kassebaum announced her support for the education reforms, after successfully amending the bill to reduce from 12 to 4 pages the requirements placed on the states in the school reform grant program. Some liberal Democratic senators raised the issue of equalizing funding among school districts, but unlike their House counterparts, they did not press the question by offering rigorous amendments dealing with opportunity-to-learn standards ("Senate Panel Passes," 1993).

The Senate committee proceeded to approve Goals 2000 (without the job skill standards) by a vote of 14 to 3, with four Republicans voting with all the Democrats (Hoff, 1993b). The Republicans voting for the education portion of the bill were three political moderates—Kassebaum, David Durenberger of Minnesota, and James Jeffords of Vermont—and one conservative, Strom Thurmond of South Carolina. The three opponents were conservative Republicans: Daniel Coats of Indiana, Orrin Hatch of Utah, and Judd Gregg of New Hampshire.

The Senate was operating in a bipartisan manner on Goals 2000, and the treatment of the job skill standards shows that attitude, which so far was different from that of the House. Senator Kassebaum had agreed to the unusual procedure in which the Senate committee approved the education portion of the bill by the 14 to 3 vote and then a week later returned to consider the entire bill, including both the education and the job skill standards provisions.

At that later meeting, the skill standards portion of the bill was the subject of partisan disagreement as Kassebaum's amendment changing it was defeated by a vote of 10 to 7, with all the Republicans supporting her and with all the Democrats voting against. Then the entire bill, with both the education and the skill standards portions, was formally approved by voice vote. That formal approval opened the way procedurally for the bill to go to the full Senate. Kassebaum's willingness to allow this use of two different meetings to approve the bill and to avoid a recorded vote on the entire package, which could have resulted in no Republican support for the bill due to the skills controversy, highlighted the bipartisanship that prevailed.

The administration gained a major victory when the Senate committee approved these education reforms by such an overwhelming vote, including a majority of the Republicans, and it was a great relief to Riley and the White House because at that point they were facing an acrimonious reception in the House. Kennedy wanted to quickly move the entire bill to the full Senate for debate, but the job standards controversy had to be resolved. His move in committee to deal separately with those provisions was tactical: The opposing sides would have to resolve their differences before the bill could be scheduled in the Senate.

Although most news media attention was on the education standards proposed in Goals 2000, the legislation was also significant in asking for the development of these national job skill standards for American business and industry. Both the education standards and the job skill standards reflected a philosophical shift toward focusing on the results of education and training, with less emphasis being placed on prescribing the conditions of schooling or training.

As Secretary of Labor Robert Reich told the Senate committee in testimony on Goals 2000, America's economic future increasingly depended on the skills and abilities of all its workers, so the country had to commit itself to a major campaign of investment in improving those proficiencies. But, he added, "Without a method of measuring those skills, we run the risk of squandering that investment" (*Education Goals and Standards,* 1993).

National business organizations agreed: The skills needed in various areas of employment had to be identified so that workers could be helped to improve their job competencies and also so that schools and other institutions could gear their training efforts to creating those competencies. The next step after these job competencies were developed, according to several major proponents of this approach, was to move to awarding people who took proficiency tests for various skill areas with certificates that would be accepted by business and industry as verifications of skill levels. Employers felt a need for such certifications of skill proficiencies based on national standards because Americans are so mobile, moving from one local area to another and from one state to another, and businesses need to know if prospective employees have mastered the necessary skills to perform a job.

Despite this widespread and bipartisan agreement about the need for national skill standards, there were disputes over the details of developing them. Some experts wanted a few broad categories of job classifications; others wanted more and narrower listings. Some business groups wanted business representatives to have a majority on any national board created to encourage these activities; other business organizations did not want all the positions designated for employees on such a national board to be filled by representatives of organized labor—the unions. Some labor unions representing employment areas where standards had already been developed (e.g., the automobile industry) did not want any new national board telling them that they had to redo criteria already agreed on by the companies and unions in these industries (Miller & Olson, 1993).

A special problem revolved around the issue of job skills and racial and ethnic minorities. Some civil rights organizations were afraid that national job skill standards would be used not to hire minorities because the skill levels would be set so high; conversely, some business groups felt that a federal law could lead to their not being able to use standards as a defense in a lawsuit against hiring someone because the skill levels set in national standards might be lower than a particular company felt that it needed to have in its employees.

These varying perceptions about the effects of national skill standards on minorities were described in several national newspapers. In June, the *Wall Street Journal* ("Skills Standards," 1993) contained a warning from an employment expert that these new standards set by the National Skill Standards Board as envisioned in Goals 2000 could lead to employers' being vulnerable to civil rights litigation. This expert argued that because high standards could lead to many members of minority groups not being able to qualify, the board would set lower standards to help minorities, and thus any industry that wanted higher skills would be open to lawsuits for violating the board's minimal requirements. Seeing the opposite problem of the standards being set at a high level, former President Bush's legal counsel wrote in the *Washington Post* that employers could be sued for using the high national standards and then having a disparate effect on different groups in society (Gray & Kemp, 1993).

These concerns, as well as the belief that business should control the Skills Board, led Kassebaum and the other Senate Republicans to write to Reich and Riley in mid-June threatening to withdraw their support from Goals 2000 unless changes were made. They said, "It would be a shame to jeopardize this bipartisan support [for the bill] because of our remaining concerns on skill standards" (quoted in "GOP Fires Warning," 1993, p. 1). The administration and Kennedy took the threat seriously and worked on a compromise with the Republicans that would give business a greater voice on the national board through increased representation and also a guarantee that the first chair would be from business.

The other issues were also resolved, mostly through negotiations between the Department of Labor and representatives of business, the unions, and the civil rights community. The results of their efforts were to ensure that the bill was neutral with regard to its effects on civil rights. This meant that whatever the federal civil rights laws required or whatever the courts determined them to mean would not be affected by these new standards.

These negotiations were time-consuming but resulted in a substitute for the committee's approved bill that Kennedy agreed to offer when the bill was taken up by the Senate. Kassebaum was satisfied and expressed her support for the entire bill ("Kassebaum Endorses," 1993). The way was now clear for Kennedy to try to secure time on the Senate's schedule for debate on the legislation.

The *Washington Post* (Swoboda, 1993) reported on this agreement about the national job skills standards and quoted the representative of the National Association of Manufacturers saying that her group was enthusiastic about the national standards because "we have to shift to a new way of doing things. . . . We're talking about a new language of jobs" (p. G1). The article added:

> If adopted by industry, the skills board plan could force a major shift in U.S. education policy, which traditionally has left teaching priorities to state and local governments. But it reflects the dramatic changes that have forced unskilled American workers to compete with the low-wage workers of the world's underdeveloped nations. (p. G1)

This news report illustrates the reason for such strong business support for the idea of national standards, not only for jobs but also for education. Major business leaders and their organizations felt that the United States was lagging in the world in upgrading American schools and training institutions and that other nations were being much more aggressive in improving the education and job skills of their citizens. This was why business groups supported Goals 2000 consistently, even though many business people were Republicans and some Republican leaders in Congress were urging them to back away from the bill because of its identification with President Clinton.

In late July, Kennedy tried to bring Goals 2000 to the full Senate for a vote because the obstacle dealing with the skill standards had been removed, but scheduling difficulties arose because the White House began to push for the national service bill to be considered. After discussions with the Senate Democratic leadership, the national service bill was scheduled and the Goals bill was delayed, because bipartisan support was perceived as slipping for the national service bill while it was holding for Goals, due to Kassebaum's endorsement. That delay for Goals put the earliest date for floor action into September because the Congress almost always takes an August recess.

While awaiting the chance to bring the bill up in the Senate, Kennedy received a letter from Governors Roy Romer and Carroll Campbell (July 20, 1993) stating the preference of the National Governors' Association (NGA) for the Senate bill over the House bill, which they called "unacceptable." However, the NGA requested several changes in the Senate bill to clarify that no state would have to meet any standards adopted as part of Goals to qualify for any other federal aid and that states would have flexibility in carrying out any opportunity-to-learn provisions. The letter seemed to be meant at least as much to chide the House for its version of the legislation dealing with opportunity to learn and "corrective action" as to ask for minor changes in the Senate bill.

While awaiting action on the bill, the Senate conducted a hearing on the issue of bringing about greater equity in the distribution of resources that are available to different local school districts (*An Examination,* 1993). At that hearing, Marilyn Gittell of the City University of New York attacked Goals for not involving the public in setting the education standards and for not emphasizing equity. She asserted that "the only way to achieve excellence for a wider spectrum of the population is to pursue equality" (p. 211) and that the bill had taken the wrong tack by pursuing excellence and not having a direct commitment to equality. Joseph Fernandez, the former chancellor of schools in New York City, representing the large city school districts of the country, supported Gittell's point of view and argued that it was not enough to set academic standards; some resources had to be provided to implement them.

The liberal Democratic senators who were sympathetic to this point of view, however, could not agree among themselves on the best way to address the issue. Some wanted separate legislation that would focus on bringing about greater equity in the distribution of state and local resources for education, and some wanted to use the Goals bill as a way of nudging states in that direction through strong provisions dealing with opportunity-to-learn standards. Because there was no such agreement, this hearing seemed to have had little effect on the Senate consideration of the bill. It appears noteworthy only in showing some commentary on the bill from more liberal segments of the population, for most of the pointed statements on the legislation from outside Congress came from more conservative members of society.

In September and early October, the Senate considered appropriations bills, as it usually does at that time of year, so there was no time on the schedule for Goals. Then the end of the legislative session in early November was fast approaching ("Kennedy Upbeat," 1993). Kennedy tried to squeeze the bill onto the agenda for the final days of the session, but Senator George Mitchell (Dem.-Maine), the majority leader, was reluctant because he felt that the bill would be controversial and that without an agreement on the amount of time the Senate would devote to it, the bill would consume too many days and not leave enough time for other bills. The Senate has loose rules governing the time to be used for debate; therefore, most controversial legislation is considered only after there has been achieved among the senators unanimous consent on the number of hours the Senate will deliberate the matter. Kennedy and Kassebaum tried to secure such a time agreement, but some conservative Republicans refused. As a consequence, Goals was deleted from the Senate's schedule for 1993, with a promise from Mitchell that it would be one of the first bills to be considered in early 1994.

These delays in scheduling in the Senate show how important timing is in the legislative and policy agenda. It is always easier to delay than it is to take action, so whenever a controversy arises, the tendency is to put off the issue. The result of the Senate's inability to consider Goals in 1993 was that the bulk of Clinton's school reform agenda had to be considered and concluded in 1994, which was a congressional election year—always a more difficult time to legislate than a year when no national elections occur. It also meant that the clock almost ran out on these bills, with the amended Elementary and Secondary Education Act (ESEA) barely making it through Congress in the last days of the session.

While the actors waited for the new year, they continued to debate the worthiness of Goals. In various speeches and appearances, Riley asserted that the legislation was necessary to establish one set of tougher academic standards for all students and not to limit high standards to those who are expected to attain a college degree. He believed that if students were given different goals based on their perceived abilities, the achievement gap would widen between white and minority children. Thus, he argued that "when [poor children] need our help the most, we give them a watered-down curriculum that doesn't prepare them for anything but washing dishes and flipping hamburgers. This is a conspiracy of low expectations, and it cannot continue" (quoted in Hoff, 1993c, p. 1). He repeatedly pointed to his experiences in South Carolina, where he said the problem was one of low expectations for many children; the reform program he had enacted in that state when he was governor raised standards and gave schools the help they needed, with the consequence that thousands of African American children took advanced placement courses when few had before (Riley, 1993).

The opponents were also busy. For instance, the *Detroit News* ("Education's Trojan Horse," 1993) editorialized that "Goals 2000 is a Trojan Horse for more wasted education spending and federal intrusion into the local control of schools" (p. A6). That newspaper, which is known for a conservative bent in its editorials, chastised former Republican President Bush for starting the whole debate. According to the editorial, Bush had tried to use the Goals process to give more choices in schools, but this laudable objective was misguided because it now had led to a "meddlesome campaign to federalize the education system" (p. A6). This description of Bush's intention to embark on a course of using national goals to bring about greater parental choice of schools does not square with the facts (see Chapter 2), but it shows that some conservatives did not want to acknowledge that Bush and the governors began the movement for national standards when they promulgated national goals.

The Heritage Foundation also continued to blast Goals because in its view, Goals would slow reform by emphasizing money and not results and by creating bureaucracies that were likely to obstruct change (Lauber, 1993). The alternative reform strategy for many of these politically conservative opponents of Goals was to encourage the use of vouchers for tuition paid at private schools.

Seeming to buttress the administration's push for higher standards for schoolchildren, a poll released in December by the New Standards Project ("Listening to the Public," 1993) showed that 82% of the public supported the idea of national standards for education and 81% favored increasing rigor in schooling. However, the same poll lent some credence to the arguments of the conservative opponents because the public opposed the federal government's imposing any set of standards. The concerns of the liberal critics were also supported by these findings because the public wanted students not meeting the standards to get extra assistance, and that seemed to be what the Reed amendment in the House and the debate over the opportunity-to-learn standards were about. The public seemed to have varying views on these issues, and each slice of its views was advocated by a segment of the political spectrum.

The National Education Goals Panel used the interim period awaiting Senate action on Goals to try to defuse concerns that standards meant federal control or outcome-based education. At the urging of Congressman Goodling, a member of the panel, a policy statement was adopted saying that the group would approve only standards that were voluntary on the states and local school districts and would oppose any attempt to require their use. It would also approve only academic standards and would avoid value-laden criteria or the "fuzzy stuff," as another panel member, Governor Roy Romer, called it ("Goals Panel," 1993, p. 4).

In Washington, D.C., the new year for policymakers begins when the president addresses Congress on the state of the union and then submits his budget for the upcoming year. On January 25, 1994, Clinton in his speech ("State of the Union Address," 1994) urged passage of the Goals legislation, saying that the nation must set "tough, world-class academic and occupational standards for all our children and give our teachers and students the tools they need to meet them" (p. A12). He described his bill as allowing schools to do whatever they wanted as long as they were measured by one high standard. The budget he submitted to Congress called for increased funding for programs in the Department of Education, one of the few areas of federal spending he selected for a substantial boost in spending because his budget was overall trying to restrain spending to reduce the federal deficit.

Following the president's speech, Senator Mitchell kept his word to Kennedy and Kassebaum and scheduled Goals 2000 as one of the first items of business in the new year. On February 2, the Senate began debate on the legislation ("Goals 2000: Educate America Act, Senate Debate," 1994a) with Senator Kennedy, the floor manager, noting that the bill would help to establish a system of education based on high content and performance standards for all students and that it would coordinate federal, state, and local efforts to achieve that goal.

The two ranking Republicans on the education committee, James Jeffords of Vermont and Nancy Kassebaum of Kansas, supported the bill. Kassebaum pointed out that the bill contained many of the same elements as President Bush's America 2000 and then asserted:

> For those of you who may be hearing opposition to this bill, let me tell you at the outset that this bill does not: federalize education, establish a national curriculum or school board; require that states adopt national standards or submit standards for government approval; tie any other federal education funds to compliance with Goals 2000 provisions; dictate to states how much they need to spend per pupil, how to license their teachers, the proper teacher-pupil ratio, which textbooks to use, et cetera; impose unfunded mandates on the states, and mandate or encourage value-based education or the establishment of school-based clinics. ("Goals 2000: Educate America Act, Senate Debate," 1994a, p. S611)

Kassebaum's speech was meant to reassure fellow Republicans that the bill was based on the same principles as was Bush's and that it would not lead to federal control of education or impose on states or school districts any of the other things that groups such as the Heritage Foundation were alleging. In other words, she was concerned that the amendments proposed by many conservative Republicans were designed to "fix" issues that were not in the legislation. In response to Kassebaum's speech, Senator Larry Pressler (Rep.-S. Dak.) said that he felt reassured by both Kassebaum and Kennedy that the bill did not contain any outcome-based education because he opposed that.

To nail the coffin shut on such allegations made by conservative opponents, Kennedy offered eight amendments that had been proposed by Gregg, prohibiting any connection between the receipt of Goals funds and the participation in any other federal program and barring any mandates on school

districts regarding their class sizes, teacher certifications, instructional practices, equalized spending, building standards, or curriculum content or requiring any state to have any standards certified at the national level. These
amendments were easily passed.

Even though most of his amendments had been adopted, Gregg, who had
been the governor of New Hampshire when the national goals for education
were first proposed in Charlottesville in 1989, opposed the bill, saying:

> This bill, although having an innocuous term, reaches well beyond just the
> definition of the goals or the attempt to assist the states. It is a significant
> power grab by the federal government for the structure to try to obtain
> control—control is maybe too strong a word—but to try to obtain a significant
> and dominant role in the manner and methodology of education of our
> children in the elementary-secondary school systems. ("Goals 2000: Educate
> America Act, Senate Debate," 1994a, p. S613)

Kassebaum tried to reassure Gregg that the bill did not have that effect,
but Gregg was not satisfied, so he offered an amendment that would have
stricken from the bill any reference to opportunity-to-learn standards. The bill
as it stood before the Senate required states to have school improvement plans
if they wished to receive funds, but it did not require that a state had to have
any standards at all as part of this plan, so no state had to have content, student
performance, or opportunity-to-learn standards to receive federal school reform monies under the Senate bill. Such standards were mentioned as types
of activities that states could undertake as part of their reform activities if they
wished, but states were not required to undertake them.

Despite the absence of any requirement for any state to have any standards, Gregg tried to delete outright any reference, even suggestive, of
opportunity-to-learn standards. His amendment lost, with 42 in favor and 52
opposed. Kennedy led the opposition to Gregg, using a convoluted strategy
that he had worked out with two liberal senators who wanted stronger equity
provisions. Senators Wellstone and Simon offered an amendment that required states to have opportunity-to-learn standards, and Kennedy opposed
that amendment with a substitute that permitted the secretary of education
to only offer states technical assistance on finding fairer ways of financing
their schools. Kennedy's substitute for technical assistance was adopted, and
then the Wellstone and Simon amendment was withdrawn. This gave Kennedy
the pretext to argue that it was now clear that no state had to have opportunity-to-learn standards, so that a mention of them in the legislation was not

harmful and should not be totally eliminated as proposed by Gregg. That elaborate strategy of amendments and counteramendments is typical of the Senate and succeeded when Gregg lost his amendment.

The next day, the Senate resumed consideration of the bill ("Goals 2000: Educate America Act, Senate Debate," 1994b). Senator Jeff Bingaman claimed that if Goals was adopted, it would be recognized by future generations as one of the main achievements of that Congress because it would lead to such improvement in American schooling. The vote the day before on the Gregg amendment showed that there was strong bipartisan support for the concepts contained in the bill (although maybe not as strong as Bingaman's) and that even divisive issues such as the opportunity-to-learn standards were not going to shake that support. Consequently, most of the remaining education-related amendments were negotiated off the Senate floor and placed in a package of over 40 amendments that Kennedy later offered to the bill.

At this point, the conservative opponents of the legislation, seeing the broad support for standards-based reform, shifted their tactics and became more vigorous in forcing the Senate to confront a variety of socially related amendments. The first set of amendments, and the most controversial, dealt with prayer in the public schools.

At the beginning of the debate on February 3, Senator Jesse Helms (Rep.-N.C.) offered an amendment to require that school districts permit "constitutionally protected" prayer ("Goals 2000: Educate America Act, Senate Debate," 1994b, p. S723). Helms spent many hours arguing his position that prayer in the schools was needed to restore morality in the country. Several senators pointed out that his amendment either meant nothing because only a court could determine constitutionality or was mischievous to local school districts because they would have to go to court to see if what they did regarding prayer was legal. After much debate, Helms's amendment was approved by a vote of 75 to 22.

Some senators, however, did not want Helms's language to be the final word on the issue because they had different opinions on the proper approach to this difficult issue. Therefore, Senator John Danforth (Rep.-Mo.) offered an amendment urging schools to offer a moment of silence during the school day. Danforth's amendment was not binding on school districts but was more a statement of intent, and the Senate adopted it.

Then, on February 4, Senator Carl Levin (Dem.-Mich.) offered an amendment that a school district could not be denied federal funds if it had a policy that was constitutional regarding school prayer ("Goals 2000: Educate America Act, Senate Debate," 1994c). Levin's amendment turned Helms's provision around by placing the burden on a complainant to go to court to show that what a school district was doing was not constitutional, instead of requiring the school district to prove that it was acting constitutionally.

The Senate adopted Levin's proposal. Thus, the Senate bill now had three different amendments dealing with prayer in the public schools, and to most observers those amendments not only were complicated in their effects but also seemed to be in conflict.

On another socially related issue, Senator Helms offered an amendment that would have prohibited the use of funds to support the distribution of contraceptives to unemancipated minors without the prior written consent of the parents. That amendment lost with 34 in favor and 59 opposed. Then Kennedy and Jeffords offered an amendment to ensure that all federally funded programs that distributed contraceptives had to develop procedures to encourage the participation of families in such programs. That amendment passed 91 to 2.

The Senate also adopted an amendment to require schools to expel students who brought guns into school. Easy passage was ensured after many senators spoke about recent incidents involving the use of weapons in school.

An amendment to fund a demonstration of vouchers for private school tuition was defeated, with 41 in favor and 52 against. This was an important vote for the national organizations representing public education, for they had worked hard at defeating the amendment. All the senators in favor of the amendment were Republicans, except for five Democrats who supported it, and all the senators opposed to the idea were Democrats, except for five Republicans.

After days spent debating all these various socially related amendments, Senator Dale Bumpers (Dem.-Ark.) concluded that the real purpose behind offering these amendments was to embarrass the sitting senators politically so that their opponents would have some issues on which to run against them. In a similar vein, the *Congressional Quarterly* (Katz, 1994) noted that although the debate was to be on the new, philosophical framework for federal aid to education, much of the time was spent on revisiting old issues about school prayer and private school choice. It speculated that the conservatives had diverted the debate to those issues because they knew that there was wide bipartisan support for the education bill.

The Senate did indeed spend most of the time allotted to the bill on these intense debates on the social amendments and on the amendments seeking to bar federal control of education. Except for the descriptions of the bill offered by Kennedy, Kassebaum, and Jeffords, there was little discussion of the underlying educational issues presented by the legislation, especially of the idea of using standards and assessments as a principal means of improving the schools.

Senator Patrick Moynihan (Dem.-N.Y.) was an exception, and his views were offered at the end of the debate on the bill, almost as an afterthought. Moynihan said that the bill was missing the main point by dwelling on goals and that its adoption would in a way divert the nation from a realization of what was truly affecting the poor performance of American children. He pointed to research showing that the conditions of family life were the main determinants of whether a child would succeed in school. Moynihan said that he would vote for the bill but that its passage might divert the country from dealing with these elemental factors and that it might in fact lead to the government's "legislating an official lie" by concentrating on these goals ("Goals 2000: Educate America Act, Senate Debate," 1994c, p. S926). Moynihan's remarks, though provocative, sparked no debate because it seemed that the Senate had exhausted itself in arguing about social issues tangentially related to schooling.

Thus, after many days of debate, much of it spent on school prayer and other social issues, the Senate brought itself to a final vote on the legislation on February 8 ("Goals 2000: Educate America Act, Senate Debate," 1994d). When all was said and done, Goals 2000 passed overwhelmingly, 71 in favor and 25 against. All those voting against were Republicans, but 17 other Republicans joined the Democrats in voting for the bill.

The *Washington Post* ("Education: The Next Step," 1994) hailed the action and said that both the House and the Senate had

> preserved the original plan's precarious balance between educational stan-
> dards that are rigorous enough to do some good (which usually brings up the
> question of some kind of enforcement mechanism) and standards that are
> voluntary and work through incentives (thus avoiding the dread specter of
> national control of the curriculum). (p. A26)

According to that newspaper (Dewar & Cooper, 1994b), the Senate vote broke through "years of deadlock over education policy" because the Goals bill went back to Bush's initiative, which had died because of his support of vouchers and because of partisan wrangling (p. A7).

The *Wall Street Journal* (Sharpe, 1994) reported on the Senate passage of the bill and said that it encouraged school reform but did not mandate anything, although the word *voluntary* had to be inserted 75 times to assure people that in fact there was no compulsion. The *Los Angeles Times* (Shogren, 1994) noted that the initiative had grown from ideas advanced by the nation's governors and former President Bush in 1989 and that passage of the legislation "culminates a five-year movement for national education reform, which started when the nation's governors, fearful that the country's children were falling behind their counterparts in other countries, agreed with Bush on six national education goals" (p. A1). That newspaper believed that the bill signaled "a radical new role in education for the federal government, which until now restricted its involvement to allocating money to help states in specific areas, such as educating poor and disabled students" (p. A1).

After passage of the bill, the usually laconic Senator Jeffords trumpeted, "This could turn out to be one of the most important days in the history of the country if we follow through . . . on these goals" (quoted in Harrison, 1994, p. 2). Senator Kennedy, who had steered the bill to passage through all these difficulties, said that the bill's acceptance meant that education was now at the top of the nation's agenda (Harrison, 1994).

▓ The Conference Committee

The Goals 2000 bill had now passed both the House of Representatives and the Senate—two essential steps on the way to final enactment of the federal government's effort to help to raise standards in the schools. But there were several more obstacles to be overcome before the bill could be placed on the president's desk to be signed into law: A conference committee had to meet to reconcile the different House and Senate bills, and then final votes had to occur in the House and the Senate on that conference committee's decisions on the bill.

When the House of Representatives passes one version of a bill and the Senate passes a different version, the two legislative bodies create a joint committee to resolve their differences. Most decisions of these Senate-House conference committees are not changed because, as a rule, the Senate and the House accept the conference reports on "up or down" votes (with some exceptions for appropriations bills). Consequently, the product of these conference committees is usually the last word in the legislative decision-making process. Needless to say, the work of these committees is very important because their decisions are generally what becomes the law.

The Senate appointed its members to the conference committee at the same time that it passed the school bill on February 8. The House followed on February 23, but only after adopting by a vote of 367 to 55 a motion "instructing" the House conferees to accept the Helms school prayer amendment during their deliberations with their Senate counterparts ("Goals 2000: Educate America Act, House Debate," 1994a).

When a member of the House feels strongly that the conferees from his or her body should accept an amendment adopted in the Senate, a motion to "instruct" the conferees can be offered, but actually such motions are not binding on the House conferees—they are merely advisory. Further, although such votes can be useful in showing the temper of the legislators, they are frequently abused by being used politically to put the elected representatives on the spot on a difficult issue, such as school prayer. Recognizing this political use of motions, conferees will often vote for these motions, knowing full well that when the crunch comes with the Senate in the conference, they will have to change or delete the amendment in question.

In this conference, the first controversies revolved around the issue of education standards. The Senate-passed bill required states to have school improvement plans to meet the national education goals but did not require that these plans had to have standards of any kind. The House-passed bill, on the other hand, reflected the administration's position that states should adopt, if they wished to receive federal funds for reform, standards of high academic content as well as student performance standards and opportunity-to-learn standards.

According to Mark Pitsch (1993) in *Education Week,* the administration's bill was changed by the Senate to delete the requirement for standards because some senators wanted to make it easier for their states that did not have standards to qualify for funding. Regardless of whether that was accurate, the Senate certainly knew that the House and the Clinton administration would insist on states' having to have academic content and student performance standards if they wished to receive funding for school reform. Such provisions would seem to be the minimal requirements for eligibility if standards-based change was to be encouraged, as promoted by Clinton, the national business organizations, and others.

Kennedy and other Senate leaders had deleted the requirement for *any* standards at the state level to help to get the bill through the Senate. Because they knew that the House and the Clinton administration would insist on academic standards, the absence of the requirement for any standards gave them a further advantage: a bargaining chip to insist that the opportunity standards be deleted. That was the real issue to be faced in conference with the House: whether standards to ensure a student's opportunity to learn would be required as a condition of state eligibility to receive federal funding for school reform. The Senate wanted to be in a good position to oppose that requirement from the House bill while accepting the provision for academic and student standards.

The liberals had been defeated in the House in requiring states to take concrete action to ensure that adequate resources would be available for education (the Reed amendment), but they were successful in having some attention paid to the issue of whether students were being educated under the proper conditions to meet the academic standards established by the state. These provisions were all that was left of the price that the administration had paid for the House liberals to go along with the concept of standards-based reform.

The House-passed bill required states to establish strategies and timetables for adopting opportunity-to-learn standards that would be consistent with the states' content and student performance standards. States would also have to ensure that the needs of all students were being met and that every school was making progress toward meeting those standards. Finally, states had to assess periodically the extent to which such standards were being met throughout their boundaries and to report to the public regarding the progress being achieved toward providing all students with a fair opportunity to learn.

The Senate bill was different and far simpler on this issue: States had to establish strategies for providing all students with an opportunity to learn, but they did not have to work toward establishing opportunity-to-learn standards of any kind. It was generally understood that developing "strategies" was meant to be a far looser requirement than developing "standards" for the opportunity to learn (U.S. Senate, 1993).

This was the biggest difference between the House and the Senate bills, and that difference obscured the fact that both bills shared many similarities in the area of opportunity to learn. For instance, both the Senate and the House provided for the establishment of voluntary *national* opportunity-to-learn standards, but neither bill required that states or school districts had to adopt such national standards. Neither did either bill require that any state standards or strategies dealing with opportunity to learn had to be submitted for any certification or approval at the national level. So the issue came down to whether a state had to have standards for students' opportunity to learn, whether a state would have to have a timetable for implementing such standards, whether such standards would address the needs of all students, and whether the states would assess schools' progress toward meeting those standards (Stedman, 1994).

President Clinton weighed in on the side of the Senate in this dispute. South Carolina Governor Campbell, who had been the cochair of the National Council on Education Standards and Testing, had written to him on March 1 to express his "deep concern and disappointment about what is happening with the education goals/standards initiative." Campbell said that tying federal programs to opportunity-to-learn standards "threatened to turn the clock back on four years' worth of bipartisan teamwork and focus again on system inputs instead of student performance."

Two days later, Clinton wrote back to Campbell, saying that he believed the key to long-term education reform lay in clearly stated national goals coupled with maximum feasible flexibility for states and localities to devise and implement their own plans for achieving those goals. The president said that "schools should be held accountable for results—not for complying with a discouraging maze of micromanaged bureaucratic prescriptions." The president, therefore, was instructing his staff to support the principles and framework of the Senate bill on this issue. Clinton did say, however, that he believed in other standards and so was insisting that states had "to incorporate challenging content and performance standards in their reform plans, so that federal and state efforts together focus on student performance."

The Democratic members of the House who were serving on the conference committee with the Senate were not pleased that the president had intervened on behalf of the other side, especially in answer to a letter from a conservative Republican governor, but not many voices were raised in favor of the House position, and the opponents of the House bill were plentiful. The major national business groups urged the conferees not to require any opportunity-to-learn standards but rather to leave that issue to the states. The Business Coalition for Education Reform supported a "performance-driven education system based on academic standards and assessments" (letter from William Kolberg and Michael Jackson of the Business Coalition to Sen. Edward Kennedy and Cong. William Ford, March 14, 1994).

The public meetings of the House-Senate conference committee could not be scheduled until mid-March due to the pressure of other business. This delay was unfortunate because the bill faced an unusual deadline: It had to be signed into law by the last day of March, or there would be no funding for it that year. In the previous year, the congressional appropriations committees had departed from their usual rules against funding a program not yet authorized by law and had provided, at the urging of the Clinton administration, some modest funding for the implementation of Goals. But the appropriations committees attached a condition to this funding: It was available only if the bill authorizing the program was signed by the President before April 1, 1994 ("Goals 2000 Conferees," 1994).

That "conditional" appropriation proved to be the driving force behind Congress's abandoning its usual lengthy legislative process and expediting the bill to passage. The deadline placed a burden on Ford and Kennedy, the two chairmen of the respective sides in the conference committee, to resolve as fast as possible the differences between the House and the Senate bills, but it also gave them a good excuse to force agreements among their colleagues, decisions that usually take a much longer time. The deadline also helped the Clinton administration because Riley and the White House could use it to focus congressional attention on finishing the bill and because once the bill was signed into law, it would receive immediate funding.

Knowing that time was short, the Senate and House conferees quickly resolved most of the issues in dispute. Provisions that had delayed consideration for months, such as the battles over the composition of the National Education Goals Panel and of the National Skill Standards Board, were resolved relatively easily. The conferees also agreed on two new national goals dealing with teacher preparation and parental participation. One of these additional goals came from the House and the other from the Senate. These two goals were then added to the original six national education goals adopted by former President Bush and the governors, and all of them were placed in law ("Conference Report," 1994).

The conferees agreed on amendments giving the secretary of education, for the first time, the authority to waive provisions of federal rules and regulations if states and local school districts requested such waivers to operate their programs better. In addition, a Senate amendment that proposed to experiment with allowing six states to waive federal rules and regulations in education programs was also adopted. These waiver provisions were agreed to on the theory that local educators ought to have greater flexibility with federal funds once the states had identified what results they wanted from students through their establishment of high academic and performance standards (Hoff, 1994c).

Despite reaching agreement on many issues, the two sides were far apart on the key question, what to do about opportunity-to-learn standards, and the clock was ticking away toward the April 1 deadline. The conferees broke up their meetings several times and tried to fashion various compromises. The key factor for Kennedy, the leader of the Senate conferees, was that he had to find a compromise that would give him enough votes to overcome a filibuster.

During recent years, the Senate has faced unlimited debate or threats of filibusters on practically every major bill coming before it. It is necessary to have 60 votes of the 100 in the Senate to cut off such delaying tactics by invoking cloture and to pass legislation. During 1994, the Democrats in the Senate had a maximum of 56 members, so they needed a minimum of four Republican votes to pass most major legislation.

Therefore, Kennedy had argued forcefully earlier in the conference for several amendments that had been offered by Republican senators because he needed their support for cloture. For instance, Senator Mark Hatfield (Rep.-Ore.) wanted the amendment allowing states to waive federal rules and regulation, and Kennedy pushed very hard for its acceptance by the House. Generally, the House conferees would yield to the Senate on those issues because they understood the need for those 60 votes in the Senate ("Conference Report," 1994).

Kennedy had to be especially careful on the issue of opportunity-to-learn standards because he had been warned by Jeffords and others that there would not be the votes for cloture if the House provisions were retained in the conference. So whenever a compromise on opportunity-to-learn standards was offered in the conference committee, Kennedy had to take soundings among his colleagues, especially the Republicans, to find out if he could secure enough support to pass such a provision through the Senate.

An additional complicating factor for Kennedy was that his state of Massachusetts had adopted a broad school reform law that had academic standards but did not have opportunity-to-learn standards. State officials from Massachusetts contended that the law addressed equity issues through provisions ensuring a fairer distribution of funding for education among school districts, but they were concerned that those provisions would not be enough to satisfy the requirements of the House-passed opportunity-to-learn standards. Massachusetts, therefore, opposed the House's provisions and asked Kennedy to delete them from any final agreement. Kennedy paid close attention to their concerns because he was up for reelection and faced the most difficult race of his political career.

Finally, after numerous false starts, the conferees on March 17 softened the provision enough to ensure adequate Senate support. The agreement was that states had to have such standards *or* strategies to ensure an opportunity to learn and that states would have the discretion to include whatever elements in these standards or strategies they thought best as long as all students were assured a fair opportunity to achieve the knowledge and skills described in the states' content standards and student performance standards. To underscore the flexibility written into this provision, the conference agreement stated that the implementation of such standards or strategies had to be voluntary on the part of states, school districts, and schools; it also explicitly provided that no equalized funding or national building standards could be inferred from this provision. The compromise also deleted the House's provisions for a state to have a timetable to carry out the standards and for an assurance that schools were moving to meet the standards ("Conferees Reach Agreement," 1994).

The Senate won on the opportunity-to-learn issue because the House liberals saw that Kennedy could not get around a filibuster in the Senate if he were to accept the House's provisions and that Kennedy himself was opposed to them because of the situation in Massachusetts. The Senate conferees, however, did yield to the House on the requirement that states had to have content and student performance standards if they wished to receive federal school reform funds. Riley and the Clinton administration were pleased that academic standards were required and not opportunity-to-learn standards—it was a double victory for them.

Once the main provisions dealing with school reform were completed, the conferees turned their attention to the various amendments affecting social issues. The most troublesome dispute centered on the three school prayer amendments adopted by the Senate: a Helms amendment barring funds from school districts having policies prohibiting constitutionally protected prayer, a Levin amendment barring funds from being denied to school districts having a constitutional policy regarding prayer in schools, and a Danforth amendment expressing the sense of the Senate that schools should encourage a daily period of silence.

The conference committee deleted all three of the Senate-passed amendments on the grounds that they contradicted one another and instead included in their place a provision contained in another law that no federal funds could be used by school districts to develop policies that prevented voluntary prayer and meditation in schools. Senator Kassebaum offered this substitute for the three overlapping Senate amendments, and her offer was quickly accepted by the other conferees ("Conference Report," 1994).

The Senate-House conference was then concluded, and the final agreement was presented to the House and the Senate. Although losing on the opportunity-to-learn issue, the House liberals remained in support of the bill, so all the Democratic conferees from the House and the Senate signed that agreement. The more moderate Republican conferees also signed, including Congressmen Goodling and Gunderson and Congresswoman Susan Molinari from New York, and Senators Kassebaum, Jeffords, and Durenberger. Even though the more conservative Republican conferees did not sign the report, the presence of the moderate Republicans and the unanimity of the Democrats boded well for the success of the final bill (Hoff, 1994b).

With the deletion of the House opportunity-to-learn provisions, the issue of federal control, which had plagued the bill from the beginning, was mostly quieted. The accusations of the far right about a national school board, promotion of outcome-based education, and distribution of condoms were blunted and not having much effect on anyone but their normal followers. But the bill in its final stages still faced some very high hurdles to overcome due to the handling of the school prayer amendments (Wells, 1994).

■ Final Agreement

Once the conference agreement was reached, the reports were filed in both the House and the Senate, but then the decision had to be made about which legislative chamber would move first to consider the final bill. Kennedy and Ford, the two chairmen, agreed that it would be the House of Representatives because the House seemed to be more securely under the Democrats' control than the Senate, where filibusters always threatened. But the House proved to be a difficult forum because of the timing of the vote on the conference report.

On the same days that the House-Senate conference committee was meeting on Goals 2000, the House had been considering another major education bill: the revisions to the ESEA (which will be discussed in the next chapter). During consideration of that bill, a school prayer amendment was adopted on March 21 by a vote of 345 to 64, and this amendment was the exact language of the Helms amendment that the Goals 2000 conference the week before had recommended rejecting in favor of the Kassebaum amendment (Cooper 1994; "Elementary and Secondary Education," 1994).

The conference report on Goals 2000 was scheduled for a vote within the next few days after that vote in the House on the Helms school prayer amendment, so members of the House would be asked to vote against the Helms prayer amendment when they voted on the conference report on Goals 2000, even though they had just accepted it overwhelmingly as an amendment to the ESEA. If the House did not agree to change its collective mind on that issue, the Goals bill would be sent back to the conference committee and in all likelihood would be bogged down and would miss the March 31 deadline.

The Clinton administration made the passage of Goals 2000 a top priority and began to line up the major national organizations behind the conference report. Riley made the argument to them that if the bill were delayed, the funding would be lost because the conditional appropriation lapsed on April 1, and no one knew what the fate of the bill would then be (Hoff, 1994a). The National Conference of State Legislatures, the nation's major national business organizations, and the major education organizations were persuaded, and all joined in support of the bill (letter from Sen. R. Connor and Rep. K. McCarthy, National Conference of State Legislatures, to House of Representatives, March 21, 1994).

The *Washington Post* of March 23 had a front-page story (Jordan, 1994) that was very helpful in impressing on Congress the importance of the legislation. The *Post*, the major newspaper in Washington, is read by most national leaders even if they disagree with its liberal editorial slant, so its articles and editorials have a major daily influence on the policy debate.

The *Post* cited the origins of the bill in the summit conference that Bush had had with the governors in 1989 and the historic nature of the United States' creation, for the first time, of national standards for education, a major departure from the tradition of local control of schooling. According to the article, Riley saw the bill as the "North Star" (p. 1) because it would guide so many other classroom changes, from new textbooks and exams to the retraining of teachers. Goals 2000, according to the newspaper, was designed to rescue a public education system widely viewed as failing to produce globally competitive students.

In addition to the attention brought to the bill by the *Post,* several letters circulated in the House emphasizing the importance of the legislation. Congressman Goodling sent a "Dear Colleague" letter (March 21, 1994) to the Republican members showing his support for the conference report. That letter was helpful in showing Republicans that the final bill was better from their point of view than the House-passed bill, especially on the issue of the opportunity-to-learn standards. The National Conference of State Legislatures wrote reassuringly that "each state can include in its education reform plan those strategies that it alone determines appropriate" and that states were safeguarded from unfunded federal mandates and preemption of state and local authority to govern public schools (letter from Sen. R. Connor and Rep. K. McCarthy, National Conference of State Legislatures, to House of Representatives, March 21, 1994).

Al Shanker of the American Federation of Teachers also endorsed the report as "an essential piece of legislation for turning around our nation's schools" because it gave the country a rational system of education similar to what competitor nations already had: clear and high academic standards, assessments based on those standards, and eventually clear consequences for achievement (letter from Al Shanker to House of Representatives, March 21, 1994). From California, the state school superintendent pressed for passage of the legislation because California needed the $10 million provided by the legislation for its curriculum and professional development and for technologies (press release, "State School Superintendent Urges Enactment of Goals 2000 This Weekend," California Dept. of Education, March 24, 1994).

From the right side of the political spectrum came the same type of opposition to the conference report as had come to the initial passage of the bill. For instance, the Family Research Council ("Alert" to Congress, "Protect School Prayer," c. March 24, 1994) asserted that Goals would "nationalize America's education system, putting more power in the hands of Washington bureaucrats."

On March 23, the House took up the conference report with a muted debate occurring on the opportunity-to-learn standards ("Goals 2000: Educate America Act, House Debate," 1994b). Republican Congressman Dan Miller of Florida attacked the compromise language as a "massive federal mandate, any way you look at it" (p. H1923), as did his Republican colleague, Congressman John Boehner of Ohio, who called the new version better than what had passed the House but still "confusing" (p. H1924). Congressman Ford of Michigan, the floor manager of the report, reminded the House that earlier Congresses had passed basically the same bill twice under Bush and that this House had overwhelmingly passed its own bill the year before.

Congressman Goodling claimed that he had been successful in ensuring that the bill did not "micromanage" the schools through the opportunity-to-learn standards or other provisions (p. H1926). He had worked for 6 years to shepherd this bill through Congress, he said, because "even though this is a very little program, a very small program, it might be one of the most effective things we have done perhaps in the history of this Congress in relation to bringing about quality in education rather than just access" (p. H1926). The current federal programs try to ensure better access to schooling, but it turns out to be "access to mediocrity" because there is no emphasis on quality, and improving quality is what Goals 2000 is about, he asserted (p. H1926).

Goodling was backed up by another Republican, Steve Gunderson, who said, "This is it. Either today you vote for education reform or you go back home and admit you're not really in support of it" (p. H1927). Gunderson repeated Goodling's assurance that there was not one mandate in the final bill, that it was "the framework for education reform, nothing more, nothing less" (p. H1928).

Congressman Kildee, who had introduced the original bill, emphasized the support from the business community, inserting a letter from the Coalition for Education Reform, which was composed of the Chamber of Commerce of the United States, the National Alliance of Business, and the National Association of Manufacturers. The coalition claimed that the bill would lead to a performance-based and results-oriented system of education and training essential to building a world-class workforce (p. H1927).

Despite the endorsement of the bill by the nation's major business groups, by the state legislatures, by the major national education organizations, and by some moderate Republicans, many conservatives were not convinced. Republican Richard Armey of Texas said that the bill would mean more power for the National Education Association and less discretion for parents.

The liberals who had fought so hard for opportunity-to-learn standards and for the corrective action amendment in the subcommittee, the full committee, and the conference committee and had then seen their work blunted by the opposition of the Clinton administration, the states, and the Senate were good soldiers and lined up in support of the legislation. Congressman Reed, referring to the "frank and vigorous discussions" that had resulted in "conscious recognition of the importance of local control of school policy," asserted that the result was that the bill was now fashioned "to provide a federal catalyst to help those local reformers" ("Goals 2000: Educate America Act, House Debate," 1994b, p. H1928). Within this framework, Reed hoped that the states would ask the hard questions about the adequacy of resources for schooling. Congressman Owens of New York called the bill "monumental" (p. H1929).

The immediate test facing the bill in the House was a motion to send the bill back to conference with the Senate to accept the Helms prayer amendment. This was the same provision that the House had adopted as an amendment to the ESEA a few days before and that the Goals conference committee had deleted with the two other Senate prayer amendments and replaced by the Kassebaum amendment barring the use of federal funds to develop policies that prevent voluntary prayer.

During the debate in the House on sending the bill back to conference with the Senate, the proponents of the Helms amendment pointed out that the Senate had adopted the provision 75 to 22, that the House had instructed its conferees on the Goals bill to accept the Senate amendment by a vote of 367 to 55, and that the House 2 days earlier had adopted the same amendment in the ESEA bill by a vote of 345 to 64. These advocates also argued that school officials were forbidding students from praying in school and that prayer was needed to restore the moral fiber of students.

There was not any debate against the Helms amendment on the merits of the issue. Instead, two arguments were made against the motion to send the bill back to conference. First, Ford and others said that if the conference had to reconvene, there would be no way that its work could be concluded before the end of the week and the funds set aside for the program would be lost. Second, the ESEA bill was being considered by the House at the same time, and the Helms amendment was in that bill, so the issue could be resolved in that piece of legislation without having to slow down the work on Goals. Congressman Gephardt of Missouri, the Democratic majority leader, took the floor and emphasized the latter point. Because someone in his position usually does not speak on bills unless they are of great importance, his speech meant that the House leadership took this bill very seriously and would be working hard to secure the votes for it.

The Clinton administration, the national education and business organizations, and the House Democratic leadership worked hard lining up support for the bill. The motion to recommit lost by a vote of 195 to 232, with enough Democratic members changing their votes from 2 days before to create that majority. Then the House adopted the conference report by a vote of 306 to 121. Goals again made its way through the House despite the strident opposition of the far right.

The *Wall Street Journal* ("House Clears Cornerstone," 1994) reported that the "cornerstone" of Clinton's education agenda had passed the House and that it would lead to the creation of voluntary national academic standards. It added, "Goals 2000 encourages school overhaul, but doesn't mandate anything" (p. A16). Despite that assurance, the bill still had one last and very large roadblock to overcome: delaying tactics and a filibuster in the Senate. This obstacle seemed so serious that some press accounts said that Goals could not get through the Senate by the end of the week and that the funds would be lost and the program delayed for a year ("Goals 2000 Compromise," 1994).

On March 23, the same day that the House approved the conference report, the Senate took up the bill ("Goals 2000: Educate America Act, Senate Debate," 1994e) and immediately became embroiled in an acrimonious debate on the prayer issue. Senator Mitchell said that the Republican leadership had notified him that the minority would filibuster the bill and also insist on the clerks' reading the entire conference report, something that had not happened for 22 years. Mitchell said he understood that this reading would take 6 to 7 hours but that he would keep the Senate in session until late into the night to accomplish it so that he could then file a cloture motion to cut off further debate on the report. Senator Robert Dole of Kansas, the Republican leader, said that Senator Helms was insisting on the reading because his amendment had been deleted.

Senator Kennedy explained that the Senate had adopted three different school prayer amendments and that the conference had decided to include in lieu of all three Senator Kassebaum's provision, which restated a 1982 law comporting with the sense of the Senate's three amendments. He urged the Senate to accept that decision because otherwise the appropriation for Goals would be lost. He also reminded the Senate that the ESEA bill was still to be considered and that the issue could be revisited there.

Senator Helms took the floor and said that he was "getting a little sick and tired of one Senator presuming to speak for all the rest of us when he does not represent the opinion of the rest of us" (p. S3532). Then he reviewed the voting on his amendment in the Senate and in the House and said that the conference committee, in a 60-second "prearranged one-act play" by Kennedy and his House colleagues, had done away with the amendment and "put in this do-nothing amendment" (p. S3532).

Kennedy reviewed the consideration of the amendment by the conference committee and the notices that had been given to Helms and his staff; then he pointed out that no senator who had been present had objected to the compromise offered by Senator Kassebaum. Helms countered with his version of the chronology, which he asserted showed that it was a "setup job" to eliminate the amendment and that the substitute was "one of these 'CMF' amendments, meaning 'cover my fanny' " (pp. S3532-S3533). Dole and Helms tried to get Kennedy to amend the conference report to insert Helms's amendment, but Kennedy refused.

The Senate therefore spent 6 hours reading the entire conference report—231 pages. Finally, after midnight, Mitchell moved that the Senate proceed to consider the report from the conference. That motion was approved by a vote of 60 to 31. Mitchell then filed motions to cut off further debate.

Under Senate rules, a motion to invoke cloture cannot be considered until after 2 days' lapse, so the first opportunity to vote on Mitchell's motions would occur after 1 a.m. Saturday morning. The Senate had been scheduled to recess for the Easter/Passover period on Friday so that the Jewish senators could get home before sunset on Friday night to observe Passover. By insisting on the reading of the conference report and by filibustering, Helms delayed that recess and threatened the plans of some Jewish senators to leave Friday afternoon.

Again, the driving force behind the vote on cloture and on final passage having to occur that week was that the bill had to be signed by the president before the end of the month due to the conditional appropriation that had been provided for Goals. Kennedy had been able to assemble 60 votes to bring the bill up for a vote, and this indicated that he would have the same number to cut off debate if he could keep them all in town when the key votes were to occur, but this was now after the recess was supposed to begin and would be into the night on Saturday. Kennedy had counted correctly in his checking on the compromises adopted in the conference on the opportunity-to-learn dispute and on the other issues, but he, Mitchell, and the Clinton administration faced a formidable task in keeping their allies in Washington for those final votes.

Senator John Chaffee (Rep.-R.I.), for instance, was a Republican supporter of the conference report who had to return home on Friday night for a campaign fund-raiser that could not be canceled. Senator Joseph Lieberman (Dem.-Conn.), an orthodox Jew, was another supporter, but he would not stay for the vote on Saturday because he had to return home before sundown on Friday.

The next day, the *Washington Post* (Dewar & Cooper, 1994a) reported that "[a] bitterly divided Senate screeched to a halt during the night as Republicans blocked a major education initiative to force approval of a contested school prayer provision" (p. A18). The *New York Times* (Clymer, 1994) noted "the bad tempers and displays of some of the silliest rules any parliamentary body ever developed" and then observed, "Democrats are anxious to leave for this recess with some record of accomplishment, and Republicans are trying to thwart them" (p. A19).

An editorial in the *New York Times* ("Mr. Helms," 1994) tried to bring the debate back to education issues when it noted that the bill was the most ambitious legislative attempt yet to put into action the promise of the 1989 conference establishing national goals and that deciding what students should know and how to help them learn had become an integral part of the national school reform movement. For that reason, according to the editorial, voluntary national standards were being developed.

On Friday, the Senate finally took up the conference report and resumed the debate ("Goals 2000: Educate America Act, Senate Debate," 1994f). Kennedy, focusing on the importance of the bill for improving schooling, noted that federal assistance would be provided for the first time in history for locally developed reform plans for all children. He also highlighted the program's encouragement to develop content and student performance standards, which he asserted would end "the confusion about what parents should expect and what makes a good school—it is a school where all students are learning what the standards describe" (p. S3862). The regulatory flexibility the bill would give helped in this effort to have communities meet their own needs, he added.

Senator Jeffords also supported the report because it would help to meet the problems in American education that the *Nation at Risk* report and the governors had identified: low expectations for students, a watered-down curriculum, minimal requirements for graduation, and a shortage of high-quality, experienced teachers. Jeffords, like Kennedy, stressed that if the report was not approved, the states would lose a year's worth of assistance to address these problems, and he urged Republicans to support the report because 22 of the 26 Republican-sponsored amendments had been retained. States did not have to adopt opportunity-to-learn standards, he emphasized; rather, they could use any strategies they wished.

Senator Kassebaum, the Republican leader on the Labor and Human Resources Committee, surprised the supporters by opposing the bill after she had supported it for so long. She said she would vote against the bill because in the conference committee the slimmed-down Senate bill had been changed to incorporate too many requirements on the states and local school districts. She gave her view, however, that the danger of the legislation was not that it would lead to a uniform, federally controlled system of education, but rather that these burdensome requirements would distract schools from improving education.

Another Republican, Slade Gorton of Washington State, said he would support the bill because although it was seriously flawed, it represented "at least a halting step forward in American educational policy" (p. S3867). Gorton said that teachers in his state needed the assistance and that the bill did not represent a federal takeover of the schools because states and schools controlled the decisions. The conference report also contained an amendment that Gorton had offered that provided for harsher treatment than in current law for disabled students who were threatening teachers or other students. The inclusion of this provision shows how Kennedy worked hard to keep in the report the amendments of various senators, especially Republicans, so that they would support the final report and give it the 60 votes needed for passage.

The debate then turned to the prayer issue. Kennedy noted that although he had voted for the Helms amendment, it had problems such as the total cutoff of federal funds for noncompliance and therefore was opposed by the major national education associations, including the National School Boards Association. Senator Coats, who was a member of the conference committee but did not attend the crucial sessions, attacked the conference report and Kennedy's handling of the prayer issue, repeating Helms's assertions about the lack of attention to the issue and about the conference's contravention of the majority votes in the House and Senate. Several other conservative senators also complained about the loss of the Helms amendment and remained on the Senate floor to object if Mitchell or Kennedy were to try to obtain unanimous consent to bring the report up for a vote before 1 a.m. Saturday.

Senator Barbara Mikulski (Dem.-Md.) noted the irony that Helms professed to be protecting people who wished to exercise their religious beliefs through prayer in the schools yet then brushed aside concerns expressed by Jewish senators that his tactics were resulting in their having to choose between their religious beliefs and staying in Washington to vote for a bill they supported. Mikulski chided Helms for using the "tools and tactics of the U.S. Senate to prevent something called prayer in the home" (p. S3917). These arguments had no effect on Senator Helms and his supporters, who persisted with their strategy of delaying the vote until late into the night on Saturday, hoping that enough senators would leave town and that the conference report would be defeated.

Finally, the hour arrived after midnight on Friday when the full Senate could express its sentiments, and the filibuster was cut off by a vote of 62 to 23. Enough supporters of the legislation stayed in Washington to vote for the bill, and Helms's strategy failed. Then the vote occurred to approve the conference report; it passed 63 to 22, with 15 senators not voting, including Senator Helms, who had gone home to North Carolina earlier in the day. Nine moderate Republicans crossed the party line and voted with all but one of the Democrats to ensure passage. That sole dissenting Democrat later became a Republican.

Eleven years after the *Nation at Risk* report and 5 years after the Charlottesville summit on setting education goals, a national school reform bill was finally on its way to the president to be signed. The federal government, after years of standing on the sidelines, was about to enter the fray of battle over improving the schools.

Secretary Riley led the chorus of praise for passage of the bill: "Today will be remembered as the day the United States got serious about education. . . . We have finally broken the gridlock" (quoted in Dewar, 1994a, p. A7). *USA Today* ("How National Standards," 1994) editorialized that although it was well hidden amid acrimony over school prayer and other more controversial issues, "Congress has written the rules for better schools, it's time for states to start playing the game" (p. 12A). The legislation, according to the editorial, "wrote into law the radical notion that every child should be expected to acquire certain knowledge and skills before leaving school" (p. 12A). Further, the newspaper said, parents were given a new weapon to judge the quality of their children's education with passage of the landmark education reform bill because the country would now know what schoolchildren ought to be taught and tested on in certain subjects (Henry, 1994).

The *Washington Post* commented on the 4-year odyssey of Goals 2000, which had ended "in a blaze of pure silliness" at 1:01 a.m. with the cloture vote "in accordance with arcane rules" ("Everything but Education," 1994, p. C6) and "after delaying tactics that were bizarre even by Senate standards" (Dewar, 1994b, p. A8). However, the passage of the bill was lauded as a significant step toward reforming education, and it was noted that the bill was the product of 5 years of effort by two presidents, most of the nation's governors, and lawmakers of both parties (Dewar, 1994b).

The NGA did not endorse the final bill, although the governors had worked on it for years. According to Secretary Riley's chief of staff, the reason was that Governor Campbell of South Carolina "single-handedly derailed the process by trying to get other Republican governors and some Democratic governors who had supported the bill to withhold their support" and that Campbell's motivation was that he wanted to be president himself and did not want Clinton to succeed (Associated Press wire, "Clinton Signs Bill With Money for State Education Reforms," April 1, 1994).

Despite all the politics and all the roadblocks placed in front of the legislation in Congress, on March 31, President Clinton finally was able to sign the bill into law (Goals 2000: Educate America Act of 1994). On that occasion, he said, "This is the beginning. It is the foundation. Today we can say America is serious about education" (p. 657). Surrounded by children at a school in San Diego, California, where the ceremony took place, Clinton (1994) asserted: "[Goals 2000] sets world-class education standards for what every child at every American school should know in order to win when he or she becomes an adult. We have never done it before. We are going to do it now because of this bill" (p. 657).

It was a happy day for Clinton, Riley, and the supporters of the idea of setting high standards for schoolchildren as a way to reform the schools. Due to the conditional appropriation, the president and his secretary of education were able to begin working immediately with the states on their initiatives to create higher standards for education. The work that President Bush and the governors had begun in 1989 finally reached a conclusion in 1994: The nation's leaders said that it was time to raise standards in the schools. But another important step had to be taken in Congress, and that was to refashion the federal programs that had been created over the course of 30 years to buttress this new national strategy for changing education.

During that debate on revising the ESEA, the same issues were to be revisited: shaping a new approach to raise standards, but with the liberals still wanting to address the financial resources available for education and with the conservatives still wanting to substitute tuition vouchers for private schools. This debate on ESEA was an echo, though fainter, of the debate on Goals and shows how Washington is a continuous debating society: There is rarely a final conclusion to the policy discussion; the arguments continue on. But this debate on amending ESEA also demonstrated how the political right was becoming better organized to fight this new idea of standards-based reform and foretold the troubles that the new concept would have in the suc-ceeding Congress, which was to be dominated by conservative Republicans.

6

The Elementary and Secondary Education Act

*How Other Federal Programs
Were Refashioned to Raise
Standards, and How This Victory
Further Hardened the Opposition
of the Political Far Right*

The Goals 2000: Educate America Act called for the development of national standards for education, for tests to measure
the achievement of those standards by students, and for aid to
states and local school districts to raise their standards. With
congressional and presidential approval, and with the support of the country's
major business and education organizations, the national government was
finally moving to help states to raise the quality of public education.

The new framework for federal aid that Clinton and Riley had advocated
was finally in place. Other forms of federal aid, however, had to be realigned
to be supportive of encouraging higher academic standards. The most important
of these was the Elementary and Secondary Education Act of 1965 (ESEA).

In 1994, at least 70% of America's public elementary schools and 20%
of secondary schools were aided by ESEA programs, making that act the most
significant form of federal aid to the schools. Over $10 billion of aid was
provided that year to nearly every school district in the country for remedial
education programs for disadvantaged children, for teacher training, for
funding of innovative programs, for general assistance to school districts
losing local tax revenue due to federal activities, and for scores of other

purposes. If ESEA could be refashioned to support higher standards, the effects of those efforts would be greatly strengthened.

▩ Need for Change

The ESEA and related programs created during the 1960s and early 1970s grew out of a concern about the inadequate education being provided to children with special needs. Therefore, these federal programs focused on aiding such children, with the result being a narrowing during the next two decades of the gap in educational achievement between advantaged and disadvantaged children. In fact, while the academic achievement of most children stagnated during the 1970s and 1980s, that of more disadvantaged students rose, according to the National Assessment of Educational Progress.

As with many solutions, however, the programs that provided extra services and raised the achievement of these children created the next set of problems. In targeting dollars on children with special needs, the U.S. Department of Education was led over time to require more and more elaborate accounting from local school districts to ensure that the funds were indeed properly focused on these students and not used for general educational purposes.

The Clinton administration's concepts for refashioning the ESEA were influenced by the complaints that came from states and school districts about federal rules and regulations needed to focus on individual children, by Riley's and Clinton's own experiences with such categorical programs when they served as governors, and by the recommendations of various experts.

Typical of the thinking of experts were the opinions of Robert Slavin, a researcher at Johns Hopkins University. Slavin (1993) wrote for the *Chicago Tribune* that the greatest potential for improving the education of poor children did not rest with school choice or vouchers but rather with the reform of Title I (the largest ESEA program, also known as Chapter 1). His view was that "what matters is what happens in the classrooms every day, and choice and vouchers are not likely to change daily life for most kids" (p. 25). Slavin and other experts pushed for a refocusing of the program on prevention, not remediation, and for a greater concentration of resources on the poorest schools. Slavin concluded, "Chapter 1 has been beneficial to millions of students, but it can be much more than it is today" (p. 25).

Marshall Smith, the undersecretary in the Department of Education, told Congress in 1994, "Operating as a separate supplemental program, Chapter 1 has gone about as far as it can go in raising the skills of at-risk children" (*The Current Status of Chapter 1,* 1994, p. 115). Smith's views were important because he was the major architect of the Clinton administration's new approach to federal aid. Another influential actor was Thomas Payzant, assistant secretary for elementary and secondary education, who had been the long-time superintendent of the San Diego, California, city schools. Payzant, widely respected in the education community, brought to the Department of Education a deep knowledge of the practicalities of operating schools, and his views were clearly imprinted on the administration's recommendations for change.

Secretary Riley's main concern with ESEA was the same as it had been with schools in general as reflected in the debate on Goals: Too many children were being held to low expectations, and the country would not succeed without changing that. His particular problem with Title I was that too many schools used the funds to provide low-skill, rote learning to disadvantaged children and did not try to get them to achieve to high standards and to learn higher-order thinking skills (as the educators put it).

In a speech in May 1994, on the 40th anniversary of *Brown v. Board of Education,* the U.S. Supreme Court decision that had led to the desegregation of the public schools, Riley asserted that the country had "so focused on the physical desegregation of schools in the 1960s and 1970s that we did not do justice to the issue of excellence and high standards which was always the primary goal." He particularly pointed to the "enormous negative impact on many of our children" of low expectations and of the use of watered-down curricula. He summed up his opinions as follows:

> I believe that there can be no equality in this nation without a renewed commitment to excellence . . . that educating every child to use his or her God-given talent is the precondition for full equality in this great country of ours. In 1954, it would have been "unfair" to talk about high standards. Now in 1994, it would be "unfair" not to talk about high standards. Excellence and equality have to be seen as one. Excellence and equality are not incompatible—we've just never tried hard enough to put them together for all of our children. (Riley, 1994)

▓ Ideas for Change

These findings led Riley, Smith, Payzant, and the Clinton administration in the direction of fundamental changes in Title I and in other similar programs.

"In my view, it is essential that ESEA become one unified, comprehensive endeavor for helping students to reach high academic standards," asserted Riley (letter from Richard Riley to William Ford, January 31, 1994). To achieve that end, the administration began work on a proposal it believed "would transform current ESEA programs and, for the first time, focus federal support directly on reinforcing state and local school reforms to improve student learning." In other words, the federal programs would be refashioned to back up the approach used in Goals 2000 to assist states and school districts in raising their educational standards for all children.

During the first part of 1993, the administration had sent to Capitol Hill its Goals legislation and was navigating the treacherous legislative waters in an attempt to secure that bill's enactment, as has been described in the previous chapters. At the same time Smith, Payzant, and others worked on the ESEA changes to fit those programs into the overall structure of standards-based reform.

The Goals bill had a difficult time in Congress, as already noted, but the Clinton administration focused singlemindedly on achieving its enactment, as symbolized by Riley's doggedness. In the House, the controlling Democrats would have preferred to begin work on the ESEA bill early in 1993 because that was the set of programs that immediately meant more to them and their school districts than did standards-based reform, but the administration did not want to send them an ESEA bill until Goals was safely enacted because of a fear that the House would set Goals aside in favor of ESEA. The problem was that Goals took much longer to enact than the administration had anticipated, and the clock was running on the time left in the 1993 congressional session to consider other legislation.

The *Washington Post* criticized the department for not submitting to Congress a bill renewing ESEA. On May 27, an editorial ("Reform School," 1993) opined:

> It's odd, in a way, that the administration sent up a separate reform bill before delivering its proposals for Chapter 1, because Chapter 1 already sets the standards and drives the testing programs for most elementary schools and a lot of secondary schools. (p. A24)

The *Post* suggested that because the Goals bill was so similar to Bush's America 2000 legislation that never made it through the last Congress, it too might not make it through so that it might make sense to look at the ESEA bill as a way to spur reform.

Instead of pushing the administration into submitting ESEA, this editorial and other criticisms confirmed in the minds of Clinton's strategists that an ESEA bill would surely divert attention away from Goals. Consequently, the administration continued along the path of delaying as long as it could the completion of its ESEA draft legislation. Finally, in September, after the legislative clock had ticked for most of the 1993 congressional session and after much prodding from different sources, including Congressman Kildee, who would have the responsibility for carrying the bill in the House, the Clinton administration's ESEA reauthorization proposal was submitted to Congress (H.R. 3130, 1993; S. 1513, 1993).

The two principal purposes of the proposal were to raise standards for all children, including those with special needs, and to have federal programs back up state and local reform efforts. Those objectives were broader than the purposes of the original federal programs, but it is easy to see the relationship that the administration sought to form between the overall reform strategy of Goals and the separate federal programs, such as Title I, each focused on an individual group of children or a particular purpose. This is why the administration had repeatedly described Goals as the new "framework" for federal aid to elementary and secondary education, with the other programs being refashioned to fit into that scheme.

Consequently, the administration's legislation had the following features for a state to receive ESEA funds: Each state would have to have standards for academic content and student performance; student progress toward achieving those standards would be measured using the state's regular assessment system; and many more schools would be given freedom to use federal aid to improve whole schools. The program then in effect differed in that no state had ever had to have education standards to qualify for federal aid, school districts were required to conduct certain federally prescribed testing to measure the progress of children being served, and schools in general had to separately account for the aid to be sure that they focused on certain types of children. In effect, the administration proposed a trade-off of more flexibility in the use of federal aid if a state adopted high education standards and measured student progress toward achieving that academic content.

Riley, Smith, and Payzant also asked that the separate federal programs be coordinated better to reinforce one another and to fit into this scheme of emphasizing results and lessening the prescriptiveness of current federal rules and regulations. Their legislation asked that each major program be tied into a state's standards-based reform and that there be a blending of federal aid instead of the separation of programs then generally prevailing.

Education Week hailed the administration's proposals for Title I as "the most significant revision of the flagship federal education program since it was enacted in 1965" (Miller, 1993, p. 1). The primary focus of that program, the newspaper asserted, would be shifted from remedial help for individual children to efforts to transform high-poverty schools. The plan would also require, it was noted, that the progress of schools be evaluated on the basis of progress toward achieving each state's standards, thus giving a strong push for the states to adopt standards-based reform as proposed in Goals.

"The Clinton administration wants to make federal aid to elementary and secondary schools contingent upon state adoption of goals and standards for what children should learn," concluded the *Congressional Quarterly* (Zuckman, 1993, p. 2394). This approach to overhauling federal aid, it continued, would in effect force states to join the standards movement. Payzant disputed that assertion and pointed out that most states were already developing their own standards for what children should know. "This is going to pick states up where they are and provide support and encouragement for them to keep moving in that direction," he said (quoted in Zuckman, 1993, p. 2394).

▓ Congressional Reaction

Congress proved receptive to these ideas, partly because the representatives and senators had heard complaints back home about the burdensomeness of federal rules and were ready to rethink federal aid if it meant more flexibility for local school districts and schools. In addition, the idea of using standards to improve education had gained credibility from the previous 4-year discussion of the national role in school reform. While grappling with Bush's two school reform proposals from 1990 to 1992 and debating Goals 2000 in 1993, Congress had heard consistently from governors and businesspeople that federal programs were too narrowly focused on procedures to ensure that the aid reached the targeted children and were not concerned enough about the educational results that they should achieve.

Indicative of congressional support for the administration's bill were the remarks of two key leaders in the House. Congressman Kildee, the Democratic chair of the relevant subcommittee, said, "I think this is one of the most comprehensive approaches to make more meaningful the federal role in education since Lyndon Johnson first began this program" (quoted in Zuckman, 1993, p. 2394). And Congressman Goodling, the education committee's ranking Republican, said that he particularly liked the link to school reform because "the whole idea of excellence is one I've been pushing for ages" (quoted in Zuckman, 1993, p. 2394).

In the Senate, the reaction was similar. Senator Kennedy labeled the bill "well-thought out and impressive" ("Improving America's Schools Act," 1993, p. S12928), and Senator Pell, the other Democratic education leader, said that the proposal put "the teeth of the federal education dollar squarely behind the education reform movement already taking place throughout our land" (p. S13022). Senator Jeffords, a key Republican, observed that this "thoughtful" proposal built on work already begun in the states calling for higher standards and greater flexibility (p. S13023).

The principal Republican leaders in the House and Senate wrote in September to Secretary Riley endorsing the overall reform themes of the proposal (letter from Sen. Kassebaum, Sen. Jeffords, Cong. Goodling, et al. to Secretary Riley, September 24, 1993). It is of interest that the Senate and House committee and subcommittee chairs in the next Congress—Senators Kassebaum and Jeffords and Congressmen Goodling, Cunningham, and McKeon—were signers of that letter in the 1995-96 Congress when they were senior or ranking members of committees, rather than the chairs, because the Democrats were then the majority.

In endorsing the concepts in the bill, the joint House and Senate Republican letter noted that "many of these ideas—such as increased flexibility, program consolidations, and high achievement standards—have historically been supported by Republicans." These members of Congress said that for too long, schools, teachers, and students had been encouraged to do only enough to get by because of minimum federal, state, and local guidelines encouraging minimum performance. The ESEA ought to be revised, they believed, to challenge all teachers, administrators, and especially children to do their best. They said that they supported high standards: "All education programs should be designed to meet high standards. Within the framework of rigorous content standards in key subjects, all students, parents, and teachers should know exactly what is expected of them."

This letter showed how far the debate had moved since the *Nation at Risk* report of 1983 (National Commission, 1983). A decade later, in 1994, both Democrats and Republicans were willing to endorse the idea that the national government had some role in encouraging higher standards for all schoolchildren. This statement also makes interesting reading because of the backsliding on this issue that occurred among some of those same Republicans in the following Congress.

In sum, the Clinton administration's ESEA bill was generally supported by Democratic and Republican leaders in the Congress of 1993-94 in its thrust for reform based on high standards. The legislation, however, ran into major trouble due to another issue: It proposed a new way that federal aid would be distributed among states and school districts. Of the total $10 billion of aid provided by ESEA, the Title I program allocated over $7 billion a year to nearly every school district in the country and used data on the number of children in poverty and the cost of their education as the means of disbursing these funds. Because so much money was involved, the method of distributing this aid had been controversial since the creation of the program in 1965.

During 1992 and 1993, the General Accounting Office, the Rand Corporation, and others recommended that federal aid be more targeted on those school districts with the greatest poverty. The Clinton administration took up this cause as one of the principal features of its revision of federal programs, and that proved to be the most controversial part of the legislation.

When the legislation was introduced, the *New York Times* (Krauss, 1993) noted:

> The Clinton administration proposed today to redirect federal aid from prosperous school districts to cities and poor rural areas, and at the same time require the poorer schools to raise their mathematics and reading standards to qualify for the assistance. . . . The proposal mixes traditional liberal prescriptions with moderate proposals intended to give states and localities more autonomy in carrying out government programs, reflecting a theme of the administration. (p. B15)

The *Wall Street Journal* ("Education Chief," 1993) reported that this "shakeup" of the federal government's largest education program would shift $500 million to the nation's poorest schools and would represent a 15% increase in federal education dollars for the nation's poorest counties. According to that newspaper, the rationale for this proposal was rooted in a concern about the poorest schools:

> The Education Department contends that Title I, the federal program aimed at helping disadvantaged students, is spread too thin. Currently, one-third of the children in the highest-poverty schools who score in the bottom third on reading tests don't receive special federal services, yet nearly half of the most affluent schools receive Title I money, officials said. (p. A24)

Storm clouds appeared immediately in Congress around the idea of redistributing this big pot of federal assistance. On the day the bill was released, Senator Mitchell, the Democratic majority leader in the Senate, issued a statement expressing concern about the effects of this change on Maine, which was more favorably treated under the current law. Some local school administrators began to lobby the Congress against the changes. One school administrator (Ochoa, 1993) wrote that "the shift of funds to large urban schools would decimate the universality of the program as well as the suburban ability to provide rich programs for its poor children" (memo from Carley Ochoa, Riverside Unified School District, to Jack Jennings et al., September 20, 1993). These were harbingers of battles ahead.

▓ House Consideration

When Secretary Riley appeared on September 23 before the House committee on behalf of the proposal, he urged the Congress "not to be modest in rethinking how we can reform and improve ESEA's many fine programs" and urged the elected representatives to give up "some of our old assumptions" (quoted in Pitsch, 1993, p. 22). Riley stressed that standards had to be raised for all children to move more children into the economic mainstream.

Although the bill would bring about the most far-reaching changes in the ESEA since it had been created in 1965, Riley and his proposal won generally favorable reviews in the House panel, according to *Education Week* (Pitsch, 1993). Congressman Kildee repeated his earlier praise that the proposal was the most well-thought-out reauthorization he had seen in the 17 years that he had been in Congress. Congressman Goodling, the ranking Republican member of the subcommittee, agreed to cosponsor the legislation, as did another prominent Republican member, Congressman Gunderson. The two Republican leaders, however, made clear that their endorsement of the bill did not mean that they agreed with the funding change being proposed for the Title I program or with some other provisions (Hoff, 1993).

At the same hearing, Congressman Roemer (Dem.-Ind.) and Congressman Boehner (Rep.-Ohio) both expressed concern about the effects of the funding changes on rural areas, especially on pockets of poverty in those areas. These complaints from the members led the Democratic chair of the full committee, Congressman Ford, to tell the press that the administration's formula did not have any chance of passing ("Lawmakers Find Fault," 1993).

When it seemed that all was in readiness for the House committee to move on the administration's bill, the bill was pushed off the schedule for the year. The House had spent much of October 1993 debating Goals and passing it. Then, in early November, Secretary of Labor Robert Reich lobbied heavily for the School to Work bill to be considered by the committee, and he prevailed. After those two bills, the congressional session of 1993 began to wind down, and the members were in no mood to be pushed again to gear up to consider the complex and important ESEA bill.

The administration had held back for so long on sending the ESEA bill to the Hill for fear that it would delay Goals that by the time it was sent it was too late in the legislative year, so the bill was delayed until the following year. This delay did not bode well because the second year of a congressional session, an election year, is always a more difficult time to legislate. The ESEA bill was thrown into that volatile year of political campaigning and, as we shall soon see, suffered the consequences.

As the bill awaited action in Congress, the news media noted the importance of the overhaul of the federal elementary and secondary education programs. "Big changes are ahead in federal policy toward elementary and secondary schools, if—as many expect—Congress gives the President his way," concluded Mary Jordan (1993, p. 6) in *America's Agenda*. The most significant change, she said, was that the administration wanted the money to flow to entire schools with large populations of poor children instead of directing money at individuals who needed remedial work.

Congressional and news media attention was focused on the funding changes, and the more fundamental shift in policy embodied in the bill—the federal government's insistence on high standards—was little discussed, undoubtedly because it had been so thoroughly argued during the Goals consideration. In other words, the idea that the federal government would tie the receipt of federal aid to states and local school districts to their adopting high standards for education was basically resolved during that earlier debate on Goals 2000, which was exactly what the Clinton administration had intended.

In November, Marshall Smith told standards writers and the National Education Goals Panel that he expected states to have content standards within 10 years because Goals would encourage such adoption and then the ESEA would "reinforce it with $10 billion" in aid to ensure that disadvantaged students met the same standards that other children in the state should be meeting (Licitra, 1993, p. 1). Some educators at that meeting expressed concern that this would diminish local control of education, but no major national education organization backed up such concerns with opposition to this major change in direction. The debate had clearly moved far since the adoption of the national goals by the governors in 1990, the development of the national standards under President Bush and Secretary Alexander in the early 1990s, and the writing of Bush's America 2000 and Clinton's Goals 2000 legislation. Those expressions of concern from educators, however, were warning signs that should have foretold the problems that national standards would soon face.

In January, the Clinton administration proposed an increase in funding for education, putting the Department of Education among only 5 of the 14 cabinet agencies having budget increases (Pitsch, 1994b). This suggested increase in aid, however, did not defuse the opposition against its formula change because it was not great enough to soften the effects of the funding losses on those school districts adversely affected. Adding to the fears of the opponents was a study released in mid-January by the General Accounting Office that found that rural schools would suffer the most under the administration's proposal to modify the distribution of money in Chapter 1/Title I (Hoff, 1994e). This report upset members of Congress from rural states and districts and added to the opposition to the administration's proposal.

The administration and its congressional supporters from the largest cities of the country argued strongly that many disadvantaged students in the very poorest schools and school districts were not receiving benefits from Chapter 1 while students in less disadvantaged schools and districts were. The congressional representatives whose districts would lose money countered that needy children residing in whatever area should be served. The politics of the situation were expressed by an educational organization's representative as follows: "The program, to be a viable program over the years, is going to have to touch as many politicians as possible" (quoted in Zuckman, 1994, p. 71).

In February, the House subcommittee met to consider and vote on the administration's ESEA reform bill. In that session, the subcommittee members defeated the administration's Title I funding change by a close vote of 12 in favor and 14 against. The Clinton administration and the big cities' lobbyists had worked hard and almost won, but the subcommittee proved to be the high point of their support because that particular legislative body was disproportionately representative in its membership of the large urban areas. The full education committee and the House of Representatives as a whole were less favorable to the large cities, especially since the 1990 census had led, for the first time in history, to the House's having a majority of its members representative of suburban areas. After defeating the administration's formula proposal, the subcommittee accepted a bipartisan substitute for the formula that kept the current level of funding going to the same areas and then directed a portion of any *new* funding to the poorest areas of the country, especially the largest cities ("Subcommittee Ok's," 1994).

Also during the mark-up of the bill, the Republicans argued against the repeal of a block grant program created during the Reagan administration, but they were outvoted by the Democrats, who supported the Clinton administration on that elimination. In addition, an amendment was adopted requiring school districts to expel a student for bringing a gun to school. However, the basic reforms dealing with standards and flexibility as proposed in the administration's bill provoked little discussion or controversy and were accepted. Finally, the subcommittee approved the bill by a vote of 18 to 8, with all the opponents being Republicans who disagreed with the elimination of the block grant.

A week later, the ESEA bill was considered in the full committee, where the formula issue was revisited. The large cities and the Clinton administration did not have the votes to overturn the subcommittee's decision and faced defeat again, but the winning side in the fight in the subcommittee decided to make some additional changes to broaden support for their amendment. Therefore, a compromise directing a greater portion of any new funds appropriated for the program toward the poorest areas, especially the largest cities, was accepted by a vote of 40 to 2—and that finished discussion of the funding issue in the House (Kuntz, 1994b).

Also during the full committee mark-up, the block grant program, whose deletion had led to the Republicans' opposing the bill in subcommittee, was restored to secure bipartisan support for the bill. Several other issues were fought over, including an amendment to create a program to teach "character" to students and the proposal to require the expulsion of students for bringing weapons to school that had been adopted in the subcommittee.

As in the subcommittee, there was little discussion of the fundamental reforms calling for higher standards until Congressman Owens of New York offered an amendment requiring states to have opportunity-to-learn standards in addition to content and student performance standards. As in the debate on Goals, Republican opponents asserted that its adoption would lead to federal control of schooling, and the liberal Democrats rallied around the Owens amendment as they had on the other equity issues in the Goals debate. This was an echo of the debate on Goals, with each side taking its accustomed position.

After the Owens amendment was adopted over the opposition of the Republicans, the bill was put to a final vote in the full committee and was approved by 29 to 14. All the votes against were from Republicans who objected to the opportunity-to-learn amendment.

A few weeks later, the bill was scheduled for consideration in the full House of Representatives, and the various groups began to organize for the debate on the Owens amendment, again along the same lines as with Goals. The National Governors' Association (NGA) focused on that requirement as another skirmish in its battle to ensure that the federal government's entry into school reform did not impose too much of a burden on the states. In a letter to William Goodling (February 23, 1994), Governors Campbell and Romer wrote:

> The mandate that states have opportunity-to-learn standards that address conditions in schools clearly violates the principle of state and local control in education. By prescribing the specific conditions that must be addressed by the state, the federal government is intruding on state and local decisions over the allocation of resources and is opening the door for more litigation as the courts attempt to use such standards to determine the adequacy of school programs in school finance equity cases.

In making the argument against the opportunity-to-learn standards, the governors referred to an assurance that they had been given during the debate on Goals that all national school reform efforts would be voluntary and that no opportunity-to-learn standards would be required for participation in any federal program.

Congressman Goodling began to form a bipartisan coalition to defeat the Owens amendment in the full House of Representatives ("Dear Colleague" letter, "Vote to Strike Opportunity to Learn Standards From H.R. 6" from Cong. Goodling, Condit, Gunderson, and Stenholm, February 17, 1994), but negotiations between him and Congressmen Owens and Kildee resulted in clarifying the amendment so that it was considerably weakened and made voluntary and thus acceptable to Goodling and the other opponents ("House Panel Strikes Deal," 1994). Despite the liberals' strong feeling that financial resources had to be considered when improving schools, they had learned from their experience with Goals that they did not have the votes when this issue came before the full House. Thus, they believed that it was better to compromise to keep *any* reference to the need for resources in the bill, however weak that might be. The debate on the Owens amendment, therefore, proved to be a faint echo of the far more strident argument that had occurred over the same issue during the consideration of Goals the previous year. During the remainder of the House's focus on ESEA, there was little additional attention to that issue or, for that matter, to the general issues of school reform.

The House considered the ESEA bill over the course of a month, February 24 to March 24, 1994—a very long time for any bill to be under consideration. However, the debate was not continuous. Several hours would be spent on various amendments one day and then none the next. The principal reason that the bill took so long was that it became a target, during the election year, for many controversial social issues, ranging from home schooling to immigration to a variety of sexually related questions. The debate over the Goals bill had made federal aid to education very controversial in the eyes of the far right, and they had learned during that debate to use social issues as a way to load down a bill and make it unpopular.

The first controversy involved home schooling of children ("Improving America's Schools Act, House Debate," 1994a, pp. H799-H846). Advocates for those who teach their children at home had interpreted an amendment in the ESEA bill dealing with teacher certification to mean that parents who home-schooled would be required to obtain teaching certificates. Despite the denial of the sponsor of that amendment that the provision had that effect or that he had ever intended that result, the opponents mounted a massive lobbying campaign that led to two amendments being adopted to exempt home schooling from any effects of the bill. That debate was very heated and consumed nearly the whole first day of legislative consideration, and for the several days surrounding that debate, the proponents of home schooling flooded the offices of Capitol Hill with telephone calls and visits (Kuntz, 1994a).

During the course of the next 30 days, some education-related amendments were considered, but most of the time was spent on emotional socially related questions. For instance, the House became embroiled in a long and angry debate over requiring school districts to report on the number of children in their schools who were illegal immigrants or who were legally in the country but who had parents who were illegally in the United States. Proponents argued that there were too many illegal immigrants in the country and that every means should be used to exclude them. Opponents countered that schools should not have the burden of identifying illegal immigrants and that children should not be asked to report on the immigration status of their parents. After much heated debate, that amendment was defeated ("Improving America's Schools Act, House Debate," 1994b, pp. H1015-H1034).

An amendment prohibiting federal funds to schools that did not permit constitutional prayer on school grounds was also accepted ("Improving America's Schools Act, House Debate," 1994d, pp. 1740-H1751). This was the Helms proposal that was offered in the House a few days before the Goals conference report was debated, as described in the last chapter. Another amendment was also debated requiring schools teaching sex education to emphasize abstinence from sexual intercourse as the only fully effective protection against teenage pregnancy. An amendment was rejected barring any education aid to benefit illegal aliens ("Improving America's Schools Act, House Debate," 1994e, pp. H1795-H1808). Amendments were also offered requiring that schools prohibit smoking and emphasize the dangers of smoking cigarettes. After debate detailing the health hazards of tobacco, those antismoking provisions were accepted ("Improving America's Schools Act, House Debate," 1994c, pp. H1127-H1131).

Last, funds were prohibited from being used to carry out programs supporting homosexuality as a positive lifestyle ("Improving America's Schools Act, House Debate," 1994f, pp. H2020-H2033). The debate on this particular amendment became raucous when a very conservative Republican proponent of the prohibition accused a moderate Republican, Steve Gunderson, of being gay and of having "a revolving door on his closet—he's in, he's out" (stricken from *Cong. Rec.* but quoted in "Debate on Gay Issue," 1994, p. A4). That remark was indicative of the emotionalism of much of the month-long debate on all these socially related amendments.

Finally, on March 24, after a debate spread over 4 weeks and mostly involving these divisive social issues, the House passed the ESEA bill by a vote of 289 to 128. Two hundred and forty-three Democrats voted in favor and 4 voted against; 45 Republicans voted in favor and 124 against; and the one independent in the House voted for final passage of the bill ("Improving America's Schools Act, House Debate," 1994f, p. H2151).

Secretary Riley hailed the passage of the bill as "a giant step forward in this administration's efforts to ensure that all of America's children, including our most disadvantaged, have equal access to a quality education" (quoted in Hoff, 1994f, p. 1). *Education Daily* (Hoff, 1994f) noted that the bill as passed by the House kept intact the basic outline of the legislation it had started debating a month ago. The *Congressional Quarterly* (Wells, 1994a) concluded, "While the main tenets of the measure were largely resolved a month ago, House members continued to battle over volatile issues such as school prayer and homosexual lifestyles" (p. 746).

As described in the last chapter, the same week that the House passed the ESEA bill, the House and the Senate also approved the conference report on Goals 2000 after the tense debate in the House on the prayer amendment and after Senator Helms's filibuster on the same issue was overcome in the Senate. Thus, by the end of March 1994, the Clinton administration had come a long way in moving forward its agenda for school reform. To complete that agenda, the last major piece was for the Senate to finish its work on the ESEA bill and for the House-Senate conference committee to resolve any differences between the two bills.

The approval in the House of the bill updating the federal programs of aid to elementary and secondary education was a victory for Clinton and Riley, but it was also the most divisive partisan vote on ESEA since the programs were created in the mid-1960s. In fact, a lower percentage of Republicans voted for the final bill in 1994 than had voted for the original act in 1965, when the idea of federal aid to education was new and quite controversial (see Figures 6.1a and 6.1b). That aspect of the ESEA fight in the House and the nasty battle in the Senate over the Goals conference report were not isolated events; rather, they were indications of broader trends showing increasing Republican opposition to federal aid to education.

An element in shaping this opposition was that the congressional conservatives felt energized and began to work very aggressively for what they considered vital moral and social issues. Helms's amendment dealing with school prayer was the leading example of that, but there were many others, such as those proposals affecting sex education, homosexuality, immigration, and home schooling. Republicans used votes on these social issues as a way to put Democrats in an awkward position for the upcoming election because many Democrats were more socially liberal and opposed to the harshest forms of these amendments. Many of these amendments were considered as part of the education legislation, so they helped to make those federal programs controversial.

Another element, however, was that the most conservative members of Congress were never fully comfortable with the idea of federal aid to education, and when the debates became intense about how the national government would help to raise standards in the public schools, these conservatives revived fears of federal takeover of the schools. Also the increasing influence of

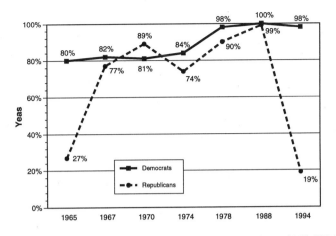

Figure 6.1a. House Votes on ESEA and Major Reauthorizations, 1965-1994
SOURCE: *Congressional Quarterly* Annual Almanacs

far-right organizations on Republican members of Congress added to the pressure on Republicans to oppose federal aid to education.

These trends will be discussed more fully in the following chapter, but it is useful to note here that Clinton, Riley, and the Democrats won their victories on this education legislation (Goals 2000 and the ESEA reforms) but that they were to pay a price in the elections of 1994 and in the next Congress. The new national role in support of school reform was successfully fashioned, but the far right was increasingly focusing on federal aid to public schools as something to be eliminated.

▓ Senate Consideration

The Senate deferred consideration of the ESEA bill until 1994 and then experienced all the difficulties of trying to move a major piece of legislation during an election year. Although the first hearing in March went smoothly with regard to the idea of encouraging higher standards, the reaction to concentrating Title I funds was far from supportive. Senator Kennedy commented, "It's a minefield of enormous proportions" (quoted in Hoff, 1994d, p. 1; see also Wells, 1994e). Not only would the Senate have great difficulty with passing a bill because of disputes over the funding changes, but Congress

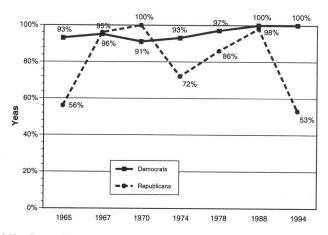

Figure 6.1b. Senate Votes on ESEA and Major Reauthorizations, 1965-1994
SOURCE: *Congressional Quarterly* Annual Almanacs

would come close to defeating the whole bill in the last days of the session due to the same controversy.

Kennedy was inclined to support an approach similar to that of the House, continuing current funding for school districts and concentrating new money on the more needy areas. Other members of Kennedy's committee, however, had different ideas, ranging from rewarding states that equalized their own funding for the schools to encouraging greater state tax efforts for education. "The formula is always the key," noted Senator Jeffords (quoted in "Senate Panel Readies," 1994, p. 6), but each senator seemed to want to use his or her own key.

In May, at the subcommittee's session to consider the bill, the administration's funding change was defeated, and Kennedy's approach mostly prevailed. After some other discussion, the subcommittee approved the bill by a vote of 17 to 0, but the issue of how to distribute the money would not go away (Pitsch, 1994d).

In June, when the bill was taken up by the full committee, the subcommittee-approved means of distributing funds was changed to concentrate larger amounts on the neediest school districts *within* states but not to concentrate funds any further *among* the neediest states. This half-step to rechanneling funds to the poorest school districts, however, did not satisfy the proponents of targeting resources to the poorer states (Wells, 1994f).

The only major dispute concerning school reform involved opportunity-to-learn standards. Senator Wellstone's amendment to include such standards in Title I was defeated after Kennedy argued that it would not prevail in the full Senate and that it would destine the bill to a long and acrimonious debate. Kennedy took up the position taken by the conservatives in the House who opposed the Owens amendment, noting that 27 states were then in court on the financing of their schools and that the adoption of this amendment would start another round of court challenges. Kassebaum also opposed the amendment and pledged her support for the bill as it stood (Wells, 1994f).

As in the House, there was little explanation about the major policy changes proposed in the legislation because there was overall agreement about these reforms. Members of Congress were ready to tie the receipt of federal aid to states' adoption of high standards for schoolchildren and to align federal programs to state and local reform efforts instead of making them separate activities within states, school districts, and schools.

The committee approved the ESEA bill by a vote of 16 to 1, with only Senator Coats in opposition. Despite this success on the basic reforms, Kennedy acknowledged during the committee meeting that the formula would remain controversial: "It's going to continue to be an issue, certainly on the floor and in conference" (quoted in Pitsch, 1994g, p. 20).

"Big Cities and Growth States Hate Senate Chapter 1 Formula," headlined *Education Daily* (Hoff, 1994a) after the Senate committee reported the bill. The newsletter noted that Texas and California, which both experienced great growth in the numbers of poor children during the late 1980s and the early 1990s, would see less Title I funding under the committee-approved distribution. The *Washington Post* ("Chapter 1, Take 2," 1994), however, praised the Senate for "signs of progress" in targeting funds on poorer districts because the committee had shifted funds to poorer areas within states, although not to needier states (p. A22).

At the end of July, the education bill was brought up for consideration in the Senate. Kennedy began the debate by noting that these were the most significant changes to be made to these programs since they had been created in the mid-1960s and that at the heart of the bill was the same idea that was embedded in Goals—namely, that all students, including those with few advantages, can meet high standards ("Improving America's Schools Act, Senate Debate," 1994a, pp. S9755-S9756).

The ranking Republicans on the committee, Senators Kassebaum and Jeffords, supported the bill. Kassebaum, who became the chair of the Senate committee in the next Congress, remarked on the contributions that ESEA had made to the improvement of education. She said:

> Years ago, efforts that I began as a volunteer to start a library in my children's school received an enormous boost when ESEA was enacted and funds became available to help establish a library in the elementary school. More recently, I have had the opportunity to visit schools throughout the state and to see that my own experience was not unique. The combination of creative teachers and a little federal funding is a powerful one, indeed.
>
> The largest of the ESEA programs, Chapter 1, provides extra help to educationally disadvantaged children, particularly in the areas of reading and math. The additional services made available under Chapter 1 often spell the difference between a child's getting a solid foundation in skills needed for future educational success or simply muddling through years of school without these skills. ("Improving America's Schools Act, Senate Debate," 1994a, pp. S9873-S9874)

The political far right did not share Kassebaum's enthusiasm for federal aid and had mounted a campaign against the bill, saying that it gave the U.S. Department of Education control over the curriculum of local schools (Hoff, 1994b). Kassebaum rebutted that claim by noting that decisions about curriculum and instructional methods would still be made by local and state officials and that there was no requirement for opportunity-to-learn standards ("Improving America's Schools Act, Senate Debate," 1994a, p. S9874).

Several conservatives broke ranks with the far right and endorsed the bill. Senator Alan Simpson (Rep.-Wyo.), for instance, made clear that he saw this bill as very different from the Goals legislation, which he had opposed, believing that it would lead to undue federal interference in local schools. He further assured the Senate that there was no encouragement of outcome-based education in the ESEA bill, although he had heard that said in his own state ("Improving America's Schools Act, Senate Debate," 1994d, pp. S10284-S10285).

With such broad support, the basic principles of the bill were ensured acceptance by the Senate. However, there was much controversy over the changes made in the distribution of funds and then, as in the House, over social issues.

With regard to money, the committee's Title I/Chapter 1 formula changes faced a "blistering barrage of criticism," according to the *Congressional Quarterly* (Wells, 1994c, p. 2148). Senator Diane Feinstein (Dem.-Calif.), unhappy that California and other high-growth states were not gaining more under the committee's formula, mounted a campaign to redress what she saw as a major injustice ("Improving America's Schools Act, Senate Debate," 1994b, pp. S10033-S10034). Senator Dale Bumpers (Dem.-Ark.), "shouting at the top of his lungs at several points," labeled the committee's changes as "one of the most perverse formulas I have ever seen" and vowed to offer amendments on behalf of the poorest states (quoted in Wells, 1994c, p. 2148). Bumpers' charges about the effects on the poorer states were echoed by Senator Thad Cochran (Rep.-Miss.). Senator Hatch also stated his intent to offer an amendment on behalf of states that were penalized because they were not considered as making enough of an effort for education according to the committee's formula.

After some initial skirmishing, it became clear that the committee's funding provisions would be defeated, so Kennedy compromised with Hatch. The net effect was that the northeastern states, which were heavily represented in the leadership of the education committee, gave up some of the funds they would have gained under the committee's revisions and allowed those funds to be spread among 38 other states. Kennedy had been correct when he had predicted months before that the formula was a minefield ("Improving America's Schools Act, Senate Debate," 1994c, pp. S10153-S10157).

While this jockeying was occurring over the distribution of funds, the Senate spent a great deal of time arguing about social issues. Senator Helms offered his school prayer amendment, which would have required "constitutionally protected" prayer to be offered in the public schools ("Improving America's Schools Act, Senate Debate," 1994a, p. S9890). This was the same amendment that he had offered and the Senate had accepted on Goals but that had been deleted in the Senate-House conference committee on Goals. As described in the last chapter, Helms was so angry about that elimination that he had unsuccessfully filibustered the Goals conference report and then vowed to bring the same amendment back to the Senate at a later date. The ESEA bill was that occasion. Helms realized that because the House version of ESEA contained this same amendment, he would lock it in if he could get the Senate to agree to it again as it had on Goals ("Improving America's Schools Act, Senate Debate," 1994a, p. S9887).

Senator Kassebaum, however, was prepared with an alternative to Helms's amendment. Her amendment would fine school officials if they willfully violated a court order to permit prayer in school. She argued that school officials were ill prepared to decide what was constitutionally protected and that therefore they should be penalized only if they willfully decided not to obey an order from a court. Her goal was to have a judge, rather than school officials, determine what prayers in school were permitted by the Constitution.

After much debate, the Senate rejected Helms's amendment 47 to 53 (reversing itself from the Goals vote) and then approved Kassebaum's amendment by a vote of 93 to 7. There were certainly many twists and turns that year as Congress debated prayer in the schools.

The *Congressional Monitor* ("Senators Walk," 1994) asserted that the senators were walking a "narrow line" on prayer in school. Senator Gorton, after hearing the debate on the various amendments, concluded that

> even though I do not think that the Helms amendment will change very much in its present form, and even though I have serious questions about whether or not the Kassebaum amendment is positively negative, destructive, I intend to vote for both of them. ("Improving America's Schools Act, Senate Debate," 1994a, p. S9901)

The reason he gave for his votes was that he hoped something good would come of them.

Additional social issues were considered by the Senate. An amendment was adopted that forbade the uses of federal funds to encourage the teaching of homosexuality as a positive lifestyle, and then a broader amendment was also adopted barring the uses of funds for the promotion of any sexual activity ("Improving America's Schools Act, Senate Debate," 1994c, pp. S10185-S10197). The intent stated later was that this broader provision would somehow bring reason to bear on the adoption of the antigay amendment. Another amendment was adopted barring the use of federal funds to distribute condoms among schoolchildren, although no evidence was produced that any federal funds were in fact then being used for that purpose ("Improving America's Schools Act, Senate Debate," 1994d, p. S10233). Violence by youth was also addressed, as was the need to teach values to youth ("Improving America's Schools Act, Senate Debate," 1994a, p. S9822; 1994b, p. S10023).

A move to permit federal funds to be used to pay for tuition at private schools was defeated by 45 to 53, and a provision was adopted allowing the use by school districts of private companies to perform some of their management functions ("Improving America's Schools Act, Senate Debate," 1994a, p. S9915; 1994b, p. S9987). An experiment allowing all-boys' schools as a means to motivate inner-city black males to do better in school was put forth by Senator John Danforth (Rep.-Mo.) and adopted ("Improving America's Schools Act, Senate Debate," 1994c, p. S10163).

Finally the Senate finished its work, and on August 2, it approved the bill by a vote of 94 to 6, with all the negative votes coming from Republican conservatives ("Improving America's Schools Act, Senate Debate," 1994d, p. S10316). Now the last stage of the process could begin, the Senate and House conference committee, but the experience in the Senate had shown that the conservatives were increasingly turning to social issues as a way to burden education bills and to embarrass politically the proponents of federal aid to education ("Senate Passes $12 Billion," 1994).

▨ Conference Committee

The predictions were that the conference committee on ESEA would be difficult because of the large differences between the House and the Senate on the Title I/Chapter 1 funding distribution (Wells, 1994g). It is clear, said *Education Week* (Pitsch, 1994f), that "the bloodiest battle in upcoming House-Senate negotiations will be an old-fashioned tussle that decides which regions will receive more federal money and which will receive less" (p. 27). The newspaper predicted that the greatest task facing the lawmakers would be devising a Chapter 1 formula that could pass in both chambers.

As it worked out, resolving the differing Senate and House amendments dealing with social issues proved as formidable a task. A prime example was the amendment permitting all-boys' schools. The national organizations supporting civil rights for women were strongly opposed to this amendment because they viewed it as discrimination against girls and as the first weakening of the federal law forbidding such discrimination. On the other side were some prominent African Americans who supported the idea as a way to improve the education of inner-city black boys. For instance, William Raspberry (1994), the nationally syndicated columnist, wrote that the amendment ought to pass because single-sex education improves the performance of some children. The battle over that amendment would be only one of many disputes over social issues that would have to be resolved, for the two bills also had amendments dealing with school prayer, homosexuality, condom distribution, and school gun policies—all of which engendered as much emotion and controversy as the all-boys' schools provision.

The Senate passed its version of ESEA on August 2 and then went on its summer recess. Therefore, the conference committee could not meet until mid-September. Because the Congress was to adjourn in early October for the elections, there were only 3 weeks to resolve the differences between the House and the Senate bills and to pass a conference report—after overcoming the expected filibuster and other delaying tactics of the opponents. It was a very tight schedule to accomplish all of that, especially because the bill was very complicated and affected a wide range of programs with provisions consuming over 1,000 pages of legal text.

A major factor helping to push the bill toward passage was the demise of comprehensive health care reform. By the start of the August summer recess, it was clear that Clinton's prime initiative for the year was not going to pass in any form; therefore, the time that the congressional leaders had set aside in September and October for the consideration of that issue was released to be used for other legislation. Furthermore, Democratic members felt that the education bill and other legislation needed to be passed to make up for their failure to enact health care reform. As they prepared to go to their congressional districts and states to campaign for reelection, they needed to point to some successes.

As the time for the members' meeting approached in mid-September, various interest groups mobilized to influence the decisions. The far right sent letters and telegrams in support of the antigay, anticondom, and pro-school-prayer amendments. The national gay organizations urged citizens to contact the conference committee members to support the weaker provisions of the antigay amendments. The *Washington Post* editorialized in favor of a Title I formula composed of a "Mix and Match on Education" (1994), by which it meant that certain provisions ought to be taken from the House and Senate bills and blended together to create a more focused formula providing additional aid to poorer school districts.

The NGA wrote that the House and Senate bills "support ongoing state reform initiatives and help provide a consistent message for schools from both the federal and state government about the importance and direction of reform" (letter from Govs. James Hunt and Christine Hoff to conferees, September 19, 1994). As expected, however, the letter repeated the NGA's opposition to the opportunity-to-learn standards required for Title I in the House bill and to any unfunded federal mandates. The letter helped in perpetuating the bipartisan tone that had been maintained for much of the ESEA debate.

Because the Senate had already appointed its conferees when it passed the bill in August, the House acted on September 20 to name its members to the conference committee. Outmaneuvering a more conservative Republican who wanted to offer a motion on an antigay provision, Congressman Gunderson offered a motion to instruct the House conferees to stand by the school prayer amendment requiring school officials to permit "constitutionally protected" prayer. Gunderson's motion was adopted by a vote of 369 to 55 ("Elementary and Secondary Education Amendments," 1994a).

After the House members were appointed, the House-Senate conference committee began its meetings. The political dynamics were that the House could probably pass most versions of the conference report because of the 78-vote Democratic margin in that 435-member body but that the Senate had to have 60 votes of the 100 in that chamber to pass any version of the report due to the probability of a filibuster, and the Democrats at that point in time had only 54 votes. This was the same dynamic that was present during the consideration of the Goals bill.

Senator Kennedy, the chair of the Senate side of the conference committee on ESEA, was always aware, as he had been on Goals 2000, that he had to find at least six Republican votes to pass any conference agreement. An additional complicating factor was that Kennedy was facing a very difficult race for reelection. He was thus unusually anxious to settle disputes during the ESEA conference to secure a victory on education that he could take home as he campaigned for reelection.

An example of Kennedy's quest to find 60 votes was a provision inserted by Senator Gregg to forbid any unfunded mandates imposed on states by the federal government as a result of the enactment of the bill. During the course of the conference meetings, Congressmen William Ford and George Miller asserted that there were no "unfunded mandates" in the bill, and they challenged Gregg to list any, which they would then remove ("ESEA Bill Conferees," 1994, p. 4). Gregg responded that although he could not identify any such provisions, adopting the amendment was good insurance if any were found later. The House members felt frustrated because the adoption of Gregg's amendment would implicitly give credence to assertions that federal aid leads to unfunded mandates. Kennedy, however, prevailed on the House members to accept the amendment (with some minor modifications) because he had Gregg's promise to vote against any filibusters and to support the final conference report. Gregg proved true to his word and later voted to invoke cloture on the filibuster mounted by many of his fellow conservatives.

The contrary outcome came about with the amendment permitting all-boys' schools. Senator Danforth, with a record of support for civil rights laws, argued passionately for his amendment in the conference committee, but due to adamant opposition from civil rights and women's groups, the amendment was deleted. Danforth, who would probably have voted for cloture on any filibuster, then opposed the final conference report and sided with the conservatives despite his moderate reputation. The Gregg and Danforth amendments demonstrated how hard it was for Kennedy to secure the votes of 60 of the 100 senators, especially in the last tiring and emotional days of the congressional session.

During the first week of their meetings, the conferees also agreed to require local school districts to adopt a policy expelling students who brought a gun to school. The Senate-passed school prayer amendment offered by Kassebaum was accepted by the House, even though the House members had been instructed to stand by the House-passed, more stringent Helms provision. In a compromise crafted by Gunderson and Kennedy, the specifically antigay amendments were deleted, and a broader provision was accepted that forbade the use of any federal education funds to encourage sexual activities or to distribute condoms or obscene materials. As part of that prohibition, there was a requirement that if any federal funds were used for health education or for AIDS education, information on the health benefits of abstinence had to be included.

More than half of the time that the lawmakers had spent in the week-long Senate-House conference was on issues such as gun possession in schools, school prayer, condom distribution, and sex education, according to *Education Week* (Pitsch, 1994e). Social issues were used to score political points back home, according to that article, especially against the backdrop of a fierce campaign season that was occurring as the ESEA conference met. In retrospect, the controversies engendered by conservatives were at least partially responsible for producing a new Congress that was to be the most conservative in decades.

This strategy to produce a more conservative Congress meant, however, that conservatives were proposing that the federal government require states and school districts to act in certain ways on social issues, and these aggressive actions would seem to be at odds with the view of a limited federal government. As one lobbyist noted about social issues, "This Congress has been more willing than ever to be the county council, the mayor's office, or the school board, and less willing to be the Congress" (Bruce Hunter, quoted in Pitsch, 1994e, p. 22).

On one of the few school reform issues that was in dispute, the conference deleted the House-passed requirement that the states had to have opportunity-to-learn standards in their Title I programs. This was the amendment offered by Congressman Owens, which was strongly opposed by the National Governors' Conference even in its weakened form. Senator Kassebaum made clear her own opposition to that requirement because she felt that it focused only on "inputs," but she also made known that this was one issue that would endanger the whole conference report because the Republican moderates would not support any requirement for opportunity-to-learn standards.

On another education issue, the House accepted the Senate-passed limitation included by Kassebaum that the standards that states had to adopt in Title I would be limited to reading and mathematics because these were the subjects in which students received help through Title I. Under that provision, states could voluntarily include additional standards. Kassebaum, who had a history of being a supporter of federal aid and of ESEA, had to be watchful about charges from more conservative Republicans that this bill was a "back door" for Goals 2000 and for standards to be forced on the states.

The conferees turned their attention several times to the most contentious issue, the Title I funding scheme, but they could not reach agreement, despite the fact that the Congress would soon adjourn for the election. Newspapers in fact reported that the conference was deadlocked due to the funding issue ("ESEA Conferees Deadlocked," 1994; Wells, 1994b).

The House and Senate leadership of the conference committee finally had to resort to a closed-door meeting from which they excluded most of the other conferees so that they could fashion a compromise. Then, when the leaders produced their compromise, the excluded conferees took their revenge by voting down the proposed agreement ("House Conferees," 1994). Soon, however, reason prevailed, and the leaders' compromise was accepted as the only alternative in the final hours of the conference ("Conferees Reach Deal," 1994).

"Few members of the conference committee were overjoyed with the formula, which was the last piece to be fit into the puzzle," reported *Education Week* (Pitsch, 1994a). "But they were forced to wrap up their deliberations last week because the ESEA programs were set to expire on Sept. 30, and Congress is poised to adjourn for the year" (p. 18). Once again, as with the

April 1 deadline for Goals, a deadline was seen as an essential pressure to achieve a legislative compromise.

The final agreement reached by the conferees on the Title I formula meant that most school districts would receive the same amount of money as they had in the past. If there was to be any new money, the poorer areas would receive more funding. In addition, schools in states spending more for education and spending these funds equally among school districts could qualify for some additional funds. Last, faster growing states would gain funds. Although complicated, this agreement was supported by enough of the members of the conference committee to reach a final conclusion (Sharpe, 1994).

▨ House Action on the Conference Report

As with the Goals bill, the congressional leaders agreed that it was more prudent to bring the ESEA conference agreement up first in the House, where the Democrats enjoyed a greater majority and where there was no threat of a filibuster. Despite that 78-vote Democratic majority, the atmosphere in the House was tense because the election was only 5 weeks away and the Republicans seemed on the ascendancy.

Adding to the tension, some socially conservative organizations lobbied strongly against the conference report because of the deletion of the Helms school prayer and the antigay amendments. The Family Research Council (1994), for instance, distributed an "Alert" letter ("Retain Pro-Family Provisions in HR 6," September 1994) to the membership of the House alleging that the conference committee had "stripped two pro-family amendments" from the report and had instead incorporated "unworkable and meaningless language."

Republican members sent "Dear Colleague" letters opposing various features of the legislation and therefore urging support for any motion to recommit to the conference because they knew that the acceptance of such a motion would kill the bill in the last days of the Congress ("GOP Readies," 1994). The letter from Congressman Cliff Stearns of Florida (September 29, 1994) objected to the compromise effecting the removal of disabled students who become violent in the classroom and advocated a harsher remedy than the one agreed on. That of Congressman Armey (September 29, 1994) recited a litany of reasons to recommit the report: "bogus school prayer language," too many new programs, "Robin Hood equalization," "groundwork for federalization," "social engineering," and "racial discrimination." Congressman

Tom Bliley of Virginia (September 29, 1994) contended that the report would somehow forbid adoption of children across racial lines. And Congressman John Boehner (September 29, 1994) contended that the federal government would be "unaccountable" if the report passed.

The Democratic supporters of the ESEA conference report were also busy sending letters to the members of the House, and they concentrated on the issue of school prayer because that would be a difficult vote for many of the Democrats. Congressman Gene Green of Texas (September 29, 1994) asserted that the compromise on school prayer respected local control of education and that the Helms amendment would have centralized the decision on what was constitutionally permitted in the hands of the Washington bureaucracy. Congressmen Sawyer and Reed (September 29, 1994) told the House that the prayer compromise avoided "creating a federal prayer czar in the Department of Education to make legal decisions on the right to pray in schools." Chairman Ford (September 29, 1994) reminded the members that the agreement would cut off federal funds to a school district if a court determined that the right to prayer had been violated.

Some other Democrats in their letters reminded members of other features of the omnibus legislation. Congressman Owens (n.d., c. September 29, 1994) noted that the programs funding drug education and school safety measures were renewed. Congressman Pat Williams of Montana (September 29, 1994) assured members from rural areas that the new Title I formula would assist their school districts. Congressman Eliot Engel of New York (n.d., c. September 29, 1994) wrote about the arts education program, and five other members (Patsy Mink et al., September 29, 1994) outlined the assistance given to school districts with military-connected children. Twenty-one members (Lynn Woolsey et al., September 29, 1994) wrote a joint letter enumerating all the various ways the bill aided education.

Because the ESEA bill extended the life of dozens of programs that were providing approximately $10 billion of aid every year to nearly every school district in the country, it was a more difficult bill for many members of Congress to vote against than was the Goals bill, which was creating a new program proposing more modest amounts of aid. Adding to the pressure for the bill, the U.S. Department of Education (letter from Judith Winston to William D. Ford, September 28, 1994) issued an opinion that no funding would be available for any of these programs after October 1 if the conference report was defeated. The proponents could now argue that funding would be lost in scores of local schools unless members of Congress overcame doubts about various provisions of the report and voted to approve it.

Another helpful argument came from the national business community. The National Alliance of Business, the Chamber of Commerce of the United States, the Committee for Economic Development, and the American Business Conference wrote a joint letter to the House (to Congressmen William Ford and William Goodling, September 30, 1994) urging approval of the conference report because "ESEA passage will guarantee that for the first time in this nation's history there will be a comprehensive framework and the appropriate federal incentives to support widespread systemic reform efforts." Passage of ESEA, they said, will ensure that the objectives of Goals 2000 become a reality: namely, high standards for all students, first-rate professional development, and unprecedented flexibility to design and operate educational programs. The business organizations urged the members of Congress "to put partisan differences aside and pass ESEA to help support the long term educational progress and economic security of our nation's future workforce."

The U.S. Catholic Conference wrote urging members to vote against any attempt to recommit the bill to conference because "any delay in the enactment of ESEA will jeopardize the implementation of the essential improvements to American public and nonpublic education that are contained in this critical legislation" ("Letter to Representatives," 1994c, p. H10404). The Baptist Joint Committee also wrote against a delay in approving the bill, as did the Council on American Private Education, which represents many denominational schools ("Letter to Representatives," 1994a, 1994b). Those letters were helpful to members of Congress who were nervous about voting for a conference report without the Helms school prayer amendment.

The *Washington Post* ("Sideshow," 1994) weighed in with an editorial criticizing "stagy amendments" having nothing to do with the central purpose of the legislation—to improve education (p. A28). The conference report deferred to local authorities on both the school prayer and the homosexual "lifestyle" issues; therefore, the editorial asserted, "You might think that such deference to local wishes would appeal to Republicans" (p. A28). Instead, the newspaper said, the Republicans were posturing and ought to back off and let the bill pass.

As the time approached for the consideration of the conference report, the Democrats feared that they would not have the votes to beat the motion to recommit on the prayer issue, according to *CongressDaily* ("Democrats Fear," 1994). The national education organizations mounted a comprehensive lobbying campaign in support of the bill because there were so many programs in the bill that benefited the teachers, students, parents, and schools they represented. The result was a well-coordinated campaign that had a major impact on the House's vote and then was continued through the Senate's voting.

On September 30, the House took up the conference report on the education bill ("Elementary and Secondary Education Act Appropriations Extension," 1994). Democratic supporters quoted from the Department's opinion that the bill was needed to continue the programs beyond their termination that very day; Republican opponents asserted that some way would be found to continue the aid provided by the programs. Supporters said that if there was a delay resulting from the adoption of the motion to recommit on school prayer, the bill would die because there was not enough time left in the session to reconsider all the complicated issues that would be reopened once the Senate-House conference committee met again. Opponents countered that no bill should be adopted in such haste and that members could not read the whole text, consisting of 1,200 pages. Democrats alleged that the Republicans were using any excuse they could to kill the bill because they wanted to show that a Democratic Congress could not do the nation's business; Republicans shot back that the bill contained so many provisions extending federal control over the schools that it should not be approved.

The intensity of the debate shows the problem with bringing a major bill up for approval at the very end of a congressional session, especially one before an election—and the 1994 election in particular held very high stakes for both parties. In September and October, the Republicans had polls showing that they could potentially take over the Congress, so they did not want to do anything that would blunt their advantage. The Democrats had their own polls showing their potential losses and wanted legislative achievements to help them counter accusations of ineffectiveness. Added to this tension were the emotions that were stirred among segments of the population about the various social issues linked to the education bill.

Congressman Kildee, the prime sponsor of the bill, noted that it was the most important reauthorization since the mid-1960s, when most of the programs in the ESEA were first created. Federal programs were being refashioned to encourage high academic standards for all students, and schools were being given unprecedented flexibility in the use of federal funds. "The heart of the legislation," he concluded, "is to demand greater educational achievement in exchange for more freedom in the use of federal funds. . . . The whole bill can be summed up in two words—flexibility and accountability" ("Elementary and Secondary Education Act Appropriations Extension," 1994, p. H10384).

Several other representatives also noted the historic shift in federal aid embodied in the bill. Congressman Sawyer noted:

> The principal thrust of this really goes to the heart of what we believe most deeply about education, that it will raise the achievement levels of educationally disadvantaged students. This bill assumes that disadvantaged students can excel if they are exposed to a rigorous curriculum and well-trained teachers. (p. H10397)

Even some of the opponents conceded that the bill contained many good features that would improve education, but they pointed to other features of the bill that they found troubling, such as the new method of distributing funds in the Title I/Chapter 1 program. Goodling and Gunderson, for instance, dwelt on the uncertainty of determining allocations to local school districts after the first 2 years of the new formula; they did not attack the substance of the legislation.

The crucial vote was on the motion to recommit the report on the school prayer amendment. Congressman Johnson, who offered that motion, argued that the House had voted three times in favor of the Helms amendment, which he had offered in the House. He also cited the opinion of the Christian Coalition that the Kassebaum amendment contained in the conference agreement was meaningless because it required a person to go to court twice to force a school district to permit prayer in the school. The opponents of the motion to recommit argued that it would make the secretary of education a "school prayer Czar" because he would have to judge whether local school officials had exercised proper judgment on whether to permit prayer in the schools.

During the entire ESEA debate, the conservatives shifted their arguments for or against federal action depending on the issue involved. Congressman Ballenger (Rep.-N.C.), for instance, said that he could not vote for the conference report because it was a move to a "Washington takeover of our schools," but then he voted for the Johnson motion to recommit, which would have overridden local decision making on school prayer to require that officials permit such prayer (p. H10389). Congressman Dan Miller (Rep.-Fla.) argued against the provision in the conference report requiring that school districts have a policy expelling children for bringing guns to schools because "local principals and school boards are more capable to solve the problem" than are federal officials, but then he voted to have the secretary of education decide whether local officials had made the correct decision on whether to permit prayer in schools (p. H10394). Congressman Barret (Rep.-Nebr.) opposed the report because it meant "more mandates, more mandates, and more mandates," but then he voted to mandate that local officials permit prayer in school (p. H10396).

The Johnson motion to recommit the conference report on the school prayer issue was defeated by a vote of 184 to 215. The partisan breakout was 33 Democrats for and 204 against and 151 Republicans for and 10 against. Then the conference report was approved in the House by a vote of 262 to 132. The partisan breakout on final approval was 230 Democrats for and 4 against and 31 Republicans for and 128 against. The one independent voted with a majority of the Democrats both times.

The next day, the *Washington Post* (Cooper, 1994) reported that the House had resolved "side issues," such as the school prayer amendment, that had dominated the debate and had then passed the bill, which supported programs in nearly every school district in the nation (p. A4). Congressmen from various regions of the country were quoted on the changes in distributing funds, with those from the richer areas bemoaning the fact that they would lose money and those from the poorest locations defending the bill. The *New York Times* ("House Votes to Extend," 1994), noting that the challenge from the advocates of school prayer had been turned back, reported that the bill had finally been approved and quoted Secretary Riley that the House action was "a vote for the children of America" (p. I8).

The *Congressional Quarterly* (Wells, 1994d) said that the House's approval of the conference report set "the stage for what is expected to be high drama when the Senate moves to clear the measure" (p. 2807). In explaining the fight, that newsmagazine noted:

> With few days left before Congress adjourns and the mid-term elections drawing near, some Senate conservatives appeared ready to delay or derail the bill to highlight the chasm with Democrats over issues such as school prayer, or to deny Democrats a victory on the issue. As for the bill's prospects, a Senate aide said: "It's going to be tight." (p. 2808)

Senate Consideration

The Senate began its consideration of the ESEA conference report on the same day that the House approved the legislation, September 30, which was the day that the legal authority for all these programs expired. Because that was a Friday and late in the day, the real debate in the Senate was entered into early the following week ("Elementary and Secondary Education Amendments," 1994b).

On Monday, October 3, Senator Mitchell asked whether the Republicans in the Senate were willing to let the bill go to a vote; he was informed by Senator Helms that there would be a filibuster. Mitchell, as Senate majority leader, then filed a motion to invoke cloture, which is the procedure necessary to cut off debate—that is, end a filibuster—and proceed to a vote. Due to a rule that requires a motion to end a filibuster to "ripen" for 48 hours (as we saw earlier with the vote on the Goals conference report), the vote on the cloture motion could not occur until Wednesday of that week.

The end of the Congress in October 1994 was an especially noteworthy time for the use of the filibuster. When the ESEA conference report came back to the Senate and Senator Helms mounted a filibuster, that action created a total of five Republican filibusters simultaneously pending. Senator Mitchell remarked that in the 15 years he had been in the Senate, he had not seen a time when there were so many filibusters mounted simultaneously. As majority leader, he vowed that the Senate would stay in session even beyond its scheduled adjournment on Friday, October 7, until all these bills were disposed of.

It is interesting to note that during the entire 19th century there were only 16 filibusters in the Senate but that in the 1991-92 Congress there were 35, according to the Congressional Research Service. In fact, 48% of all Senate filibusters in American history have appeared since 1980, according to the House Democratic Study Group (1994). Clearly, the use of the filibuster has dramatically increased in the past decade and a half. As significant as the numbers, however, has been the increase in the threat of a filibuster. Just a threat can now scuttle a bill in the Senate.

During the ESEA debate, Senator Paul Simon (Dem.-Ill.) opined that the right to filibuster was being so misused by his colleagues that this privilege would in the end be eliminated.

"Any right or privilege that is abused eventually is going to get lost. And we are, in my view, abusing the right of filibuster." He added that the filibuster ought to be used "rarely . . . to protect the public" ("Elementary and Secondary Education Amendments," 1994b, p. S13901).

Simon's prediction may come true in the future, but in 1994, the supporters of the education bill had to deal with the current reality: namely, securing the necessary 60 votes to invoke cloture. As was described earlier, Senator Kennedy was keenly aware of this need for votes as he shepherded both the

Goals and the ESEA bills through the Senate during the 103rd Congress. In the Senate-House conference committees, Kennedy always tried to fashion his agreements so that there would be 60 votes supporting the final product when he returned with the conference reports to the Senate floor. He had prevailed on the Goals bill, and now he faced the same situation on the ESEA bill.

The identical issues that were involved in Goals returned to haunt the prospects for the ESEA bill: school prayer and the specter of federal control of education. A new, additional issue was the Title I formula. The opponents played on all three of these issues—the national role in school reform, funding for education, and social amendments—in trying to kill the bill.

On the first day of action on the report, Senator Helms began the debate by attacking the conference committee for dropping the House-passed prayer issue, and he repeatedly went back to the action on the prayer amendment in the Goals conference committee. He said that "a lot of high jinks have gone on" and that he was amazed about "the reckless way in which the conferees have destroyed the effect of bill after bill after bill that have passed the Senate" (p. S13900).

Senators Mitchell and Simon pointed out to him—to no avail—that the ESEA conference report was coming back to the Senate with the Senate-passed school prayer amendment intact because the House conferees had accepted the Kassebaum amendment. Senator Helms ignored that point and the fact that he had been defeated on his amendment by a vote of 46 to 54 and that the Senate had accepted instead the Kassebaum amendment by a vote of 93 to 7. Helms wanted the Kassebaum amendment to be rejected by the Senate conferees and the House-passed amendment offered by Congressman Johnson to be accepted because it was the same as his amendment that had been defeated in the Senate, so he was determined to filibuster the conference report to show his disagreement.

On Wednesday, the second day of the debate and the date for the crucial cloture vote, the speeches began early and lasted for most of the afternoon ("Elementary and Secondary Education Amendments," 1994c). Senator Helms called federal aid to education a "crazy concept" because he said that every time the federal government aided something, it moved in and took control of it (p. S14150). Senator Barbara Boxer (Dem.-Calif.) rebutted this view as extremist and cited the benefits coming to schools and children from the various federally assisted programs. She also noted that a Republican president, Dwight Eisenhower, was the initiator of the modern system of federal aid to education when he proposed the National Defense Education Act in 1958 and that he did so because he understood the link between national defense and the level of education of the people.

Senator Coats called the bill "bad legislation" and said that "this is an unprecedented federal take-over of local and state education" (p. S14148). Coats quoted from a letter sent to the Senate by former U.S. Secretaries of Education William Bennett and Lamar Alexander, both Republicans, in which they said that the bill was "pernicious legislation" that was hostile to reform because it was overregulatory and intrusive.

Senator Kassebaum rebutted these assertions of fellow Republicans Coats, Bennett, and Alexander. She said that "a great deal of misinformation" was being given out about the legislation" (p. S14150), and she sought to assure her colleagues:

> I do not think that this is a takeover of education by the federal government. As a former member of a school board, nothing is more important to me than local control in educational matters, and I think we always need to protect that here in Congress. (p. S14150)

Kassebaum proceeded to list the features of the conference report that made federal programs less burdensome than they had been formerly: allowing schools to combine programs into a unified whole, allowing common applications for federal funds to ease the paperwork burden, and permitting waivers of federal rules and regulations. She also noted the features that guarded against any federal control: namely, the prohibition against unfunded mandates (offered by Senator Gregg and accepted by the Democrats), the prohibition against the secretary of education's dictating standards and assessments or participation in the Goals program, and the absence of any requirement for opportunity-to-learn standards. She said that the bill did not mandate national standards or outcomes-based education and that "decisions about curriculum and instructional methods are properly left with state and local school boards" (p. S14150).

Kassebaum tried to steer the debate to the educational features of the bill. She pointed out that the report put in place a system that would help guard against a lower set of expectations being applied to disadvantaged students because states would have to have higher standards for children if they were to receive these funds. Kassebaum said that this fit with a strong belief of hers that children would rise to the level of expectations set for them and that the country needed to demand more of all children.

The opponents, however, were not to be deterred from the school prayer issue and the fear of a federal takeover of the schools. Like their House allies, they did not note the inconsistency in their two positions: fearing federal control of education but advocating a federal mandate that schools had to permit prayer to receive funds. The opponents added to this mix their arguments about the effects of the changes in the Title I formula.

Senator Coats asserted that 33 states, represented by 66 senators, would receive less than they were currently being allocated. Senator Harkin (Dem.-Iowa), an author of the formula compromise in the conference committee, refuted Coats and asserted that he had misrepresented certain statistics showing the effects of the formula. Using the same charts that had been provided to Coats by the Congressional Research Service, Harkin showed that 33 states would gain—rather than lose—funds over what they were then receiving under the law.

The debate about the formula went on, with both sides making differing assertions about the outcomes of the funding changes. Neither side was totally and objectively correct—or erroneous—because the final conference agreement gave all states what they had received before for 2 more years, and in the last 3 years, allocations depended on how much and how additional funding was provided. The very complexity of resolving strongly held, differing points of view in the conference committee meant that the final product was not precise and instead depended on future actions. People could make whatever assertions they liked because the future was unknown.

Early in the debate, Senator Jeffords had urged acceptance of the conference report and had predicted:

> We will soon see whether the members of the U.S. Senate will support the millions of children helped by this bill, or whether we are more interested in scoring political points against one another at their expense. Before us is the single largest education program within the federal government. Yet I predict in this debate we will hear very little about education. (p. S14152)

At the end of the debate, Jeffords, again noting his strong support for the legislation, observed that very little had been said about education in the hours of argument over the bill; opponents had instead used important social issues to "distract us from emphasizing those things in this bill which do help to do what we must to improve education in this country" (pp. S14192-S14193). He then elaborated on this theme:

We are graduating kids who cannot read, yet we are worried about whether they can pray in school. Let us let the schools try to teach them to read, and let their parents and churches worry about their religious instruction and observance.

We rank last or next to last in the industrialized world in our children's math and science ability, yet instead of worrying about how we teach science and math, we are consumed by how we deal with sexuality.

Our priorities in this debate are all wrong. We talk about one set of issues, while ignoring the more important issues. Instead of worrying so much about school prayer and sex education, we should be worrying more about how we are going to teach our children the skills they need to compete with the rest of the world. (p. S14193)

Jeffords then discussed the important educational features of the bill, including increased flexibility in the uses of funds so that teachers can find the best ways to help children to achieve more. Further, this bill "fundamentally changes the status quo by demanding high academic standards and encouraging the philosophy that all children can learn" (p. S14193). Because disadvantaged children are the beneficiaries of many federal programs, this new law can assist in giving them a better education, he asserted.

Senator Kennedy, as the manager of the legislation on the Senate floor, closed the main portion of the debate before the final vote. He claimed that the bill's significance was that it put the federal government behind the reform efforts that were taking place in states and local school districts and encouraged these reforms without dictating them from Washington.

After all the arguments for and against the bill, the Senate voted to cut off the filibuster by a margin of 75 to 24, with 20 Republicans (somewhat less than half) joining all but one of the Democrats in favor. On the final vote to approve the conference report, the legislation was supported 77 to 20 (p. S14207). All of the Democrats voted for the final bill, and the Republicans split, with all 20 votes against being Republicans and with another 21 Republicans joining Kassebaum and Jeffords in supporting the bill. The battle was over—for that Congress.

After the successful passage of the ESEA bill, Kennedy stated, "The gridlock that has affected just about every aspect of Congressional action has not affected education" ("Congressional Gridlock?" 1994, p. 6). In addition to approval of ESEA, he cited passage of an expansion of Head Start, the Goals 2000 bill, the school-to-work bill, the national service bill, and an overhaul of the college student loan program. With the passage of ESEA, the *Los*

Angeles Times (Shogren, 1994) noted that the White House had "won final approval of the last part of its education agenda, . . . overcoming unexpectedly fierce congressional opposition" (p. A14).

According to the *New York Times* (Clymer, 1994), there were two major reasons that the education bill escaped the last-minute bitterness that was dominating the Congress. One was identified by Senator Jeffords: "If you're a candidate, it's popular back home. . . . Money does talk" (p. A22). The other reason, according to the newspaper, was that Senator Kennedy carefully sought the support of Jeffords, Kassebaum, and other Republicans by adding provisions that mattered to them. Senator Gregg wanted the "no-mandates" section; Senator Pete Domenici (Rep.-N. Mex.) wanted a new program encouraging the teaching of character and values; and other Republicans were attracted by provisions for greater aid to the smallest states and by more subsidies for school districts that had many Indians or Alaska natives. Senator Mark Hatfield (Rep.-Ore.), the influential ranking member of the appropriations committee, promoted deregulation and simplification in programs, and his amendments were accepted.

Another important reason was that the education community was united and worked hard to secure enactment of the bill ("Committee on Education Funding," 1994). Senator Kennedy praised the many teachers and parents who had contacted senators in behalf of the bill and noted the effects that their lobbying had had. The national elementary and secondary education organizations pulled together as they had not for many years, and the results showed.

"The House and the Senate beat back Republican attempts to scuttle a major education bill in the final days of the Congressional session and sent the measure to President Clinton for his signature," reported *Education Week* (Pitsch, 1994c, p. 1). The Republicans launched an all-out effort just weeks before the midterm elections to smother several bills, including the education one, because they were "emboldened by the demise of the health-care and welfare-reform legislation and Mr. Clinton's waning popularity," concluded that newspaper (p. 1).

The significance of the bill, according to *Education Week,* was that it required states to have high content standards in mathematics and language arts if they wished to receive federal aid. The standards for disadvantaged children would be the standards for all children, and that was different from the past, according to *Education Daily* (Hoff, 1994c). Teachers and administrators would also have to coordinate their efforts much more than in the past because the federal programs would be merged.

▩ Presidential Approval

On October 20, President Clinton signed the bill into law at a school in Framingham, Massachusetts, a site chosen to help with Senator Kennedy's reelection. Kennedy well deserved the pay-back because of his leadership in steering Clinton's entire education legislative agenda to passage. In his remarks, Clinton said that the revised ESEA signaled that the federal government in the future would no longer prescribe how every penny of federal money should be spent. As an example, he noted that the federal government's role in the bill was restricted to setting the goals and helping develop the measurements that would determine whether schools were meeting the goals, rather than the traditional role of prescribing detailed regulations ("President Signs," 1994).

According to the *New York Times* (Celis, 1994), the bill Clinton signed was the most extensive revision of the ESEA since it had been created in 1965, and it gave educators broad freedom in how they spent federal money. The much-needed overhaul demanded high standards in exchange for flexibility. "The revamped program, now called Title I, strongly discourages the pullout program and requires that all students in schools that receive Title I money— not just those needing help in math and reading—be required to perform at higher academic standards," the newspaper noted (p. B11). Though the Title I program, the main national source of aid, received most of the public attention, other federal programs, such as bilingual education, were also affected by this reform. Overall, school districts would have much more freedom to fashion programs to meet the individual needs of children (Dillon, 1994).

At the ceremony where he signed the legislation, Clinton noted that the administration's entire education agenda had been enacted and that it represented the most significant accomplishments in education since the administration of Lyndon Johnson. Jack Anderson, the nationally syndicated columnist, and Michael Binstein called Clinton the "new education president" because he had achieved the passage of a "raft of Clinton education reforms" enacted in this Congress—nine in all, including the revision of the ESEA (Anderson & Binstein, 1994, p. C7).

"Clinton has, quite simply, set in motion a revolution in public education," concluded a *National Journal* columnist (Stanfield, 1994, p. 2485). No president can single-handedly change the nation's education system because the federal government pays for so little of the bill of supporting the schools and has no direct control over the schools, but, the *National Journal* columnist asserted, the president had profoundly shifted the pedagogical course. The capstone of that effort was the revision of the $10-billion ESEA, a piece of a package of half a dozen education measures that all fit together and reinforced the central theme of education reform.

> That theme comes down to a demand for rigorous—and univeral—academic standards. The expectation is that all students can meet those standards and that all schools should teach them to do so. That might not sound like much, but it's a change in thinking of truly revolutionary proportions. (p. 2485)

Even the *Washington Post* ("An Education Congress," 1994), which had editorialized for months, mostly unsuccessfully, about the need to concentrate more Title I funding on the poorest school districts, acknowledged that the Congress had been "highly productive in the field of education" (p. A16). Head Start had been both expanded and changed to emphasize improving the quality of programs. The Goals 2000 program found a way to set high standards without turning it into a national curriculum. The ESEA was reconfigured, although not as much as the newspaper and the administration had wanted regarding the distribution of funds. The school-to-work bill had passed with the purpose of making school more relevant to work. The national service corps had been created to let young people work off the cost of college and perform community service at the same time. And the student loan program had been restructured to save money and to make repayments by students more flexible. The conclusion was:

> The federal government isn't in the business of education so much as it is in the business of funding education in ways it hopes will lead to certain results. The goal is not to encroach upon the system but nonetheless to cause it to improve. Not easy, but each of these bills takes some steps in the right direction. Together, they represent a real achievement. (p. A16)

Several Republicans acknowledged the successes in education of the 103rd Congress and the Clinton administration. Congressman Gunderson (1995) wrote that this Congress would go down in history as "the most successful 'Education Congress' " because it had passed so much legislation that focused on reform (p. 105). Senator Durenberger (1994), a member of the Senate education committee, noted that the bundle of legislation that passed in that Congress led to the addition of a new national purpose in education and that this shift had its origins in the work begun by President Bush and Secretary Alexander. He said about Bush's effort:

> Previously, the federal government's interest and involvement in education
> focused primarily on equalizing access to opportunity for every American
> child—the traditional goal of Chapter 1, special education, and other federal
> education programs.
>
> The federal government's interest in education was now being extended
> to quality—to results—to setting goals and measuring improvement in what
> students actually learn. More importantly, the federal government's role was
> to be enabling and empowering—for states, for school districts and for
> individual schools, for parents and teachers and students—the federal gov-
> ernment setting broad goals, creating opportunities, providing modest re-
> sources—but leaving decisions on how to achieve those goals up to those who
> know best—in each local community. (p. S14752)

Durenberger attributed Bush's failure to achieve the addition of this new
national purpose in education to his insistence on including private schools in
his parental choice programs. Clinton did not make the same mistake, and he
triumphed where Bush had failed: The national government now was pursuing
the goal of quality as well as the goal of equity. But just as there were obstacles
to accomplishing this change in legislation, there would be impediments to
implementing it.

According to the *Congressional Quarterly* (Cloud, 1994),

> The Democrats began the 103rd Congress promising to govern. They ended
> it unable to deliver on much of their legislative program, blocked at every
> turn by a Republican Party confident of its election prospects and in its ability
> to exact better terms from President Clinton next year. (p. 2847)

In the closing weeks of the Congress, many major Clinton initiatives, some
of which began the year with broad bipartisan support, "smashed into procedural roadblocks erected by Republicans who grew bold in proclaiming the
virtues of gridlock" (Cloud, 1994, p. 2847).

Clinton's agenda for improving education was the exception, making it
through these roadblocks, and the president, Secretary Riley, and the education community expected to spend the next several years implementing these
reforms. Instead, the Democrats were swept out of Congress in the elections
of November 1994, and the Republicans, whose leaders had sought to block
Clinton's agenda, assumed power. The new congressional majority then
proceeded in an attempt not only to undo Clinton's accomplishments but also
to dismantle the traditional role of the federal government in education.

In other words, the new role of improving the quality of education was
challenged as an item on the national agenda, as was the older and previously

accepted purpose of encouraging equity. Thus, the battle to add a new national purpose focusing on improving the quality of education, which began in 1989 with President Bush, evolved into an assault during 1995 and 1996 on the traditional equity purpose of federal aid. The new conservatives wanted no federal role in education, whether to encourage equity *or* quality.

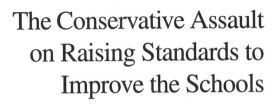

The Conservative Assault on Raising Standards to Improve the Schools

How the Conservative Opposition Tried to Undo Standards-Based Reform and Failed Because Clinton, the Business Community, and Governors Fought Back

The Elections of 1994

Going into the elections for Congress in 1994, there was a general disappointment with the performance of the Democratic Congress and with President Clinton. Although Clinton's education proposals were enacted, other initiatives that attracted much greater publicity failed. Most notably, the Congress could not pass Clinton's comprehensive health care reform. In addition, restructuring of the welfare system and major anticrime legislation both came to nothing.

Major federal budget deficit reduction and ratification of the NAFTA free trade agreement linking the economies of the United States, Canada, and Mexico were the most publicized successes of Clinton and the Congress during 1993 and 1994. Neither of those accomplishments, however, engendered much popular support, especially among groups that would be inclined to vote for the Democrats. Therefore, the electorate in the fall of 1994 was faced with what seemed to be an ineffectual Democratic Congress and an unsuccessful presidential administration.

At the same time, the Republicans were on the upswing. The pattern in American elections is that the party that wins the White House usually loses seats in Congress during the next election, so the Republicans in 1994 had this trend in their favor, in addition to the anti-Democratic and anti-Clinton mood. Republicans also had a new energy due to the increasing involvement of Christian fundamentalists in that party and the resurgence of the political right. Congressional Republicans promoted a debate on socially related issues in the House and the Senate on Goals 2000, the Elementary and Secondary Education Act (ESEA), and other legislation as a way to energize these conservative voters for the upcoming election.

As a result of these factors, the Republicans in the elections of 1994 captured control of the U.S. Congress for the first time in 40 years. Not since the first 2 years of Dwight Eisenhower's presidency in 1953 and 1954 had there been Republican majorities in both the House of Representatives and the Senate. Another indication of the Republican surge in the same elections was that 30 of the 50 state governors were Republicans after November 1994, which was a record giving that party dominance of the nation's statehouses. Republicans also achieved noteworthy successes in gaining seats in many state legislatures.

During the political campaign of 1994, many conservative organizations repeatedly attacked the Goals program and the whole idea of standards-based reform. For instance, the American Policy Center ("Fight Begins," 1995) asserted that Goals 2000 was a "diabolical assault on schools" because through it "the Department of Education is controlling local school curriculum" to change values instilled by parents (p. 1). At the Christian Coalition's conference in September before the elections, not only was there great support for prayer in the public schools and for vouchers to send students to private schools, but there were also T-shirts among the delegates with the slogan "Repeal Goals 2000" (Walsh, 1994).

The *Wall Street Journal* published in the summer of 1995 some of the more interesting assertions made about Goals 2000 by some of these groups. The author of the article (Sharpe, 1995) was trying to explain why the law that had been accepted on a bipartisan vote in the previous year was facing the prospect of no funding from the new Republican House of Representatives. She concluded, "The flexible program became a political Rorschach test, embodying for some conservatives a host of government evils" (p. A1). The following were some examples of these fears:

➡ "Goals 2000 will produce stupid children. The government plans to take over the responsibility for raising infants, toddlers and preschoolers," according to the American Policy Center in Virginia (p. A1).

➡ The law's real goals were "mind manipulation for political correctness," according to Eleanor Campbell, president of an anti-Goals 2000 group in New Hampshire. Mrs. Campbell believed that the law "would let federal workers judge parents' performance in the home and take their children away" (p. A1).

➡ The Gun Owners of New Hampshire believed that "Goals 2000 would allow the federal government to remove children from homes where guns can be found and loaded within 10 minutes" (p. A1).

Many of these same groups went further and advocated eliminating entirely the national role in assisting schools and students. The president of the American Association of Christian Schools, for example, stated that "if Congress truly desires to reform education, it must devolve the Department of Education and eliminate the federal role in education" (letter from Carl Herbester to Members of Congress, July 28, 1995).

This sentiment to eliminate the federal role in education found its most ardent advocates among the newly elected Republican congressmen, many of whom were very conservative and had been supported during their campaigns by far-right organizations opposed to Goals 2000, federal aid to education, and many other federal activities in social areas. In May 1995, a coalition of House Republican freshmen announced their plans to put the U.S. Department of Education out of business, turn over most of the funds to the states, and scatter the remainder of the programs. Not surprisingly, Goals 2000 was targeted for repeal. Representative Charles Joseph Scarborough (Rep.-Fla.), as the leader of that group, announced, "The great federal experiment in education is over. It failed. It is time to move on" (quoted in Sanchez, 1995b, p. A19).

Conservative intellectuals, who, with President Bush, Secretary Alexander, the chief executive officers of many large corporations, and many Republican congressmen and senators, had had a large role in starting this whole debate, reversed their prior positions. In some cases, there was even a rewriting of history to meet the new political reality of far-right opposition to standards-based reform.

Irving Kristol (1994) of the American Enterprise Institute, for example, tried to wash his hands of any involvement by writing:

Some of my best friends, experts in the field of education, thought it was a good idea. I was skeptical of the ability of the federal government to enact any kind of serious educational reform, but I deferred to their superior knowledge and judgment. Well, now that the Goals 2000: Educate America Act has become law, I find my skepticism vindicated. It will be an expensive disaster. (p. A14)

Bruno Manno (1995) of the Hudson Institute, who had served in the U.S. Department of Education under President Bush, saw a "hijacking." He wrote that looking at results is a good, commonsense idea: "We should judge the quality of education by focusing on outputs—on what students learn and on measurable academic results. To do this we need to set clear goals and standards that we expect our young people to meet" (p. 721). Therefore, he commended Bush and the governors for giving support to this movement in their education summit, but after 1989 he asserted that the idea had become "hijacked" by teachers who did not set exclusively academic standards for students (p. 722).

Referring to the first set of national standards for history, Charles Krauthammer (1994), a conservative columnist with the *Washington Post,* also saw a "hijacking." He said:

In the late '80's and early '90's, conservatives in the Bush administration, alarmed at the decline in American education, pushed for national standards to help restore discipline and excellence to American schools. By 1992 they had won. Congress authorized task forces to draw up national standards for core academic subjects.

Beware what you wish for. The National Standards for United States History have just been published. And, as some (most notably, the National Review) had warned at the time, they have been hijacked by the educational establishment and turned into a classic of political correctness. (p. A25)

Mr. Krauthammer was not accurate that the Congress, a Democratically controlled one at the time, had authorized the task forces to write the national standards. As noted in Chapter 2 of this book, the Bush administration avoided seeking congressional approval for the writing of the national standards because Secretary Alexander and others did not want congressional review. Instead, Alexander used discretionary funds in the U.S. Department of Education to make most of the awards and urged other federal agencies to use their own discretionary funds to make the other awards. Furthermore, Alexander and other Bush appointees were the ones who chose the organizations to write all the standards, including the history standards.

The origins of the federal government's involvement in the development of national standards, national tests, and federal aid for school reform were often ignored in 1994 and 1995 as conservatives sought to blame Clinton, the Democrats, and teachers for what Bush, Alexander, and the governors had started. The national business community proved to be the steadfast ones who had helped to originate this movement with President Bush and now stayed with it with President Clinton, thereby providing indispensable support for retaining Goals 2000 and the standards movement in general.

▓ The New Congress

In the very first month of the new Congress in January 1995, the attack on national standards and Goals 2000 began when Senator Gorton offered an amendment that would have required the National Education Goals Panel to disapprove the draft set of national history standards developed by the National Center for History in the Schools at the University of California at Los Angeles (UCLA) ("Unfunded Mandates," 1995). Gorton labeled these proposed standards—funded by a grant from the Bush administration—as an "ideologically driven, anti-Western monument to politically correct caricature" because certain historical figures and events were not mentioned or were not emphasized enough and because he detected a bias toward a liberal point of view (p. S1028).

In opposing that amendment, Senator Jeffords stressed that it was the business community that had exerted the greatest pressure for improvement of the schools through raising standards. Senator Bingaman called the amendment "an insult" to the governors serving on the National Panel because they, and not the Congress, should review the standards once they were submitted (p. S1031), and Senator Pell reminded the Senate that the standards were proposed and not as yet ready for submission to any panel.

In support of Gorton's amendment, several senators spoke against the standards for neglecting certain aspects of American history. The outcome of the debate was that Gorton's amendment was watered down and made into a nonbinding "sense of the Senate" that merely expressed the opinion of that body that those standards should be revised, without any necessary action having to be taken. That amended version then passed by a vote of 99 to 1 (p. S1040).

Although the Gorton amendment did not have any real effect, it was important symbolically. It showed that in the very first days of the new

Congress, the conservatives were homing right in on Goals 2000, the movement to raise education standards, and more generally the federal role in education. More immediately, the vote pushed the UCLA Center, which had developed the draft standards with the involvement of many scholars and teachers, to reopen the draft to changes. The Council on Basic Education, at the request of several major foundations, convened panels of historians, teachers, and citizens who reviewed the proposed standards and made recommendations for changes. The council's work, guided by its president, Christopher Cross, a former official in the Bush administration, and by a former Republican governor, Al Quie, led to those standards reemerging a year later and being quietly accepted by most of the critics of the first draft.

The next action taken in 1995 affecting Goals 2000 was the elimination by the House of the panel created by that legislation to review the voluntary submission of standards for certification. In May 1995, Congressman Goodling's bill was unanimously passed by the House committee after that council was called a "national school board" by several members (Camphire, 1995). The Clinton administration supported that bill as part of a strategy to save Goals 2000 by removing from the law a lightning rod for conservative anger. At the committee session to consider that bill, Congressman Lindsey Graham (Rep.-S.C.) moved to kill the entire program, but his amendment was ruled out of order by Goodling in his new role as the committee chair. Goodling reiterated his support for standards-based reform, saying that the standards movement "remains one of the most promising strategies for improving education for all children in our nation" (Pitsch, 1995, p. 20). The House shortly afterwards approved that legislation, but it did not move separately in the Senate; rather, it became part of an appropriations bill passed nearly a year later.

These were the initial skirmishes; the real battle over Goals and federal aid to education involved the appropriations bill. In the summer of 1995, the House voted to eliminate any funding for Goals 2000 and forbade use of any other funding for standards setting, cut the Title I program by 17%, and erased a score of other federal programs. The conservatives were well on their way to eliminating the new national role of improving the quality of the schools and were also reaching back to rescind the traditional equity role (Jennings & Stark, 1996).

The cuts in education spending by the House were called "mammoth" by David Hoff (1995a, p. 1) in *Education Daily* and "just plain dumb" by David Broder (1995, p. A25), a nationally syndicated newspaper columnist. Broder, writing from the governors' summer meeting, reported that many governors with whom he had spoken considered the strangling of Goals as "dumb," and he asked why Congress would want "to kill our best hope for setting higher standards in the schools" (p. A25). At that same meeting, Republican Governor Tommy Thompson of Wisconsin told Broder that the standards movement needed to be jump-started because so many of the governors were new since the Charlottesville summit with President Bush. Also at the same meeting, Louis V. Gerstner, Jr., the chief executive officer of IBM, urged the governors to recommit themselves to this reform.

In the Senate, where the moderate wing of the Republican party, though shrinking, was still stronger than in the House, Arlen Specter, chair of the appropriations subcommittee for education, proposed continuing to fund Goals and to mitigate the other cutbacks in federal aid. Consequently, the Senate appropriations committee cut back on federal aid for education by 9% instead of the 15% proposed in the House bill and retained most funding for Goals, while amending it to make some minor changes (Hoff, 1995b).

These lessened cutbacks were still too much for President Clinton and the Democrats in the Senate. Clinton threatened to veto any bill that contained cutbacks of such a magnitude in federal aid to education, and the Senate Democrats threatened a filibuster of the appropriations bill because of these cuts in education. Because even a threatened filibuster scuttles legislation, the Senate was not able to schedule the appropriations bill.

Prominent chief executive officers of large corporations loudly protested against these cutbacks in funding for education. The leaders of the Business Roundtable met with President Clinton to plot strategies to keep Goals 2000 alive. "If we lose this, it would set back state education reform efforts by years," said Joseph T. Gorman, chair and chief executive officer of TRW Inc., a large aerospace and automotive parts company. "The value of Goals 2000 is that it's designed to spur systematic, break-the-mold reform and hold schools accountable to clear standards" (quoted in Sanchez, 1995a, p. A4).

The *Washington Post's* Rene Sanchez (1995a) summarized business's attitude:

> Many business leaders exasperated with the state of public schools have backed Goals 2000 in the hope that it would bring more focused, national attention on an issue that throughout American history has been an almost entirely local concern. A retreat from Goals 2000, they argue, would leave school reform as muddled as ever. (p. A4)

"Will Republicans Make Clinton the Education President?" asked *Business Week* (Garland, 1995). Congressional Republicans were "targeting virtually every federal education program from Head Start to college aid to the war on drugs in schools," noted that widely read business magazine's "Washington Outlook" column in the fall of 1995 (p. 67). Corporate chieftains were worried that the "Republican cuts in education will make it difficult to maintain a highly skilled workforce," so CEOs, such as Gorman of TRW, John E. Pepper of Proctor & Gamble, Louis V. Gerstner Jr. of IBM, David R. Whitwam of Whirlpool, and Kent C. Nelson of UPS, were lobbying the Congress to reverse these cuts. "Public education is key . . . to our continued ability to compete," noted Nelson (p. 67).

The business community, which frequently sides with the Republicans on national policy issues, thus opposed the new shift of that party away from federal aid to education and from the new purpose of encouraging states and local school districts to raise their education standards. Their support was crucial for moderate Republicans in Congress who agreed with them and disagreed with their party's abandonment of the national commitment to aid public schools and students. Such Republicans included most notably Senators Kassebaum, Jeffords, and Specter, all of whom held key positions on education and appropriations committees and used their authority to seek to maintain Goals 2000 and federal aid to education.

For the next 7 months, the president and the Republicans in Congress went through a long battle over spending priorities, including these cutbacks in Goals and in education in general. Clinton vetoed their bills repeatedly, and because the Republicans did not have a two-thirds majority in either the House or the Senate, they were not able to override those vetoes. The federal government was shut down several times, but Clinton still did not give in to the Republican demands.

In the end, federal aid to education and the new, additional national purpose of raising the quality of education for all students survived. In April 1996, Rene Sanchez (1996c) commented in the *Washington Post:*

> After seven months, after a dozen temporary, last minute funding bills, after a marathon debate over the federal government's role in the nation's schools, Congress is finally on the verge of settling the Department of Education's budget for this year—and after all that, it may not change much. (p. A21)

Federal aid to education was basically retained at the same level of funding in the final appropriation. In addition, there were some minor changes to Goals 2000: The last references to opportunity-to-learn standards were removed, and local school districts were permitted to apply for funding if their states declined to participate. The Democratic liberals who had fought so hard for the inclusion of some attention to adequate funding witnessed the erasure of their remaining influence on the legislation.

Although the far right lost the battle to eliminate Goals, conservatives secured amendments that would not "permit any federal or state official to inspect a home, judge how parents raise their children, or remove children from their parents" because a school district participated in Goals 2000 (Amendments to Goals 2000: Educate America Act, 1996). Although allegations about such activities had been made by the far right, there seem to have been no documented cases of any such interference. Nonetheless, because the allegations were made, though undocumented, Congress felt that it had to forbid such activity. It was a case of fears stirred up by the far right becoming realities in people's minds and therefore having to be addressed (Pitsch, 1996).

With this small price being paid to the far right and with the removal of the last imprints of the political left, the new national purpose of improving the quality of education for all children survived the first year of the conservative Congress, as did the traditional equity purpose of federal aid (Hoff, 1996). The far right did its best, but it failed in eliminating national attention to education—and Clinton received much of the credit for trying to improve the schools. Morton Kondracke, a columnist for *Roll Call* who had been critical of the Goals bill earlier in the process, concluded in 1996 that this time a real education president was running for reelection.

The Governors and Business Leaders

While all of this controversy was occurring at the national level about standards-based reform and Goals 2000, there were echoes in many states during the period of 1994 through 1996. For instance, in the spring of 1994, Virginia, South Carolina, and New Hampshire announced that they were reluctant to apply for Goals funding because there might not be enough flexibility to continue their current reform efforts, but the press speculated that the real reason was that the Republican governors of those states did not want to be associated with a Clinton program (Hoff, 1994).

Other states, however, were less reluctant and applied for funds, although several had to overcome opposition from the far right. In October 1994, "Some 250 parents, children, and other Ohioans gathered on the Statehouse grounds here last week to declare war on the U.S. Department of Education," reported Mark Pitsch (1994, p. 1) in *Education Week.* This rally was aimed at the state board of education, which was considering applying for funds from Goals 2000, and was organized by local chapters of the Eagle Forum, the Christian Coalition, and the U.S. Citizens Alliance. Notwithstanding this protest, Ohio did eventually apply for funds and used them to implement its state and local school reform initiatives, including developing higher standards for students.

After the election of 1994, the opposition to Goals 2000 became especially fierce in many states because of the Republican gains in governorships and in state legislatures that were partially achieved with the energy provided by the far right. The Montana legislature voted not to use the funds, and the state board of education in Virginia voted not to apply. The Republican governor of Alabama withdrew his state from the program, and the Republican governor of New Hampshire vetoed a bill passed by the legislature to have the state apply for funding. Governor Pete Wilson of California would not permit that state to apply for funds while he was running for president in the Republican primaries of 1995, but after he withdrew from the race, he allowed California to participate.

The same pressures that existed at the national level were present in those states and in many others. The far right was becoming stronger in many state Republican parties, and governors and legislatures therefore increasingly reflected their views. But the business community was often a counterforce within states, with the business roundtables pressing for school reform and frequently endorsing raising education standards as the prime means of reform. Adding political weight to those arguments, Democratic officials in those states, and many public education organizations too, frequently criticized Republicans for not availing themselves of funds to improve education.

While all this political static was in the air, and frequently despite it, 48 states eventually applied for and received Goals funds during the first year of its availability, and by the end of 1996 the same number of states were participating either directly or through local school districts (U.S. Department of Education, 1996). In other words, a highly charged political debate was occurring in the states on one level, and the work of raising standards in education was proceeding on another level. A disjunction existed between political rhetoric attacking standards reform and the continued incremental progress being made in writing standards and implementing them, noted the Consortium for Policy Research in Education (Massell, Kirst, & Hoppe, 1997).

Some governors and business leaders came to believe that the movement to raise standards had to be regenerated. In 1995, Governor Thompson was quoted by columnist David Broder as convinced that the governors had to be recommitted to the concept that the states had to raise their standards for education. As noted before, Thompson observed that many governors were elected after 1989 and so were not party to the discussion that began with the summit conference on education convened by President Bush in Virginia. In 1996, Thompson moved on his convictions when he took advantage of his chairmanship of the National Governors' Conference to convene a second national summit conference on education.

The precipitating factor in calling for this summit was a speech that Louis V. Gerstner, Jr., the chief executive officer of IBM, gave at the summer meeting of the governors in 1995. Gerstner told the governors that American education was in crisis and that they had to take action. Thompson took up the challenge and called for a meeting of the governors in March 1996. To show the support for higher standards from the business community, each governor was asked to bring a business leader from his or her state. IBM's Gerstner was made the cosponsor of the meeting, which took place in Palisades, New York (Sanchez, 1996b).

Thompson explained to the press that momentum to improve the schools had been lost since the Charlottesville summit of 1989 and that the purpose of the new summit was to reach agreement on rigorous, blunt new standards for what students in every grade level should be learning in core subjects, such as reading, science, and mathematics. Thompson told the *Washington Post* that a reason for the summit was that only six of the governors had participated in the Charlottesville summit and that the rest were newcomers to the debate over academic standards. He emphasized that the distrust of the federal government on this issue was so great that the governors were the only ones who could get the movement back on track (Innerst, 1996a).

The Republican governor faced a problem from the conservative side of the political spectrum: The right was suspicious of what would come out of such a conference. As the *Washington Times* (Innerst, 1996a) noted, "Another National Education Summit looms—this time in Palisades, N.Y.—and a number of conservatives are worried what will occur during the high-powered conversation about education policy" (p. A3). Fears of "hidden agendas and politics" were mentioned, most particularly that the governors would shore up support for the Goals 2000 program and would be influenced by the "more money" ideas of some of the education experts asked to attend the meeting with the governors and the CEOs (p. A3). Governor Thompson tried to reassure them by saying that Goals was never embraced by the public because it was "a top-down initiative . . . doomed to failure" (quoted in Innerst, 1996b, p. A11). Furthermore, he assured them:

> I'm not being sucked in by anything. I want to make sure people understand this is not Goals 2000, not OBE [outcomes-based education]. It's a way to commit ourselves as governors and business leaders to go back to our states and set up standards in core academic areas like geography, science, reading and writing. (quoted in Innerst, 1996b, p. A11)

To the further dismay of conservatives, Thompson made clear that the summit would not deal with encouraging vouchers for tuition for private schools, nor with criticisms that the teachers' unions were impediments to school improvement, nor with school choice or with charter schools. Thompson said: "It won't help to spend our time bashing one group over another group" (quoted in Innerst, 1996b, p. A11). Instead, he urged that the conference focus solely on standards, assessments, and technology in education. "I do not believe you can truly improve the quality of education in America unless you raise the bar on standards and assessments," he said. "It's the glue that holds everything together" (quoted in Innerst, 1996b, p. A11).

When the summit convened in late March 1996, 41 governors attended, with 49 chief executive officers of corporations. The main tension was not between Republican and Democratic governors, as usually occurs at governors' meetings, but rather between conservative Republican governors and business leaders: an echo of the conflict that had occurred in many states, with far-right organizations opposing developing standards and with the business community pushing the legislatures or the state boards of education in the direction of raising standards.

From the business point of view, standards were absolutely essential. As IBM's Gerstner said before the summit:

> Hard as it is to believe, many school districts have no formal, written academic standards whatsoever. As business leaders, our first goal is to make sure our schools have benchmarks from which to measure student achievement. That's the first rule of business: without goals and objectives, it's impossible to measure success.
>
> Academic standards serve as a Rosetta stone for what we should expect of our schools and our students. They clearly define what students should know and be able to do in specific academic areas and at certain points in their schooling.

But setting high academic standards is just the first step. To reach them, we must push through a fundamental, bone-jarring, full-fledged, 100 percent revolution that discards the old and replaces it with a totally new, performance-driven system. We must demand better use of technology in our schools, better trained educators, improved curriculum and other changes in the organization and management of schools necessary to facilitate improved student performance. ("IBM CEO's Vision," 1996, p. 4)

Gerstner wanted high standards and then major change in American education, and in that sentiment he was joined by many other business leaders. Some CEOs, in fact, did not understand why there could not be national standards for education in the United States because they were accustomed to dealing in their businesses with national and even international standards to measure quality. At the summit, Paul O'Neill, the CEO of ALCOA and a former Republican official in the Ford administration, asked, "Why on earth can't we insist on universal standards at least for nine-year-olds? Can't a nine-year-old multiply nine by nine and get the same answer in all 50 states?" O'Neill said he was perplexed and did not understand why "we have to do the basics 50 times." Gerstner replied, "This is a political issue, Paul, not a rational issue" (quoted in Kondracke, 1996, p. 5).

Gerstner's observation proved to be on target during the sessions at the summit. Governor George Allen of Virginia insisted on several changes in the proposed policy statement: removing any wording implying an endorsement of the national education goals adopted after Bush's summit of 1989, deleting the word *collaboration* and inserting "information sharing," and objecting to the creation of an independent, privately financed, nongovernmental entity to serve as a national clearinghouse on standards (Lawton, 1996, p. 14). Allen's concerns were rooted in a fear of the federal government, as stirred up by the far right. As he was to write later about his disdain for federal assistance, "The Goals 2000 law thus treats the states and local school boards as serfs of the federal government" (Allen, 1996, p. 4). Another very conservative Republican governor, Tom Ridge of Pennsylvania, said that he supported Allen's concerns.

All of this was too much for the business leaders: Their perception of the problems facing American education was so different from that of the conservative governors and their feeling was so strong that action needed to be taken soon to raise standards that they simply could not understand why these governors were objecting so forcibly to what seemed to them to be common sense. Finally, after wrangling over these minor and major objections, Gerstner and the other business leaders became so frustrated that they walked out of one of the sessions with Allen and the other governors. The *Wall Street Journal* (Sharpe, 1996) reported on "shouting matches behind the scenes" between the business leaders and the conservative governors, with Gerstner denouncing the process as "hogwash" (p. C15).

When the need for action became clear, the CEOs and the other governors agreed to a few cosmetic changes to mollify Allen, Ridge, and their supporters. The major amendment was to delay for a few months the final agreement on the establishment of the entity created to monitor standards development. With these changes, Allen was able to go to the press and to conservative groups and say that he had caused modifications in the final document. As the *Washington Times* (Innerst, 1996c) reported, "Led by Virginia Gov. George Allen, a group of participants rewrote the policy statement to better reflect conservative views and reaffirm that the states and not the federal government play the major role in education" (p. A6).

Gerstner and the other business leaders had their own education at the summit and did indeed learn from Allen and other very conservative governors that it was politics and not reason that often seemed to drive the debate over raising standards in the schools. President Clinton, by contrast, clearly understood the political dimensions of the debate, so he stated at the very beginning of his address at the summit that the states and the governors have the constitutional responsibility for the public schools. Furthermore, Clinton (1996) assured the governors: "I accept your premise, we can only do better with tougher standards and better assessment, and you should set the standards. I believe this is absolutely right. And that will be the lasting legacy of this conference" (p. 576).

Looking back at the Charlottesville summit with President Bush that had resulted in the movement to create national standards, Clinton concluded, "Now, the effort to have national standards, I think it's fair to say, has been less than successful" (p. 576). But the debate was not entirely worthless, he suggested, and did some good. Clinton also reminded the governors of the same sentiment as did Paul O'Neill: "Being promoted ought to mean more or less the same thing in Pasadena, California, that it does in Palisades, New York" (p. 577).

Clinton asserted that the country had a special problem in education that

we should resolve, that is even prior to the standards and assessment issue, and that is that too many people in the United States think that the primary determinant of success and learning is either IQ or family circumstances instead of effort. (p. 574)

He continued:

> I believe the most important thing you can do is to have high expectations for students—to make them believe they can learn, to tell them they're going to have to learn really difficult, challenging things, to assess whether they're learning or not, and to hold them accountable as well as to reward them. (p. 576)

Therefore, the president urged the governors not only to set high standards but also to require students to pass a test based on mastering that material as they passed from elementary school to middle school, then on to high school, and then to graduation with a diploma from high school.

Clinton said that his administration had tried to do its part by seeking enactment of the Goals 2000 program, which provided assistance to the states and local school districts if they established their own high standards, and by overhauling the ESEA to take out of the Title I program the concept of lower expectations for poor children. As he said, "I don't believe that poor children should be expected to perform at lower levels than other children" (p. 576).

The last important point in the president's speech was a statement of his belief that the development of high standards and assessments of student mastery of those standards were necessary before the citizens of the country could be convinced to spend additional funds on the schools. "We cannot ask the American people to spend more on education until we do a better job with the money we've got now" (p. 579).

After Clinton's speech, the governors and the CEOs unanimously adopted an agreement that would bind both the governors and the business leaders to take immediate actions to help in implementing higher standards in the schools. The governors agreed that each one would go back to his or her state and develop "internationally competitive academic standards, assessments to measure academic achievement, and accountability systems in our states, according to each state's governing structure, within the next two years" (National Governors' Association, 1996, p. 6). The business leaders committed within 1 year to change their hiring practices so that they would use high school transcripts and other school records showing the academic achievement of applicants for jobs. The statement also included an agreement that there would be established a national clearinghouse of effective practices to improve achievement because of the savings and other benefits offered by cooperation between the states and local school districts. This entity would not be federal but rather would be "an external, independent, nongovernmental effort" (p. 6).

This second national summit on education was significant in that it committed the new governors, many of whom were elected with the support of organizations opposed to Goals 2000, to the idea that the states had to raise their standards for education. It also helped to dispel fears that through this process the federal government would somehow come in and take over education. Governor Thompson asserted, "We're not here to ask anything from Washington" (quoted in Sanchez, 1996a, p. 6). Governor Terry Branstad (Rep.-Iowa), who had also participated in the Charlottesville summit, sought to put in perspective the movement to raise standards:

> We got sidetracked after the last summit on having national education guidelines, and that has created a lot of backlash. We want to avoid that situation this time. We want to make sure that every state and local school district has rigorous standards. (quoted in Sanchez, 1996a, p. 6)

Paul Gray (1996) in *Time* magazine commented that at the summit there was "more than a little political walking on eggshells here" (p. 40) because the governors were acknowledging through calling for the clearinghouse that there was some economic and practical usefulness in the states' cooperating with one another as they developed standards and assessments but were also trying to avoid stirring up any suspicion that this cooperation might lead to national standards of any kind. Diane Ravitch (1996) and other commentators were later to write about the impracticality of avoiding any commonality in standards among the states.

After all was said and done, however, the fact remained that the governors unanimously committed themselves to developing academic standards and assessments within 2 years and that this group comprised most of the 30 Republican governors who were in office with the support of coalitions that included the very conservative organizations and individuals who were opposed to any standards development or at least to any national or state action in this area. That was a noteworthy accomplishment.

Peter Applebome (1996) of the *New York Times* commented that this summit might prove to be more important than the first one in Charlottesville because it drew on the most powerful corporations in the United States and moved forcefully toward a politically palatable agenda of tough state and local rather than national standards for the schools. He quoted President Clinton's remarks to the governors at the summit that compared the present situation to that of the early 1980s when the *Nation at Risk* report was released and of the first education summit:

> In 1983, we said we've got a problem in the schools. In 1989, we said we need to know where we're going; we need goals. Here in 1996, you're saying you can have all the goals in the world, but unless somebody really has meaningful standards and a system of measuring whether you meet those standards, you won't achieve your goals. (p. B10)

8

The Elections of 1996 and Clinton's Second Term

How the Conservatives Were Rebuffed, and How Clinton Revived the Idea of National Standards and Tests

The National Elections

By the spring of 1996, President Clinton and the Democrats, with some assistance from moderate Republicans, had succeeded in saving Goals 2000, Title I, and the other federal aid to education programs after the assault on them by the congressional conservatives. This meant that the federal government would remain involved in encouraging the states to raise their education standards, as well as in continuing with the traditional equity purpose of federal aid.

Also early in 1996, Governor Thompson, Louis Gerstner, and other governors and business leaders had succeeded in recommitting the governors to raising standards in their states. But from that education summit came the message from some governors that talk of national standards and federal involvement in raising standards was not helpful. These conservative politicians were being influenced by the far right with their accusations of federal takeovers of the schools and mind control of students by teachers, and they needed some nudging from the business community to commit themselves to raising standards in their states.

While all this was occurring, Republican primary voters were selecting Bob Dole, the Senate majority leader, to become the nominee to run against President Clinton in November. Senator Dole said that he favored as key elements of his education platform the abolition of the U.S. Department of

Education and wanted to enact a major program of federal aid for vouchers to pay for tuition at private schools. He blamed the teachers' unions for many of the problems of the public schools (Harden, 1996).

Dole's proposal for private school vouchers in 1996 was an expansion of Bush's "G.I. Bills for Students" of 1992. Dole differed from Bush, however, in that he did not favor raising standards in public schools through national aid, as Bush had 4 years earlier. To underscore this abandonment of a national commitment to raising standards in public schools, Dole said that he would pay for his $2.5-billion private school voucher program through the repeal of Goals 2000 and other federal programs aiding children in public schools (Hoff, 1996).

Clinton meanwhile renewed his opposition to vouchers for private schools and repeated his support for an expansion of parental choice of public, not private, schools. Clinton also stressed again the need to raise standards for public school students. In addition, Clinton proposed a series of new initiatives to improve education, most notably an effort to enlist volunteers to ensure that every child was literate by the end of third grade and a large expansion of aid for students in postsecondary education.

At the political parties' conventions during the summer, the Democrats and Republicans wrote platforms reflecting these varying views of their candidates. The Republicans adopted a platform on education that began with Dole's being quoted saying that the public schools were in trouble because they were being run, not by the public, but by narrow special interest groups who viewed them as political territory. The platform continued: "The American people know that something is terribly wrong with our educational system. The evidence is everywhere: children who cannot read, graduates who cannot reason, danger in schoolyards, indoctrination in classrooms" ("Improving Education," 1996, p. 2327).

The Republicans stated that because the federal government had no constitutional authority to be involved in school curricula, they would abolish the U.S. Department of Education and repeal Goals 2000 and other federal programs. Their remedies to achieve better schools were to teach abstinence education, to help parents to choose private and religious schools, to allow home schooling, and to work for prayer in the schools. They would also encourage the adoption of an education consumer's warranty to be free from educational malpractice and to have other rights.

The Democrats adopted a platform that emphasized that education is the key to opportunity; therefore, they bemoaned the congressional cutbacks in spending for education. That strategy, they said, was like cutting defense spending at the height of the Cold War. Instead, they urged that more must be done to expand educational opportunity:

> In the next four years, we must do even more to make sure America has the best public schools on earth. If we want to be the best, we should expect the best: We must hold students, teachers, and schools to the highest standards. ("Today's Democratic Party," 1996, p. 37)

The Democrats said that children must be able to read by the end of third grade, that students must demonstrate achievement to be promoted or to graduate, and that teachers must meet high standards or get out of the classroom. Further, failing public schools should be redesigned or overhauled. They urged an expansion of choice of public schools and opposed aid to private schools. Last, they urged teaching of good values, strong character, and the responsibilities of citizenship.

In the platforms of 1996, there were echoes of the positions taken by the political parties in 1992. The Republicans took a very dim view of public education, blamed the teachers' unions for many problems, urged aid to private schools, and put an emphasis on restoring moral values. The Democrats urged a reform of public schools through holding students and teachers to higher standards, endorsed teaching about character, and opposed aid to private schools.

The major difference between 1992 and the 1996 was noted by *Education Week* (Pitsch, 1996):

> In 1992, the Republican Party platform bragged about President Bush's "bold strategy" for improving the nation's schools that included "several legislative proposals" for parental choice, raising academic standards, and the creation of "break the mold" schools. . . . This year, however, the GOP platform makes clear that there should be as little federal involvement in education as possible. (p. 33)

The major exception to lessened federal involvement was the multi-billion-dollar proposal for vouchers, according to *Education Week*. Several prominent conservatives, such as Phyllis Schlafly of the Eagle Forum, were quoted as being quite pleased with this shift in philosophy between 1992 and 1996.

During the campaign, the polls showed that Clinton and the Democrats enjoyed a huge advantage over Dole and the Republicans on the issue of education. A September *USA Today*/CNN/Gallup poll showed that 59% of the voters believed that Clinton would better handle the education issue, compared with 30% for Dole and 4% for Perot (Wolf, 1996). The annual Phi Delta Kappa-Gallup poll (Elam, Rose, & Gallup, 1996) showed Clinton with a 49% to 23% margin over the congressional Republicans on the question of who was doing more to improve public education. In the same poll, the Democrats were perceived as more interested than the Republicans in improving public education by a 44% to 27% margin. Conversely, the Republicans were perceived as the party that would likely favor private schools over public schools by a margin of 59% to 37%.

The National Education Association (NEA) even raised the question of whether the party platform adopted at the Republican convention reflected the views of the rank-and-file Republicans. The NEA had commissioned a poll showing that Republican voters supported maintaining or increasing federal funding for public schools by a margin of almost 8 out of 10 (79%). The same poll showed that Republicans opposed the abolition of the U.S. Department of Education by a 54% to 34% margin (*Hearings before the Democratic Policy Committees,* 1996).

As the election approached and the poll results were reviewed, the Republicans in Congress became concerned about their prospects to retain control of the U.S. House of Representatives, and they especially worried about their vulnerability on the issue of education. Consequently, they did a complete about-face on cutting back on federal spending for education and got into a bidding war with Clinton and the congressional Democrats over how much more to appropriate for the very programs that had been targeted by the conservatives a year earlier for abolition or curtailment. After intense negotiations with Clinton and the Democrats, the final agreement resulted in the largest increase in funding for education at the federal level since the 1960s. In addition, all the legislative bills that would have eliminated or combined federal programs were killed.

By the time of the elections of 1996, therefore, Goals 2000 not only survived but had its appropriation pushed up by 40%. Further, all the traditional federal programs, such as Title I, survived intact—many with substantially increased funding. The assault of the conservatives on both the equity purpose of federal aid and the newer quality purpose not only failed but became a rout (Jennings & Rentner, 1996).

In the November elections, the Republicans retained control of the House, but by a thin margin, and increased their numbers slightly in the Senate. Meanwhile, Clinton won a convincing victory over Dole. After the elections, the post mortems were that Republicans had lost votes due to their positions on education and that Clinton and the Democrats had gained votes because of their advocacy for education.

In late November, Dan Balz (1996) reported in the *Washington Post* that Republican party officials had concluded in particular that "attacks on the Education Department cost Republican candidates crucial support among female voters" (p. A6). Governor George Bush of Texas said, "There's no question that from a political perspective, he [President Clinton] stole the issue and it affected the women's vote. . . . Republicans must say that we are for education" (quoted in Balz, 1996, p. A6).

Congressman Michael Castle (Rep.-Del.), a moderate Republican who had helped to increase the appropriation for education at the end of the Congress in October 1996, wrote the following year that the last election showed how strongly the American people felt about education. Castle said that "the message that Americans got was that Republicans did not think education was important" (Castle, 1997, p. 13). He noted:

> In my view, things got off to a rocky start last Congress on education because Republicans did not advance an education agenda that many Americans perceived as pro-education. Most of the proposals began with the words "abolish," "eliminate," or "cut." Thus, Americans were left with the impression that Republicans wanted to eliminate the federal role in education. (p. 13)

Lamar Alexander, who had run for the Republican nomination for president and lost to Dole, told the *New York Times* (Applebome, 1997) about the reaction he got when he talked about his ideas for vouchers for private school tuition as the way to reform education: "It does scare people. Sometimes when I describe it to an audience, they just stare at me" (p. B8). Alexander, though, said that he still believed that radical reform based on choice involving private schools was what was needed.

▓ National Standards Revived

While the Republicans were debating whether the way that their positions were stated was the problem or whether it was the message itself, President Clinton lost no time after the election in making education his focus of attention. In his state of the union address after he was inaugurated for a second term, he told Congress that his "number one priority for the next four years is to ensure that all Americans have the best education in the world" (Clinton, 1997a, p. 137). In that February 1997 address, he laid out a 10-point program that included the tutoring initiative and the expanded aid for postsecondary education he had promised during the campaign. He also asked for an expansion of 20% in aid for education to carry out his proposals, even while he was moving to reduce other spending so that the federal budget could be balanced.

The centerpiece of his education agenda was the development of national tests based on national standards. After the last Congress had tried to eliminate Goals 2000 and after the governors had recommitted to raising standards in their states while keeping a distance from national standards, Clinton went back to the emotional issue that had helped to generate much of the political heat of the past few years: national standards for education. Clinton was being consistent with his prior positions, but he must also have been emboldened by his electoral victory, which was at least partially due to his stance on education.

Clinton (1997a) said he wanted "a national crusade for education standards—not federal government standards, but national standards, representing what all our students must know to succeed in the knowledge economy of the 21st century" (p. 138). He urged every state and school to shape the curriculum to reflect these standards and to train teachers to lift students up to them. He pledged that national tests of student achievement in reading and math would be developed by his administration over the following 2 years to help schools meet high standards and to measure their progress toward them.

In his address, Clinton (1997a) contended that raising standards would help students and that good tests would show who needed help, what changes were needed to be made in teaching, and what schools needed to improve. Clinton said: "Tonight, I issue a challenge to the nation. Every state should adopt high national standards, and by 1999, every state should test every fourth-grader in reading and every eighth-grader in math to make sure these standards are met" (p. 138).

In the month before his state of the union address, Clinton had visited some school districts in Illinois that had participated in international tests of mathematics and science. While there, the president spoke about the need for high standards in math, science, and other basic subjects. He said that such high standards would come about only if there were standards national in scope and nationally tested but adopted and implemented locally. He added, "And we can no longer hide behind our love of local control of the schools and use that as an excuse not to hold ourselves to high standards. It has nothing to do with local control" (Clinton, 1997d, p. 79). Clinton stated that the federal government should not set the standards directly but that it would not happen "unless we get out here and beat the drum for it and work for it" (p. 79).

To buttress Clinton's argument that high standards would come about only if there were national standards, the U.S. Department of Education released data showing that many states were setting their standards too low. In a comparison of fourth-grade reading, Wisconsin said that 88% of its students were proficient, whereas only 35% were considered so on the basis of the National Assessment of Educational Progress (NAEP). Likewise, Georgia said that 67% were proficient in terms of the state standard, when only 26% were proficient in terms of the NAEP standard (see Figure 8.1).

Governor Thompson, representing one of the states that the U.S. Department of Education listed, disagreed with Clinton. In an article he wrote for the *New York Times* (Thompson, 1997), he urged that standards be left to states and local school boards. "Education is a local issue," he argued. "This is the way our parents and communities want it, and that is how it should be. After all, the states and local taxpayers are the ones who pay for schools" (p. A35). Thompson must have been concerned that after he had worked so hard to get the backing of the governors for raising standards in their states, the president was endangering that agreement by raising the issue of national standards, which might reignite the opposition of the far right to the idea of using standards to raise the quality of education.

Clinton, however, was not deterred and took his fight to the states. Early in 1997, he spoke to the legislatures in Maryland, North Carolina, and Michigan and won commitments from each of those states to use the national tests in 1999. As of June 1997, he had received commitments to administer the tests from West Virginia, Massachusetts, and Kentucky.

While visiting those states, Clinton made his case for national standards and tests. In Maryland, he told the state leaders:

> Now, already in the last week I have heard some people saying, [this] sounds like a federal power grab to me. That's nonsense. We will not attempt to require them, they are not federal government standards, they are national standards. But we have been hiding behind a very small fig leaf for very long, and the results are not satisfactory. Anybody who says that a country as big and diverse as ours can't possibly have national standards in the basics—I say from Maryland to Michigan to Montana, reading is reading and math is math. No school board is in charge of algebra, and no state legislature can enact the law of physics. And it is time we started acting the way we know we should. (Clinton, 1997e, p. 170)

EDUCATION STANDARDS

STATES VARY WIDELY IN READING GOALS

A *comparison of the academic standards in some states with the standards of the National Assessment of Educational Progress (NAEP), which samples student achievement in core subjects. This chart shows what percentage of fourth-graders meet NAEP's "proficient" standard in reading, compared with the percentage that meet state goals in reading. Often, reaching the state goal appears much easier for students.*

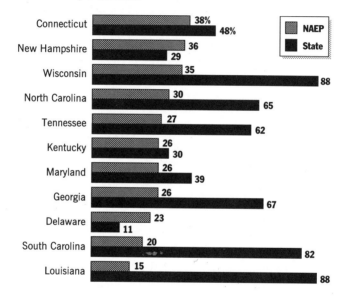

Figure 8.1. A Comparison of Some States' Academic Standards With Those of the National Assessment of Educational Progress
SOURCE: U.S. Department of Education, National Education Goals Panel. © 1997 *The Washington Post.* Reprinted with permission.

In Michigan, Clinton made the case to the state legislature and to the governor that the current way most schools test their students is not good enough. Most students are compared with one another and not to a standard of mastery of certain knowledge. That too must change, and it would in the type of national tests that Clinton was proposing. He said, "We need tests that test to the standards, that say whether you crossed the threshold of what you must know to do well in the world of tomorrow" (Clinton, 1997b, p. 295).

In North Carolina, Clinton told the legislature about his early involvement in setting national goals and standards. He said that history is what made him propose these national tests:

> In 1989, when President Bush and the governors met at the University of Virginia, I had the honor of being the Democratic governor chosen to try to write the nation's education goals. And at the time we always assumed that out of those goals there would come national standards and a system, a nationally recognized system of testing our children to see if they met those standards. Well, that hasn't happened yet. And as a result, we still don't know. We don't really know whether every child in every classroom knows what he or she needs to know when he or she needs to know it in math and in basic language skills. (Clinton, 1997c, p. 355)

In April 1997, 240 leaders of high-tech corporations met at the White House to endorse Clinton's proposed national tests. These leaders included Jim Barksdale of Netscape Communications, Steve Case of America OnLine, Louis Gerstner of IBM, and Lewis Platt of Hewlett-Packard. The Business Roundtable's education task force also endorsed the national tests (Sanchez, 1997). Thus, the country's major business leadership continued its support of national involvement in raising the quality of the schools through setting high standards that they had begun when George Bush was president in 1989.

Other leaders were more divided. Governor Thompson spoke for some governors who were opposed to the new national tests, but other governors endorsed them, including some very conservative ones. In the six states that had first committed to using the national tests, there were three Republican and three Democratic governors. Clearly, support for national tests was not strictly along partisan lines.

On Capitol Hill, Secretary Riley appeared and argued two reasons for national standards and tests in addition to those given by Clinton: First, the mobility of the population required that parents be able to measure achievement in reading and math anywhere in the country using a national standard; and second, parents in poor-performing schools where their children were being given high grades but then received low scores on these national tests would demand changes to improve the education being offered in those schools (*Hearings Before the House Subcommittee,* 1997).

At that hearing, Congressman Goodling, who had supported Goals 2000 in 1994 despite the opposition of most of his fellow House Republicans, now opposed Clinton's development of the national tests without outright congressional approval. Congressman George Miller, who had helped to precipitate in 1993 the liberal opposition to the use of content standards without their being linked to opportunity-to-learn standards, now supported the development of the new national tests.

The *Washington Post* commented in an editorial ("Standards for Standards," 1997) on some aspects of the convoluted history of the standards movement:

> The push for standards, when it began, was identified with conservative-leaning politicians who saw better measurement of student learning as the way to get past teacher-union inertia and the tendency to measure school quality by what was spent. Once Mr. Clinton embraced them, though, standards were treated as anathema by some Republican governors who feared even voluntary tests would become a lever for federal influence over the curriculum. The countervailing force this time is business leaders, who, at an education summit a year ago, were scornful of the idea that potentially employable kids in Boise or Birmingham need anything but a single, "national" standard for reading or math. (p. C1)

In September 1977, Congressman Goodling followed up on his opposition to the president's proposal by moving to block the U.S. Department of Education from proceeding with any action to develop such national tests. By a vote of 295 to 125, the House of Representatives adopted that amendment, which was offered to the annual appropriations bill for education. The Senate, however, voted 87 to 13 to allow the development of the tests to continue but to move the authority over them to an independent national council (Sanchez, 1997a). After protracted negotiations between the Congress and the president, the development of national tests for mathematics and reading was allowed to proceed, but the National Assessment Governing Board (which oversees the National Assessment of Educational Progress) was charged with the responsibility of deciding which national standards ought to be used and how the tests ought to be developed. Pilot testing of any such assessments could not occur before October 1, 1998. Another key element of the compromise was that the National Academy of Sciences was charged with determining if current tests developed by private companies and the states could have their results compared to national standards and thereby avoid the need for a separate set of national tests (Departments of Labor, Health and Human Services, and Education, and Related Agencies Appropriations Act of 1997; Pianin & Sanchez, 1997).

David Hoff (1997) in *Education Week* summarized the situation quite well:

> In the outline of a hard-fought compromise, House Republicans backed away from their demand that all testing preparations stop, and the administration agreed to slow an ambitious schedule that would have put the tests in front of students in the spring of 1999.
>
> But the agreement settles nothing for the long term. Over the next 12 months, both sides will continue the debate over whether the federal government should pay for and endorse the creation of new tests to be given to 4th graders in reading and 8th graders in mathematics. (p. 1)

Epilogue

In the period from 1989 to 1997, there were two presidents, George Bush and Bill Clinton, both of whom advocated for national standards for public schools and national tests for students. In the same period, there were two national education summits, which resulted in the nation's governors raising education standards in their states and writing tests to ensure that students met them. It is clear, however, that the path between these two presidencies and two summits has been rugged and wandering.

The country got on this path of establishing clearer standards for the schools because business, political, and education leaders believed that the public schools were not doing well enough in educating children and that setting higher benchmarks would help them to do better. Many liberals, however, felt that improving educational opportunity through increasing funding for the schools should occur first, and many conservatives felt that setting national standards would increase federal influence over the schools. The last political force, the far right, took advantage of this debate to build its own strength through making exaggerated and false statements.

By the end of 1996, opposition to the idea of setting higher standards for the schools was overcome as nearly every state wrote and was beginning to implement clearer academic benchmarks for the public schools. National standards and tests, however, seemed like an idea whose time had passed. Then, at the beginning of 1997, President Clinton raised anew the concept of using national standards and tests. Why couldn't things have been left well enough alone? Why are we still talking about national standards and tests after their seeming demise during the debates of the previous 7 years?

Clinton's proposed national tests for math and reading may—or may not—take place in 1999 or 2000, but even if they do not due to procedural or political problems, they will not be the last word from business, political, and education leaders on the need for national action to improve the schools. Remember that Senator Dole, even as he called for the abolition of the U.S. Department of Education and the repeal of Goals 2000 and other assistance for public schools, advocated the creation of a federal multi-billion-dollar program of vouchers for private school tuition.

Why *national* action? The United States has a very decentralized system of public education with 14,000 local school districts and with varying degrees of state-level influence over education. Therefore, when leaders believe that improvement must occur, as they do now, they call for national action to focus the attention of the vast number of local and state decision makers—the millions of teachers, principals, superintendents, school board members, state legislators, state board members, and union leaders.

In 1991, President Bush called for national standards and tests, and the explanation for this departure from the tradition of local control of education was that "Washington can help by setting standards, highlighting examples, contributing some funds, providing some flexibility in exchange for accountability, and pushing and prodding—and then pushing and prodding some more" (U.S. Department of Education, 1991, p. 2). In 1997 President Clinton (1997) also called for national standards and tests, and explained that higher standards would not come about "unless we get out here and beat the drum for it and work for it" (p. 79). Neither president wanted federal control of education, but both saw the need for prodding from the national level for school improvement.

Business leaders have been very consistent in seeing the need for national focusing of attention on improving the schools, so they have steadfastly stood by Bush's, Clinton's, and congressional actions to raise standards in the schools. They too understand that the federal government has very limited powers and thus can urge action only by the primary actors in education—the states and local school districts.

Why *standards and tests?* If there is a need for a national focus on school improvement, why have these leaders urged raising standards and using tests to implement these standards? Why not other remedies?

The simple answer is that a focus on what is taught and learned is the proper one if student achievement is to be raised. Many elements are important in determining whether a student learns, but the school must first be clear about what is to be learned—and American education has not always been structured in such a way that there is a clear academic goal.

Louis Gerstner of IBM was amazed to learn that schools do not always have standards to measure what is taught and learned. The National Academy of Sciences documented that teachers in local school districts are given an impossible task to define curriculum with little time or resources and thus fall back on what has been done in the past or on what is available from commercial companies. Marshall Smith and Ramon Cortines pointed out the confusion that exists in American education, with tests coming from commercial publishers, with textbooks coming from other sources, with professional development being done by yet others, and with teachers not always knowing what they will be held accountable for.

Focusing on curriculum is proper in order to raise student academic achievement, but setting clear standards and writing tests to measure their attainment is only the beginning point. Teachers must be retrained, textbooks must be improved, and students who do not do well must be assisted. Parents, too, must understand that greater emphasis must be placed on raising academic achievement. Last, employers must show that academic mastery counts when employment decisions are made.

The national debates about improving education that occurred between 1989 and 1997 showed that the idea of national standards and testing is controversial but that national action is needed to improve the schools, and setting higher standards is the proper place to start. Despite all the fighting over these ideas, when all is said and done, the attention focused on improving education by these debates over national standards has helped the country to have better schools.

References

Prologue

Immerwahr, J., & Johnson, J. (1996). *Americans' views on standards: An assessment by Public Agenda.* New York: Public Agenda.

Chapter 1

Consortium for Policy Research in Education. (1994). *Ten years of state education reform, 1983-1993: Overview with four case studies.* Philadelphia: Author.

Elam, S. (1995). *How America views its schools: The PDK/Gallup polls, 1969-1994.* Bloomington, IN: Phi Delta Kappa Educational Foundation.

Elam, S. M., Rose, L. C., Gallup, A. M. (1995, September). 26th annual Phi Delta Kappa-Gallup poll of the public's attitudes toward the public schools. *Phi Delta Kappan,* pp. 41-56.

Gerstner, L. V., Jr. (1994, May 27). Our schools are failing: Do we care? *New York Times,* p. A27.

National Academy of Sciences. (1989). *Everybody counts: A report to the nation on the future of mathematics education.* Washington, DC: National Academy Press.

National Council on Education Standards and Testing. (1992). *Raising standards for American education.* Washington, DC: Government Printing Office.

New Standards Project. (1994). Benchmarking globally for high standards locally. *New Standard,* 2(9), 1-2.

Office of Educational Research and Improvement. (1994). *What do student grades mean? Differences across schools.* Washington, DC: U.S. Department of Education.

Riley, R. W. (1993, August 16). Remarks presented at the meeting of the National Governors' Association, Tulsa, OK.

Shortfalls in 1980s reform: Refocused educational strategies on the results of schooling. (1994, July). *R&D Preview,* p. 6.

Smith, M. S., & Cortines, R. (1993, June 24). Clinton proposals will challenge students and the school systems. *Philadelphia Inquirer,* p. A15.

185

Chapter 2

Alexander, L. (1993). What we were doing when we were interrupted. In J. Jennings (Ed.), *National issues in education: The past is prologue* (pp. 6-7). Bloomington, IN: Phi Delta Kappa International.

Bush, G. H. W. (1991a, April 18). Address to the nation on national education strategy. *Weekly Compilation of Presidential Documents, 27,* 464-472.

Bush, G. H. W. (1991b, May 27). Message to Congress transmitting proposal America 2000: Excellence in Education Act. *Weekly Compilation of Presidential Documents, 27,* 648-650.

Butler, O. B. (1991, July 5). Some doubts on school vouchers. *New York Times,* p. A8.

Chira, S. (1991, July 22). A sea of doubt swells around Bush's education plan. *New York Times,* p. A12.

College Entrance Examination Board. (1994). *The College Board annual report 92-93.* New York: Author.

Consortium for Policy Research in Education. (1994). *Ten years of state education reform, 1983-1993: Overview with four case studies.* Philadelphia: Author.

Cooper, K. J. (1991, April 9). Education department in high gear. *Washington Post,* p. A4.

H.R. 5115, 101st Cong., 2nd Sess. (1990).

H.R. 1675, 101st Cong., 1st Sess. (1989).

H.R. 2435, 102d Cong., 1st Sess. (1991).

H.R. 2460, 102d Cong., 1st Sess. (1991).

H.R. 3320, 102d Cong., 1st Sess. (1991).

H.R. 4323, 102d Cong., 2nd Sess. (1992).

Heyneman, S. P. (1990, March). Education on the world market. *American School Board Journal,* pp. 28-30.

Hoff, D. (1994, February 15). Study finds little evidence of high school reform. *Education Daily,* p. 1.

In the name of choice [Editorial]. (1991, October 29). *Washington Post,* p. A22.

Jennings, J. F. (1992, December). Lessons learned in Washington, D.C. *Phi Delta Kappan,* pp. 303-307.

National Council on Education Standards and Testing Act, 20 U.S.C. § 1221-1 (1991).

National Council on Education Standards and Testing. (1992). *Raising standards for American education.* Washington, DC: Government Printing Office.

National Governors' Association. (1991). *From rhetoric to action: State progress in restructuring the education system.* Washington, DC: Author.

National test for high school seniors gains backing. (1991, January 31). *Washington Post,* p. A4.

National tests urged for public schools. (1991, January 17). *New York Times,* p. A20.

O'Day, J. A., & Smith, M. S. (1993). Systemic school reform and educational opportunity. In S. H. Fuhrman (Ed.), *Designing coherent education policy: Improving the system.* San Francisco: Jossey-Bass.

Office of the Press Secretary, the White House. (1991, April 18). *America 2000: The president's education strategy* [Fact sheet]. Washington, DC: Author.

Policy Information Center. (1994). *What Americans study revisited.* Princeton, NJ: Educational Testing Service.

Ravitch, D. (1993). Critical issues in the Office of Educational Research and Improvement. In J. Jennings (Ed.), *National issues in education: The past is prologue.* Bloomington, IN: Phi Delta Kappa International.

S. 2, 102d Cong., 1st Sess. (1991).

S. 695, 101st Cong., 1st Sess. (1989).

S. 1141, 102d Cong., 1st Sess. (1991).

Smith, M. S., & O'Day, J. A. (1991). Systemic school reform. In S. H. Fuhrman & B. Malen (Eds.), *The politics of curriculum and testing.* Philadelphia: Falmer.

Sontag, D. (1992, March 23). Teachers' leader calls for a return to tradition. *New York Times,* p. B7.

U.S. Department of Education. (1991). *America 2000: An education strategy.* Washington, DC: Author.

Yang, J. E. (1991, May 23). President unveils school legislation he says will break the education mold. *Washington Post,* p. A6.

Zuckman, J. (1992, May 23). Panel gives listless approval to scorned reform bill. *Congressional Quarterly,* p. 1451.

Chapter 3

Ambach, G. (1992). *Transition guide for "President's Program for Education."* Unpublished document.

Baumann, D. (1992, July 14). Bush, Clinton, and Perot: Where they stand on education. *Education Daily,* p. 3.

Clinton, W., & Gore, A. (1992). *Putting people first: How we can all change America.* New York: Times Books.

Clinton proposes $30.7 billion for 1994 education budget. (1993, April 9). *Education Daily,* pp. 4-6.

Clymer, A. (1991, April 14). Bush to propose broad changes in U.S. schools. *New York Times,* p. I1.

Cooper, K. J. (1993, January 30). For Democrats, a new ballgame. *Washington Post,* p. A8.

Finn, C. (1992, December 16). The education empire strikes back. *Wall Street Journal,* p. A14.

Jordan, M. (1993, September 9). Writing a new chapter in public school aid. *Washington Post,* p. A19.

Miller, J. A. (1992, October 21). Election 1992: Candidates' education and related policies at a glance. *Education Week,* p. 22.

Party stresses family values, decentralized authority. (1992, August 22). *Congressional Quarterly,* pp. 2562-2563.

Party's statement of policies mirrors Clinton's goals. (1992, July 4). *Congressional Quarterly,* p. 62.

Scully, T. A. (1993). Investing in education: The Bush record. In J. Jennings (Ed.), *National issues in education: The past is prologue.* Bloomington, IN: Phi Delta Kappa International.

Stout, H., & Murray, A. (1992, August 6). Real differences on education between Clinton and Bush came down to commitment, money. *Wall Street Journal,* p. A14.

Chapter 4

Administration's proposal for schools announced. (1993, April 22). *Washington Post,* p. A28.

Armey to push choice alternative to Clinton plan. (1993, July 22). *CongressDaily,* p. 3.

Bipartisan House education coalition collapses. (1993, May 6). *CongressDaily,* p. 3.

Celis, W., III. (1993, April 22). Administration offers plan for better schools. *New York Times,* p. A20.

Chira, S. (1993, April 21). Clinton to offer plan for change in U.S. schools. *New York Times,* p. A18.

Clinton, W. (1993a, April 21). Message to Congress transmitting the "Goals 2000: Educate America Act." *Weekly Compilation of Presidential Documents, 29,* 643-644.

Clinton, W. (1993b, July 5). Remarks to the National Education Association Representative Assembly. *Weekly Compilation of Presidential Documents, 29,* 1261-1269.

Clinton proposes $30.7 billion for 1994 education budget. (1993, April 9). *Education Daily,* pp. 1-6.

Clinton, Riley aim complaints at House Democrats for changing administration's Goals 2000 legislation. (1993, May 31). *Department of Education Reports,* pp. 1-2.

Clymer, A. (1993, June 24). Clinton bill on educational standards advances. *New York Times,* p. A19.

Cooper, K. J. (1993, January 30). For Democrats, a new ballgame. *Washington Post,* p. A8.

Del Valle, C. (1993, April 26). Why Bill Clinton is teacher's pet. *Business Week,* p. 43.

Democrats' amendment angers GOP. (1993, June 24). *Congressional Monitor,* p. 3.

The faces aren't so happy at Education. . . . (1993, April 5). *U.S. News and World Report,* p. 10.

Family Research Council. (1993, September 24). Education lobby flunks. *Washington Watch*, p. 1.

Free Congress Foundation. (1993, July). Education reform or bureaucracy reborn? *Policy Insights*, pp. 1-4.

Goals 2000. (1993, October 13). *Congressional Record*, pp. H7735-H7794.

Goodling, B. (1993, May 24). How to measure "opportunity to learn." *Roll Call*, p. 16.

Grading Goals 2000: A word from Geiger, Finn. (1993, May 24). *Daily Report Card*, p. 6.

H.R. 1804, 103d Cong., 1st Sess. (1993).

Hearings on H.R. 1804, Goals 2000: Educate America Act, Committee on Education and Labor, U.S. House of Representatives, 103d Cong., 1st Sess. (1993, April 22) (testimony of Secretary Richard Riley).

Hoff, D. (1993a, May 7). Democratic amendment sparks Goals 2000 debate in House. *Education Daily*, pp. 1, 3.

Hoff, D. (1993b, August 16). NGA says states should control school delivery efforts. *Education Daily*, pp. 1-2.

Hoff, D. (1993c, August 18). Riley says reform standards will be model, not requirement. *Education Daily*, p. 1.

House panel close to passing school reform bill. (1993, June 23). *CongressDaily*, p. 4.

House panel Democrats fix school reform plan glitches. (1993, October 4). *CongressDaily*, p. 3.

Innerst, C. (1993, April 22). Schools bill shifts focus to resources. *Washington Times*, p. A4.

Jordan, M. (1993, October 1). Riley assails lack of progress on improving U.S. schools. *Washington Post*, p. A2.

Kolberg, W. (1993, September 11). Goals 2000: Many reservations [Letter to the editor]. *Washington Post*, p. A20.

Kondracke, M. (1993a, September 27). Education reform nears floor after Clinton veto threat. *Roll Call*, p. 6.

Kondracke, M. (1993b, August 30). GOP waffles on education. *Dallas Morning News*, p. A13.

Kondracke, M. (1993c, April 5). Urgently needed: New standards, testing for schools. *Roll Call*, p. 6.

LaHaye, B. (1993, August). Educational reform! Utopia by 2,000 AD? *Family Voice*, pp. 1-10.

Leo, J. (1993, June 21). Lowering the education bar. *U.S. News and World Report*, p. 19.

Make schools better with national standards [Editorial]. (1993, April 23). *USA Today*, p. A12.

Manno, B. (1993, June 22). Deliver us from Clinton's school bill. *Wall Street Journal*, p. A14.

Miller, J. (1993a, March 31). Democrats' objections spur E.D. to delay reform bill. *Education Week*, p. 26.

Miller, J. (1993b, August 4). E.D. and House Democrats negotiate on Goals 2000 bill. *Education Week*, p. 36.

Miller, J. (1993c, April 14). Prospects brighter for administration's reform bill. *Education Week*, p. 20.

Pitsch, M. (1993a, September 29). Agreement on E.D.'s reform measure clears way for action on House floor. *Education Week*, p. 23.

Pitsch, M. (1993b, July 14). Sharply divided House panel amends Goals "2000." *Education Week*, p. 21.

Reinventing government: That means education too. (1993, September 14). *Education Week*, p. 23.

Riley, R. (1993a, July 14). Don't distort Clinton education reform [Letter to the editor]. *Wall Street Journal*, p. A13.

Riley, R. (1993b, August). Remarks presented at the meeting of the National Governors' Association, Tulsa, OK.

Riley pledges Goals 2000 bill would not mandate school funding equity. (1993, July 19). *Department of Education Reports*, pp. 5-6.

Rolling Riley [Editorial]. (1993, April 19). *Wall Street Journal*, p. A12.

Rothman, R. (1993, May 26). NGA hears range of views on opportunity standards. *Education Week*, p. 20.

S. 846, 103d Cong., 1st Sess. (1993).

Samuelson, R. (1993, April 28). Hollow school reform. *Washington Post*, p. A19.

Schools and standards [Editorial]. (1993, October 19). *Washington Post*, p. A22.

Sharpe, R. (1993a, April 16). Clinton package for schools has chance to pass. *Wall Street Journal,* p. B1.

Sharpe, R. (1993b, April 22). White House unveils $420 million plan for national standards in education. *Wall Street Journal,* p. A6.

Stanfield, R. (1993, June 19). New lesson plans. *National Journal,* p. 1515.

Tucker, A. (1993, July 14). Goals 2000: Stifling grass roots education reform. *Issue Bulletin,* pp. 1-8.

U.S. Department of Education. (1993, October 7). *Example of response to Dear Colleague letter of Congressman Armey.* Unpublished document.

U.S. House of Representatives, Committee on Education and Labor. (1993, June 23). *Mark-up of H.R. 1804 "Goals 2000: Educate America Act."* Unpublished transcript.

U.S. House passes Goals 2000: National standards move ahead. (1993, October 14). *Daily Report Card,* p. 6.

Wattenberg, B. (1993, June 8). No more something for nothing. *Wall Street Journal,* p. A16.

Zuckman, J. (1993a, April 24). Clinton's school reform plan has high hopes, low funds. *Congressional Quarterly,* pp. 1027-1028.

Zuckman, J. (1993b). House approves reform bill setting national goals. *Congressional Quarterly,* p. 2817.

Zuckman, J. (1993c, June 26). School standards approved along party-line vote. *Congressional Quarterly,* p. 1663.

Chapter 5

Clymer, A. (1994, March 25). Delaying a Senate vote, with charity for none. *New York Times,* p. A19.

Conferees reach agreement on "Goals 2000" education bill. (1994, March 18). *Congressional Monitor,* p. 3.

Conference report on H.R. 1804, Goals 2000: Educate America Act. (1994, March 21). *Congressional Record,* pp. H1635, H1677.

Cooper, K. (1994, March 22). House vote affirms voluntary school prayer. *Washington Post,* p. A4.

Dewar, H. (1994a, March 27). Education bill caps busy week. *Washington Post,* pp. A1, A7.

Dewar, H. (1994b, March 26). Weary Senate passes education bill after breaking Helms filibuster. *Washington Post,* p. A8.

Dewar, H., & Cooper, K. (1994a, March 24). GOP blocks Senate schools measure, balks at House crime debate rules. *Washington Post,* p. A18.

Dewar, H., & Cooper, K. (1994b, February 9). Senate approves administration legislation that sets goals for education. *Washington Post,* p. A7.

Education: The next step [Editorial]. (1994, February 10). *Washington Post,* p. A26.

Education goals and standards: Hearing before the Committee on Labor and Human Resources, U.S. Senate, 103d Cong., 1st Sess. (1993, February 24).

Education's Trojan horse. (1993, November 1). *Detroit News,* p. A6.

Elementary and secondary education. (1994, March 21). *Congressional Record,* p. H1750.

Everything but education [Editorial]. (1994, March 27). *Washington Post,* p. C6.

An examination of the federal role in school finance: Hearings before the Subcommittee on Education, Arts and Humanities of the Committee on Labor and Human Resources, U.S. Senate, 103d Cong., 1st Sess. (1993, August 3).

Goals panel adopts principles on national content standards. (1993, November 17). *Education Daily,* pp. 3-4.

Goals 2000: Educate America Act, House debate. (1994a, February 23). *Congressional Record,* pp. H582-H650.

Goals 2000: Educate America Act, House debate. (1994b, March 23). *Congressional Record,* pp. H1921-H1937.

Goals 2000: Educate America Act, Senate debate. (1994a, February 2). *Congressional Record,* pp. S605-S631, S634-S653.

Goals 2000: Educate America Act, Senate debate. (1994b, February 3). *Congressional Record,* pp. S699-S731, S736-S751, S756-S758.
Goals 2000: Educate America Act, Senate debate. (1994c, February 4). *Congressional Record,* pp. S835-S908, S910-S932, S936-S945.
Goals 2000: Educate America Act, Senate debate. (1994d, February 8). *Congressional Record,* pp. S1093-S1101, S1116-S1124, S1146-S1160.
Goals 2000: Educate America Act, Senate debate. (1994e, March 23). *Congressional Record,* pp. S3531-3536.
Goals 2000: Educate America Act, Senate debate. (1994f, March 25). *Congressional Record,* pp. S3845-4036.
Goals 2000 compromise passes House, is blocked in Senate. (1994, March 28). *Vocational Education Weekly,* pp. 1, 3.
Goals 2000 conferees facing deadline. (1994, March 11). *CongressDaily,* p. 1.
GOP fires warning on school reform. (1993, June 22). *CongressDaily,* p. 1.
Gray, C. B., & Kemp, E. (1993, September 19). Flunking testing; Is too much fairness unfair to school kids? *Washington Post,* p. C3.
Harrison, D. (1994, February 9). Senate wrapping up work on its Goals 2000 bill. *Education Daily,* pp. 1-2.
Henry, T. (1994, March 28). Goals 2000 act sets standards for students and schools. *USA Today,* p. 4D.
Hoff, D. (1993a, May 5). GOP criticizes reform bill for being too top heavy. *Education Daily,* pp. 1, 3.
Hoff, D. (1993b, May 20). Senate panel gains GOP votes for Clinton's reform bill. *Education Daily,* p. 3.
Hoff, D. (1993c, November 12). Standards must be set high for all students, Riley says. *Education Daily,* pp. 1-2.
Hoff, D. (1994a, March 22). E. D. keys on Goals 2000 as deadline looms. *Education Daily,* pp. 1, 3.
Hoff, D. (1994b, March 18). Negotiators build flexibility into school standards demand. *Education Daily,* pp. 1, 2.
Hoff, D. (1994c, March 16). School delivery standards snag initial House-Senate talks. *Education Daily,* pp. 1-2.
House clears cornerstone of Clinton education plan. (1994, March 24). *Wall Street Journal,* p. A16.
Jennings, J., & Stark, D. (1996). Education stalemate in the capital. *Phi Delta Kappa, Washington Newsletter, 5*(2), 1-4.
Jordan, M. (1994, March 23). Vote nears on national school goals. *Washington Post,* pp. 1, 17.
Kassebaum endorses job skills deal. (1993, July 14). *CongressDaily,* p. 1.
Katz, J. L. (1994, February 5). School prayer, choice part of Senate Goals' debate. *Congressional Quarterly,* p. 248.
Kennedy upbeat on prospects for school reform legislation. (1993, October 25). *CongressDaily,* p. 2.
Lauber, W. F. (1993, November 16). Goals 2000: The "Washington knows best" approach to school reform. *Issue Bulletin* [Heritage Foundation], pp. 1-9.
Listening to the public. (1993, December). *New Standard,* pp. 1-3.
Miller, J., & Olson, L. (1993, May 26). Senate panel approves Clinton's Goals 2000 bill. *Education Week,* pp. 20, 22.
Mr. Helms vs. the Education bill [Editorial]. (1994, March 25). *New York Times,* p. A28.
National skills standards: Hearing before the Subcommittee on Elementary, Secondary, and Vocational Education, U.S. House of Representatives, 103d Cong., 1st Sess. (1993, May 18).
How national standards can improve schools [Editorial]. (1994, March 28). *USA Today,* p. 12A.
Pitsch, M. (1993, November 17). New "Goals 2000" bill excises state standards requirement. *Education Week,* p. 15.
Riley, R. (1993, October). The Clinton administration's education agenda. *Dialogue* [Phelps-Stokes Fund], pp. 1-4.
Senate panel passes education bill with GOP support. (1993, May 19). *CongressDaily,* p. 3.

Sharpe, R. (1994, February 9). Clinton's education reform package, school-to-work legislation clear Senate. *Wall Street Journal,* p. A16.

Shogren, E. (1994, February 9). Senate OKs two major school reform efforts. *Los Angeles Times,* p. A1.

Skills standards: Could Goals 2000 lead to litigation? (1993, June 3). *Daily Report Card,* pp. 2-3.

State of the Union Address. (1994, January 26). *Washington Post,* pp. A12, A13.

Stedman, J. (1994, February 18). *Selected opportunity to learn options.* Unpublished document, Congressional Research Service.

Swoboda, F. (1993, July 14). U.S. nears effort to set national job skill standards. *Washington Post,* pp. G1, G4.

U.S. Senate, Committee on Labor and Human Resources. (1993, November). *Goals 2000: Educate America Act, question and answer sheet.* Unpublished document.

Wells, R. (1994, March 19). Conferees reach agreement on Goals 2000 bill. *Congressional Quarterly,* p. 678.

Chapter 6

Anderson, J., & Binstein, M. (1994, October 16). The new education president. *Washington Post,* p. C7.

Celis, W. (1994, October 18). Schools to get wide license on spending federal money under new education law. *New York Times,* p. B11.

Chapter 1, take 2 [Editorial]. (1994, June 29). *Washington Post,* p. A22.

Cloud, D. S. (1994, October 8). End of session marked by partisan stalemate. *Congressional Quarterly,* pp. 2847-2849.

Clymer, A. (1994, October 6). Lobbying bill caught in partisan wrangle. *New York Times,* p. A22.

Committee on Education Funding. (1994, October). Education community bands together to help push ESEA reauthorization through in the last days of the 103rd Congress. *Committee on Education Funding Newsletter,* pp. 10-13.

Conferees reach deal on ESEA bill. (1994, September 28). *CongressDaily,* pp. 1, 7.

Congressional gridlock? Not when it comes to education. (1994, October 7). *Daily Report Card,* p. 6.

Congressional Quarterly. (1965, 1967, 1970, 1974, 1978, 1988, 1994). *Congressional Quarterly annual almanac.* Washington, DC: Author.

Cooper, K. (1994, October 1). $13 billion education bill clears House; Senate is likely to vote on it next week. *Washington Post,* p. A4.

The current status of Chapter 1, Senate Committee on Labor and Human Resources, 103d Cong., 2nd Sess. (1994, March 16) (testimony of Marshall Smith).

Debate on gay issue gets personal. (1994, March 25). *Washington Times,* p. A4.

Democratic Study Group, U.S. House of Representatives. (1994, June 13). *A look at the Senate filibuster: Special report.* Unpublished document.

Democrats fear lack of votes to beat recommit motion. (1994, September 29). *CongressDaily,* p. 3.

Dillon, S. (1994, October 20). Report faults bilingual education in New York. *New York Times,* pp. A1, B4.

Durenberger, D. (1994, October 7). Final passage of ESEA conference committee agreement and general comments on education reform. *Congressional Record,* pp. S14751-S14754.

Education chief plans shift in aid for poor schools. (1993, September 15). *Wall Street Journal,* p. A24.

An education Congress [Editorial]. (1994, October 18). *Washington Post,* p. A16.

Elementary and Secondary Education Act, 20 U.S.C. § 2701-3386 (1965).

Elementary and Secondary Education Act appropriations extension. (1994, September 30). *Congressional Record,* pp. H10391-H10409.

Elementary and Secondary Education Amendments. (1994a, September 20). *Congressional Record,* pp. H9249-H9253.

Elementary and Secondary Education Amendments, conference report. (1994b, October 3). *Congressional Record,* pp. S13899-S13905.

Elementary and Secondary Education Amendments, conference report. (1994c, October 5). *Congressional Record,* pp. S14147-S14209.

ESEA bill conferees stalled over unfunded mandates. (1994, September 22). *CongressDaily,* p. 4.

ESEA conferees deadlocked on Chapter 1 formula. (1994, September 26). *CongressDaily,* p. 2.

GOP readies at least two motions to recommit ESEA. (1994, September 28). *CongressDaily,* pp. 2, 3.

Gunderson, S. (1995). The Chapter 2 program. In J. Jennings (Ed.), *National issues in education: Elementary and Secondary Education Act.* Bloomington, IN: Phi Delta Kappa International.

Hoff, D. (1993, September 24). GOP leaders join Democrats in sponsoring education department's ESEA bill. *Education Daily,* pp. 1, 2.

Hoff, D. (1994a, June 17). Big cities and growth states hate Senate Chapter 1 formula. *Education Daily,* pp. 1, 2, 4.

Hoff, D. (1994b, July 25). Christian family group garners opposition against Senate bill. *Education Daily,* pp. 3, 4.

Hoff, D. (1994c, October 7). Coordination is the key to making ESEA work, state officials say. *Education Daily,* pp. 1, 3.

Hoff, D. (1994d, March 3). Education department's Chapter 1 formula gets cool Senate reception. *Education Daily,* pp. 1, 2.

Hoff, D. (1994e, January 13). Education department's Chapter 1 proposal would hurt rural schools, GAO says. *Education Daily,* pp. 1, 2.

Hoff, D. (1994f, March 28). House passes basic ESEA bill with only few revisions. *Education Daily,* pp. 1, 3.

House conferees vote down ESEA Chapter 1 deal. (1994, September 27). *CongressDaily,* p. 3.

House panel strikes deal on controversial standards. (1994, February 24). *CongressDaily,* p. 1.

House votes to extend education financing. (1994, October 1). *New York Times,* p. 'I8.

Improving America's Schools Act. (1993, October 4). *Congressional Record,* pp. S12928, S13021-S13023.

Improving America's Schools Act, House debate. (1994a, February 24). *Congressional Record,* pp. H798-H897.

Improving America's Schools Act, House debate. (1994b, March 3). *Congressional Record,* pp. H1006-H1051.

Improving America's Schools Act, House debate. (1994c, March 9). *Congressional Record,* pp. H1093-H1134.

Improving America's Schools Act, House debate. (1994d, March 21). *Congressional Record,* pp. H1684-H1754.

Improving America's Schools Act, House debate. (1994e, March 22). *Congressional Record,* pp. H1794-H1809.

Improving America's Schools Act, House debate. (1994f, March 24). *Congressional Record,* pp. H2020-H2153.

Improving America's Schools Act, Senate debate. (1994a, July 27). *Congressional Record,* pp. S9754-S9925.

Improving America's Schools Act, Senate debate. (1994b, July 28). *Congressional Record,* pp. S9981-S10043.

Improving America's Schools Act, Senate debate. (1994c, August 1). *Congressional Record,* pp. S10153-S10213.

Improving America's Schools Act, Senate debate. (1994d, August 2). *Congressional Record,* pp. S10233-S10317.

Jordan, M. (1993, Fall). Capitol improvements. *America's Agenda,* p. 6.

Krauss, C. (1993, September 15). Clinton aims to redirect school aid to the poor from wealthy districts. *New York Times,* p. B15.

Kuntz, P. (1994a, February 26). Home schooling movement gives House a lesson. *Congressional Quarterly,* pp. 479-480.

Kuntz, P. (1994b, February 12). Panel shifts funds slightly to target poorer schools. *Congressional Quarterly,* pp. 328-331.

Lawmakers find fault with new education aid formula. (1993, September 24). *Congressional Monitor,* p. 4.

Letter to Representatives from J. Brent Walker, General Counsel, Baptist Joint Committee. (1994a, September 30). *Congressional Record,* p. 10398.

Letter to Representatives from Joyce McCray, Executive Director, American Council on Private Education. (1994b, September 30). *Congressional Record,* p. 10404.

Letter to Representatives from Sister Lourdes Sheehan. (1994c, September 30). *Congressional Record,* p. 10404.

Licitra, A. (1993, November 17). Leaders mull voluntary nature of national academic standards. *Education Daily,* pp. 1, 3.

Miller, J. (1993, August 4). Change in course eyed for flagship federal program. *Education Week,* pp. 1, 52.

Mix and match on education [Editorial]. (1994, September 8). *Washington Post,* p. A18.

Pitsch, M. (1993, September 29). Education department officials begin task of marketing their proposal to reinvent E.S.E.A. Education Week, p. 22.

Pitsch, M. (1994a, October 5). Accord struck on Chapter 1 fund formula. *Education Week,* pp. 1, 18.

Pitsch, M. (1994b, January 12). Clinton likely to seek budget increase for education. *Education Week,* p. 20.

Pitsch, M. (1994c, October 12). Congress fends off GOP attacks, backs E.S.E.A. *Education Week,* pp. 1, 20.

Pitsch, M. (1994d, May 25). ESEA reauthorization clears Senate panel. *Education Week,* p. 6.

Pitsch, M. (1994e, October 26). In political season, "social issue" add-ons bulk up E.S.E.A. *Education Week,* p. 22.

Pitsch, M. (1994f, August 3). Senate passage of E.S.E.A. measure expected this week. *Education Week,* p. 27.

Pitsch, M. (1994g, June 22). $12 billion E.S.E.A. bill clears Senate panel. *Education Week,* p. 20.

President signs major education bill. (1994, October 21). *Business Currents,* p. 1.

Raspberry, W. (1994, August 9). A sensible provision for same-sex classes. *Washington Post,* p. A19.

Reform school [Editorial]. (1993, May 27). *Washington Post,* p. A24.

Riley, R. (1994, May 17). *Remarks of Richard Riley on the 40th Anniversary of* Brown v. Board of Education. Georgetown University Law Center, Washington, DC.

Senate panel readies for its part in education spending battle. (1994, May 6). *Congressional Monitor,* p. 6.

Senate passes $12 billion in federal education aid. (1994, August 3). *Washington Post,* p. A3.

Senators walk narrow line on prayer in school. (1994, July 28). *Congressional Monitor,* pp. 1, 5.

Sharpe, R. (1994, September 28). Conferees approve $10.5 billion plan for aid to schools. *Wall Street Journal,* p. A5.

Shogren, E. (1994, October 6). Education reform bill okd after filibuster is thwarted. *Los Angeles Times,* p. A14.

Sideshow on the schools [Editorial]. (1994, September 30). *Washington Post,* p. A28.

Slavin, R. (1993, October 20). To educate the poor, put money in the right place. *Chicago Tribune,* sec. 1, p. 25.

Stanfield, R. (1994, October 22). An A for effort—and achievement. *National Journal,* p. 2485.

Subcommittee ok's elementary, secondary measure after defeating Clinton bid to refocus Chapter 1 funds. (1994). *Congressional Monitor,* p. 7.

Wells, R. (1994a, March 26). Elementary-secondary aid bill passes House, 289-128. *Congressional Quarterly,* p. 746.

Wells, R. (1994b, September 24). Funding formula compromise holding up conferees. *Congressional Quarterly,* pp. 2691-2692.

Wells, R. M. (1994c, July 30). Funding formula, prayer issue hold up Senate action. *Congressional Quarterly,* pp. 2148-2149.

Wells, R. (1994d, October 1). House gives its approval to school aid measure. *Congressional Quarterly,* pp. 2807-2808.

Wells, R. (1994e, March 5). More funds to poorer schools likely to be rejected. *Congressional Quarterly*, p. 552.

Wells, R. (1994f, June 18). Senate panel easily approves $12.7 billion measure. *Congressional Quarterly*, pp. 1632-1633.

Wells, R. M. (1994g, August 6). Senate passes school aid bill but shifts funding formula. *Congressional Quarterly*, pp. 2256-2258.

Zuckman, J. (1993, September 11). Clinton would tie federal aid to learning standards. *Congressional Quarterly*, p. 2394.

Zuckman, J. (1994, January 15). Clinton's Chapter 1 formula runs aground in House. *Congressional Quarterly*, pp. 70-73.

Chapter 7

Allen, G. (1996, May 13). With Goals 2000, state and local school boards become "serfs" to an intruding federal bureaucracy. *Roll Call*, p. 4.

Amendments to Goals 2000: Educate America Act, 7 U.S.C. § 706 (1996).

Applebome, P. (1996, March 28). An education conference with a corporate agenda. *New York Times*, p. B10.

Broder, D. (1995, August 2). Just plain dumb. *Washington Post*, p. A25.

Camphire, G. (1995, May 11). House panel moves to kill standards council. *Education Daily*, pp. 1, 2.

Clinton, W. (1996, March 27). Remarks at the National Governors' Conference Education Summit. *Weekly Compilation of Presidential documents, 32*, 573-581.

Fight begins to abolish federal department of education. (1995). *Insider's Report: Newsletter of the American Policy Center, 2* (4), 1.

Garland, S. (1995, September 25). Will Republicans make Clinton the education president? *Business Week*, p. 67.

Gray, P. (1996, April 8). Debating standards. *Time*, p. 40.

H.R. 1045, 104th Cong., 1st Sess. (1995).

Hoff, D. (1994, May 27). Three states unsure of Goals 2000 commitment. *Education Daily*, pp. 1, 3.

Hoff, D. (1995a, August 21). House bill sets historic course for ED reductions. *Education Daily*, pp. 1, 3.

Hoff, D. (1995b, September 13). Specter looks to amend Goals 2000 in spending bill. *Education Daily*, pp. 1, 3.

Hoff, D. (1996, April 30). Goals 2000 changes would lessen ED oversight. *Education Daily*, pp. 1, 3.

IBM CEO's vision of high expectations, achievement for America's schools: Interview with Louis Gerstner. (1996). *Work America, 13*(2), 1, 4, 5.

Innerst, C. (1996a, March 11). Conservatives wary of slant in education summit agenda. *Washington Times*, p. A3.

Innerst, C. (1996b, March 22). Most divisive issues kept off Education Summit's agenda. *Washington Times*, p. A11.

Innerst, C. (1996c, March 28). Summit policy position altered. *Washington Times*, p. A6.

Jennings, J., & Stark, D. (1996). Education stalemate in the capital. *Phi Delta Kappa, Washington Newsletter, 5*(2), 1-4.

Kondracke, M. (1996, April 11). This time, a real "education president" runs for re-election. *Roll Call*, p. 5.

Krauthammer, C. (1994, November 4). History hijacked. *Washington Post*, p. A25.

Kristol, I. (1994, April 18). The inevitable outcome of "outcomes." *Wall Street Journal*, p. A14.

Lawton, M. (1996, April 3). Summit accord calls for focus on standards. *Education Week*, pp. 1, 14.

Manno, B. (1995, May). The new school wars. *Phi Delta Kappan*, pp. 720-726.

Massell, D., Kirst, M., & Hoppe, M. (1997). *Persistence and change: School reform in nine states*. Philadelphia: Consortium for Policy Research in Education.

National Governors' Association. (1996, March 27). *1996 National Education Summit: Policy statement*. Washington, DC: Author.

Pitsch, M. (1994, October 19). Critics target Goals 2000 in schools "war." *Education Week,* pp. 1, 21.

Pitsch, M. (1995, May 17). House committee passes bill to eliminate standards council. *Education Week,* p. 20.

Pitsch, M. (1996, May 1). To placate conservatives, measure alters Goals 2000. *Education Week,* p. 19.

Ravitch, D. (1996, April 11). 50 ways to teach them grammar. *Washington Post,* p. A23.

Sanchez, R. (1995a, September 26). GOP's power of the purse put to test: Education goals program targeted for early demise. *Washington Post,* pp. A1, A4.

Sanchez, R. (1995b, May 25). House Republicans' proposal would end much of federal role in education. *Washington Post.*

Sanchez, R. (1996a, March 27). Business leaders urge governors to make higher school standards a priority. *Washington Post,* p. 6.

Sanchez, R. (1996b, February 8). Governors will repeat academic course. *Washington Post,* p. A23.

Sanchez, R. (1996c, April 11). Most programs emerge from arena unscathed. *Washington Post,* p. A21.

Sharpe, R. (1995, August 30). Federal education law becomes hot target of wary conservatives. *Wall Street Journal,* p. A1.

Sharpe, R. (1996, March 28). Governors promise tougher standards for education. *Wall Street Journal,* p. C15.

Unfunded mandates. (1995, January 18). *Congressional Record,* pp. S1025-S1040.

U.S. Department of Education. (1996, April 30). *Goals 2000: Increasing student achievement through state and local initiatives.* Washington, DC: Author.

Walsh, M. (1994, September 28). Christian Coalition puts education at heart of education agenda. *Education Week,* p. 10.

Chapter 8

Applebome, P. (1997, February 19). New call for support of Clinton on schools. *New York Times,* p. B8.

Balz, D. (1996, November 27). Stands on education cost GOP among women, governors told. *Washington Post,* p. A6.

Castle, M. N. (1997, June 2). Republicans really are a pro-education party. *Roll Call*(Suppl.), p. 13.

Clinton, W. (1997a, February 4). Address before a joint session of Congress on the state of the union. *Weekly Compilation of Presidential Documents, 33,* 136-144.

Clinton, W. (1997b, March 6). Remarks to a joint session of the Michigan legislature in Lansing, Michigan. *Weekly Compilation of Presidential Documents, 33,* 290-299.

Clinton, W. (1997c, March 13). Remarks to a joint session of the North Carolina state legislature in Raleigh, North Carolina. *Weekly Compilation of Presidential Documents, 33,* 351-360.

Clinton, W. (1997d, January 22). Remarks to the First in the World Consortium in Northbrook, Illinois. *Weekly Compilation of Presidential Documents, 33,* 74-80.

Clinton, W. (1997e, February 10). Remarks by the president to the Maryland General Assembly in Annapolis, Maryland. *Weekly Compilation of Presidential Documents, 33,* 165-175.

Elam, S. M., Rose, L. C., & Gallup, A. M. (1996, September). The 28th annual Phi Delta Kappa/Gallup poll on the public's attitudes toward the public schools. *Phi Delta Kappan,* pp. 41-59.

Harden, B. (1996, July 18). Dole hits "monopoly" and its "pliant pet." *Washington Post,* p. A8.

Hearings before the Democratic Policy Committees on the impact of the Dole economic plan on education, 104th Cong., 2nd Sess. (1996) (testimony of David Glover, National Education Association).

Hearings before the House Subcommittee on Early Childhood, Youth, and Families, Committee on Education and the Workforce, 105th Cong., 1st Sess. (1997) (testimony of Richard W. Riley, U.S. Secretary of Education).

Hoff, D. (1996, July 19). Dole revives Bush's school choice proposal. *Education Daily,* pp. 1, 2.

Hoff, D. (1997, November 12). White House, GOP craft agreement on testing. *Education Week,* pp. 1, 23.

Improving education. (1996, August 17). *Congressional Quarterly,* p. 2327.

Jennings, J., & Rentner, D. S. (1996). Educators triumph: Efforts for increased funding succeed. *Phi Delta Kappa, Washington Newsletter, 6*(2), 1-2.

Pianin, E., & Sanchez, R. (1997, November 6). Compromise reached on testing plan. *Washington Post,* p. A12.

Pitsch, M. (1996, September 4). Four years later, GOP platform takes new tack on education. *Education Week,* p. 33.

Sanchez, R. (1997, February 23). The hard truths of higher standards. *Washington Post,* pp. A1, A8, A9.

Sanchez, R. (1997a, September 17). House votes down Clinton plan for national reading, math achievement tests. *Washington Post,* p. A20.

Sanchez, R. (1997b, April 3). Schools chief, CEOs back national tests. *Washington Post,* p. A4.

Standards for standards [Editorial]. (1997, February 9). *Washington Post,* p. C1.

Thompson, T. G. (1997, February 21). Leave standards to the states. *New York Times,* p. A35.

Today's Democratic party: Meeting America's challenges, protecting America's values. (1996, September 4). *Education Week,* p. 3.

Wolf, R. (1996, September 25). Dole, Clinton courting votes with education proposals. *USA Today,* p. 5D.

Epilogue

Clinton, W. (1997, January 22). Remarks to the First in the World Consortium in Northbrook, Illinois. *Weekly Compilation of Presidential Documents, 33,* 74-80.

U.S. Department of Education. (1991). *America 2000: An education strategy.* Washington, DC: Author.

INDEX

About the Author

John (Jack) F. Jennings is the director of the Center on Education Policy in Washington, D.C. That center, which is foundation funded, is an independent national, nonpartisan advocate for improved public schools. The center works directly with states, school districts, and organizations to improve education and also communicates with teachers, parents, and the general public through presentations, books, pamphlets, and brochures.

From 1967 to 1994, Mr. Jennings worked in the area of federal aid to education for the U.S. Congress. He began his career as Staff Director of the subcommittee responsible for elementary and secondary education and ended it as General Counsel for the Committee on Education and Labor. In his work with Congress, he was involved in nearly every major education debate held at the national level over the course of those three decades. He was influential in the drafting of every significant federal education law, including the Elementary and Secondary Education Act, the Vocational Education Act, the School Lunch Act, the Individuals With Disabilities Education Act, and the Higher Education Act. As the chief expert on education for the U.S. House of Representatives, he has spoken at hundreds of meetings in the United States and has traveled to China, the former USSR, Italy, and several other countries representing the United States. In addition, his activities have included editing several books, writing a national legislative newsletter, and publishing numerous articles.